THE POLICE FOUNDATION

Roadcraft
The Police Driver's Handbook

Did you know that *Roadcraft* is also available as an app?

and as an e-learning course with a certificate?

The Stationery Office
London

Contributing authors: Penny Mares, Philip Coyne, Barbara MacDonald.
Current author: Mark Rylander.
Design: Adam Ray.
Illustration: Original illustrations created by Nick Moxsom.
Additional design by Adam Kimberley.
Front cover photography: Rob Brown and Adam Kimberley. Vehicle courtesy of Norfolk Constabulary.
Project manager: Catherine Saunders, The Police Foundation.
Project advisor: Daniel Whittle, TSO.

The Police Foundation

The Police Foundation is an independent charity that researches, understands and works to improve policing.

For further details of the Police Foundation's work and other related *Roadcraft* publications, contact:

Email: roadcraft@police-foundation.org.uk
Website: www.roadcraft.co.uk

Charity Registration Number: 278257

© The Police Foundation 2025

Although the author and publisher have made every effort to ensure that the information in this publication was correct at the time of press, neither the author and/or the publisher assume and hereby disclaim any liability to any party for any loss and/or damage caused by any errors and/or omissions, whether such errors and/or omissions result from negligence, accident, and/or any other cause. This publication is not intended to be a substitute for the advice of qualified emergency services driving instructors. The reader should take independent advice relating to their driving ability from persons with appropriate qualifications.

The publication may include hyperlinks to third-party content, advertising, or websites, provided for the sake of convenience and interest.

The publishers do not endorse any advertising or products available from external sources that are contained or referenced in this publication.

NO AI TRAINING NOTICE: unless expressly permitted and/or denied by applicable law (including under Crown Copyright/Open Government Licence), the material and the contents in the Work cannot be used for any form of Artificial Intelligence ('AI') training and/or any training of generative AI models without the prior written consent of TSO which is to be obtained on an each and every occurrence basis. Applications should be made to permissions@tso.co.uk

Other essential guides to safe driving and riding also published by The Stationery Office include:

Motorcycle Roadcraft – The Police Rider's Handbook (2025)
ISBN 978 0 11 709505 2

Roadcraft and *Motorcycle Roadcraft* e-learning courses
https://www.safedrivingforlife.info/shop/roadcraft-elearning

To order or find out more about these or any other driving titles, please refer to the contact details printed inside the front cover of this book.

Applications for reproduction should be made in writing to
The Stationery Office Limited, 18 Central Avenue,
St Andrews Business Park, Norwich, NR7 0HR

New edition 2025

ISBN 978 0 11 709504 5

SD000315

Acknowledgements

This edition of *Roadcraft* has been approved by the National Police Chiefs' Council (NPCC) and Police Scotland, which are satisfied that it reflects current best practice in police driver instruction and takes into account the relevant views of civilian experts.

The Police Foundation would like to thank the many individuals and organisations who gave so freely of their time and expertise in the preparation of this new edition of *Roadcraft*. Particular thanks go to Dr Gemma Briggs, Professor of Applied Cognitive Psychology at the Open University; Craig Arnold, Technical Lead at the Transport Research Laboratory; Dr Helen Wells, Director, Roads Policing Academic Network; and Jason Powell, Fleet Lead, National Police Chiefs' Council. Some sections of material in Chapters 1 and 4 are adapted from *Human Aspects of Police Driving* by kind permission of Dr Gordon Sharp and Police Scotland.

The Police Foundation would also like to thank Norfolk Constabulary for their kind assistance in arranging the cover photography.

The Police Foundation would like to thank Drivetech for providing a financial contribution towards the cost of producing the handbook.

This new edition of *Roadcraft* was produced with the strategic oversight of a Standing Advisory Board with representatives from major police and civilian driving organisations, to whom we are most grateful.

Standing Advisory Board

Mark Bull, Regional Senior Examiner, Royal Society for the Prevention of Accidents (RoSPA)

Jon Curtis, Roads Policing Business Manager, College of Policing

Roger Gardner, Chairman, National Police Chiefs' Council National Driver Training (Practitioners) Group

Richard Gladman, Chief Examiner, IAM Roadsmart

Bob McNay, Head of Road Policing and Driver Training, Scottish Police College, Police Scotland

Rick Muir, former Director, The Police Foundation (Chair)

Stuart O'Neill, Metropolitan Police Driver Training Academy

Colin Stewart, Assistant Chief Driving Examiner and Driver Training Policy Manager, Driver and Vehicle Standards Agency (DVSA)

It was undertaken with the dedicated help of a Reflective Practitioners group of senior police, fire, ambulance and civilian instructors, whose contribution to the detailed editorial and updating process has been invaluable.

Reflective Practitioners

Byron Chandler, Specialist Skills Manager and Chief Driving Instructor, Gloucestershire Constabulary

Iain Cook, Driver Training and Development, West Yorkshire Police

Kevin Dell, Emergency Response Driver Specialist, National Fire Chiefs Council

Donna Kidd, Road Policing and Driver Training, Scottish Police College, Police Scotland

Nick Lambert, Head of Education, East Midlands Ambulance Service

Peter Mosdell, Head of Specialist Skills, Education and Training, Babcock International Group

Peter Rodger, former Inspector, Metropolitan Police Driving School and former Chief Examiner, IAM RoadSmart

Colin Stewart, Assistant Chief Driving Examiner and Driver Training Policy Manager, DVSA

Matthew Thomas, Head of Driver Training, Dyfed-Powys Police

Editorial and Project Management Board

Lisa Daniels, Account Director, TSO

Mark Rylander, Editor and Technical Writer

Catherine Saunders, Communications and Publications Manager, The Police Foundation

Daniel Whittle, Content Development Manager, TSO

Foreword

In its 70th year, *Roadcraft* remains the backbone of police driving, providing a valuable reference and learning tool for police drivers.

The first edition of *Roadcraft* was published in 1955 and known as *The Police Drivers' Manual*. Over the years, it has been used more widely by the emergency services and members of the public, who acknowledge its benefits in providing a system of safe driving.

UK police driving is held in very high regard and seen as the best across the policing world. The skills and standards of police drivers are extensively used and tested daily, demonstrating the value of quality training. I am confident that the experience and qualifications of our trainers using the curriculum supplied by the College of Policing, and supported by *Roadcraft*, will continue to enable police officers and emergency response drivers to meet the challenges they face.

Each year sees a growth in the number of road users and advancements in vehicle technology, which create new challenges for road safety. The reduction of road casualties and the safety of all road users remains paramount. It is the driver who is best placed to achieve this and I would encourage all drivers to use the principles outlined in this publication to further enhance their skills and safety on the road.

Deputy Chief Constable Terry Woods,
NPCC Lead Police Driving

Roadcraft is endorsed by the following organisations:

Contents

Acknowledgements	iii
Foreword	v
Preface to the new edition	xix
About *Roadcraft*	xxi

Chapter 1 Becoming a better driver — 1

Becoming a better driver	2
What makes a good driver?	3
The hierarchy of road users	3
Competences for police drivers	4
Your vulnerability as a driver	6
What are the commonest causes of collisions?	6
Who is most likely to be involved in a collision?	7
Critical learning from experience	8
Develop awareness of your personal vulnerability	10
Human factor risks for emergency services drivers	13
Distraction due to multi-tasking	13
Driving stress	13
Operational stressors	14
Time pressure and the purpose of your journey	16
'Noble cause' risk-taking	16
'Red mist'	16
How you learn	17
Training, practice and feedback	17
Overconfidence after training	18

Self-assessment will help you continually improve	19
Be honest	20
Check your understanding	22

Chapter 2 Advanced driver-assistance systems — 23

What are ADAS?	24
How do ADAS work?	24
Why do ADAS matter?	25
ADAS features at a glance	26
ADAS features in more detail	28
Autonomous vehicles	32
Check your understanding	33

Chapter 3 The system of car control — 35

The need for a system of car control	36
Integrating a range of competences	36
What is the system of car control?	37
How the system works	38
The importance of information	39
Mirrors and signals	39
The system of car control	40
Information	40
Position	41
Speed	41
Gear	41
Acceleration	41
Use the system flexibly	42

Applying the system to a left-hand turn	44
Applying the system to a right-hand turn	45
Applying the system to a roundabout	46
Re-applying the system to leave the roundabout	47
Applying the system to a potential hazard	48
Overlapping braking and gear changing	**49**
Brake/gear overlap – an example	50
Incorrect use of brake/gear overlap	51
Check your understanding	**52**

Chapter 4 Information, observation and anticipation — 53

Processing complex information	**54**
Improving your information processing	55
Tips to improve information processing	58
Why observation and anticipation are essential for better driving	**58**
What is a hazard?	59
Planning	**60**
Anticipate hazards	62
Prioritise hazards	63
Decide what to do	64
Forward planning beyond the next hazard	64
Improving your observation	**65**
Scanning the environment	65
Looking but not seeing	66
Peripheral vision	68

Zones of visibility	69
Your choice of speed	71
Keep your distance	74
Human factors that affect observation and anticipation	**76**
Alertness	76
Tiredness	76
Other physiological factors	78
Check your understanding	**80**

Chapter 5 Anticipating hazards in the driving environment 81

Night driving	**82**
You	82
Your vehicle	82
Your lights	82
Following other vehicles at night	83
Information from other vehicles' lights	84
Dazzle	84
Reflective studs and markings	85
Other ways to improve observation at night	85
Weather conditions	**86**
Using lights in bad weather	87
Using auxiliary controls and instruments in bad weather	87
Observing when visibility is low	88
Micro climates	88
Road surface	**89**
Road surface irregularities	90

The road surface in winter	92
Driving through water	92
Road signs and markings	**93**
Local road knowledge	**97**
Making observation links	**97**
Check your understanding	**100**

Chapter 6 Acceleration, using gears, braking and steering — 101

Developing competence at controlling your vehicle	**102**
The tyre grip trade-off	103
Vehicle balance and tyre grip	104
Technology to help keep control of the vehicle	105
Using the accelerator	**105**
Retarders	106
Regenerative braking	106
Acceleration and vehicle balance	107
Acceleration and balance on different types of vehicle	107
Developing your competence at using the accelerator	108
Acceleration sense	109
Using the accelerator on bends	110
Key points	113
Fuel/power source affects acceleration and engine braking	113
Using the gears	**113**
Moving off from stationary	114
Accurate use of the gears	114
Key points	116

Vehicle transmission systems — 117

- Automatic transmission — 118
- Using the features of automatic systems — 119
- Developing your competence at using automatic systems — 120
- Electric vehicle transmission — 120
- Developing your competence at using EV transmission — 122
- Road conditions — 122

Slowing down and stopping — 123

- Releasing the accelerator – engine braking — 123
- Using the brakes — 124
- Normal braking (tapered braking) — 124
- Braking, tyre grip and balance — 125
- The safe stopping distance rule — 126
- Overall safe stopping distance — 127
- The two-second rule — 128
- Braking for corners and bends — 129
- Braking as you approach a hazard — 130
- Emergency braking — 131
- Using the parking brake — 132

Steering — 132

- Steering technique — 133
- Seat position — 133
- How to hold the steering wheel — 134
- Pull–push — 134
- Rotational steering — 136
- Key points — 137

Check your understanding — 138

Chapter 7 Manoeuvring at low speeds — 139

Developing your competence at low-speed manoeuvring — 140

Using the system — 140

    Observation — 141

    Planning — 142

    Steering — 143

Reversing in a confined space — 144

    Manoeuvring with a guide — 146

Parking — 146

Check your understanding — 148

Chapter 8 Maintaining vehicle stability — 149

Controlling your vehicle's stability — 150

    Attitudes to vehicle safety technology — 151

How active safety systems work — 151

    Anti-lock braking systems — 152

    Traction control systems — 153

    Electronic stability programmes — 154

    Centre of gravity and electric vehicles — 154

    Key points — 155

Avoiding skidding — 155

    How does a skid happen? — 156

    How to minimise the risk of skidding — 157

Recognising the cause of a skid — 158

    Cause: driving too fast for the circumstances — 159

    Cause: harsh acceleration — 159

    Cause: excessive or sudden braking — 159

Cause: coarse steering	160
Understeer and oversteer	160
Aquaplaning	**162**
Check your understanding	**163**

Chapter 9 Driver's signals — 165

Developing your competence at using signals	**166**
The purpose of signals	166
Key points	167
Interpreting signals given by others	167
The range of signals	**168**
Using the indicators	168
Using hazard warning lights	169
Brake lights	170
Using the horn	170
Flashing your headlights	171
Arm signals	172
Using courtesy signals	172
Responding to other people's signals	173
Check your understanding	**174**

Chapter 10 Positioning — 175

Developing competence at positioning your vehicle	**176**
Positioning for advantage	**177**
Safety position on the approach to hazards	**178**
Roadside hazards	178
Improving the view into nearside road junctions	180
Following position	181

Position on bends	182
Position for turning	182
Position at crossroads	184
Position for stopping behind other vehicles	185
Position for approaching the brow of a hill	186
Position at pedestrian crossings and traffic lights	186
Check your understanding	**187**

Chapter 11 Cornering — 189

Developing your competence at cornering	190
Using the system to corner safely	190
Key principles for safe cornering	190
Cornering forces	191
Vehicle characteristics	193
Roadworthiness	193
Vehicle specification	193
Understeer and oversteer	193
Camber and superelevation	194
Summary of factors affecting cornering	195
Assessing the sharpness of a bend	196
The limit point	196
The double-apex bend	204
Using a cross view	206
How to use the system for cornering	207
Information	207
Position	208
Speed	210

Gear	211
Acceleration	211
Check your understanding	**213**

Chapter 12 Overtaking — 215

Developing your competence at overtaking safely	216
Passing a stationary vehicle	217
Overtaking moving vehicles	220
The vehicle in front	221
The vehicles behind	221
Other hazards to consider before overtaking	222
A single-stage overtake	223
A three-stage overtake	226
Stage one: following position	226
Stage two: overtaking position	228
Stage three: overtaking	229
Overtaking vehicles in a line of traffic	230
Other overtaking situations	233
Overtaking on a single carriageway	233
Overtaking on bends	234
Overtaking on single carriageway roads marked with three lanes	236
Overtaking on multi-lane carriageways	237
The range of hazards	238
Cyclists, motorcyclists and horses	238
Road layout and conditions	239
The road surface	240
Human factors in overtaking	241

Helping other road users to overtake	241
Overtaking: key safety points	242
Check your understanding	243

Chapter 13 Driving on motorways and multi-lane carriageways — 245

Driving on multi-lane carriageways	246
Layout of the carriageway	247
New motorway layouts	248
Joining the motorway	248
Use the system	249
Driving on the motorway	250
Overtaking	251
Motorway junctions	255
Using the hard shoulder	256
Entering or leaving the hard shoulder	256
Leaving the motorway	257
Bad weather conditions on fast-moving roads	258
Fog	259
Rain	260
Snow, sleet and ice	260
High winds	260
Bright sun	262
Other hazards	262
Debris	262
Lane closures	262

Additional hazards on fast-moving multi-lane carriageways   263
Human factors in motorway driving   263
Check your understanding   265

Chapter 14 Emergency response   267

What is an emergency response?   268
Using the national decision model   269
Risk assessment   269
Responding to an emergency   270
    Use of emergency warning equipment   270
    Speed limits   271
    Approaching traffic light-controlled junctions   272
    Approaching traffic light-controlled pedestrian crossings   275
    Contravening keep left/right signs   276
    Positioning to see and be seen   276
    Approaching and passing vehicles   277
    Interpreting other drivers' signals   280
    Stationary vehicles at or near an incident   280
    Responding on multi-lane roads   281
    Approaching roundabouts   282
    Passing on the nearside of other vehicles   283
    Multi-vehicle response   284
    Vulnerable road users   285
Check your understanding   287

Appendices — 289

Appendix 1 Are you fit to drive? — 290
    I AM SAFE checklist — 290

Appendix 2 Is your vehicle fit to drive? — 291
    Roadworthiness/pre-driving checklist — 291
    POWDER checklist — 292
    Inside the vehicle checklist — 293
    Testing the brakes — 294

Appendix 3 Fuel-efficient driving — 295
    Key principles of fuel-efficient driving — 295

Appendix 4 Goals for Driver Education — 296

Bibliography — 299

Index — 303

Preface to the new edition

This new and fully updated edition of *Roadcraft* is the result of sustained consultation with experts in the theory and practice of advanced driving.

The last edition of *Roadcraft* was published in 2020 and featured major updates to the overtaking and limit point sections, as well as other significant changes designed to reflect the changing state of advanced driving practice.

The 2025 edition seeks to maintain this tradition by explaining the purpose of advanced driver-assistance systems (ADAS). As well as a general introduction to the core concepts, the text features clear explanations of common types of ADAS and their functions, supplemented by updates to the electric vehicles section in Chapter 6.

This emphasis on technology is due, in no small part, to the way that police vehicles have changed since the last edition went to press. With the development of electric cars and the rapid increase in assistance technologies, it's become essential to deal with the fundamentals of these systems and recognise their primary role as a tool to assist drivers, not a replacement for good judgement.

To support the development of advanced observation skills, this edition also contains a new section on using cross views to take information on bends. This forms part of a series of complementary techniques, including understanding zones of visibility and using observation links to gather information about the road environment.

As in previous editions, *Roadcraft* specifically focuses on addressing human factors in police driving. Central to this theme has been the work of psychologist Dr Robert West (1997 edition), occupational physician Dr Gordon Sharp (2007 edition) and psychologist Dr Lisa Dorn (2007 and 2013 editions) with additional contributions made by Dr Gemma Briggs and Dr Julie Gandolfi (2020 edition) and Dr Gemma Briggs, Dr Helen Wells and Craig Arnold for the current edition. Each has contributed a range of insights to equip students to recognise, manage and reduce risks arising from these human aspects. And, as understanding of the psychological factors that influence driving behaviour evolves, new developments in this field – including the way that in-vehicle technology affects the relationship between the driver, the vehicle, and the environment – will continue to inform future editions of *Roadcraft*.

This edition of *Roadcraft* includes an updated emergency response chapter that demonstrates nationally formalised response advice. As well as its value in an operational context, it is considered to be useful for the public to be informed about response driving and riding so they are better prepared to react when they encounter an emergency vehicle.

About *Roadcraft*

How can *Roadcraft* help you become a better driver?

Roadcraft is the handbook for police and other emergency services drivers undertaking driver training. In driver training, *Roadcraft* is combined with practical instruction. This edition is designed so that it can be used for self-study either before or during a course, and for ready reference afterwards.

The aim of *Roadcraft* is to improve your driving ability. Your safety and that of other road users depends on your awareness of what's happening around you and your ability to control the position and speed of your vehicle relative to everything else on the road. A collision or even a near miss is often the result of a lapse in driving skill. *Roadcraft* aims to help you become a better driver by increasing your awareness of all the factors that affect your driving – your own capabilities, the characteristics of your vehicle, and the road and traffic conditions.

The system of car control aims to increase your safety by providing a systematic approach to hazards.

What vehicles does *Roadcraft* cover?

You can apply the principles of *Roadcraft* to any vehicle you drive, whether a modern car or larger or older vehicles.

The basic design and the supplementary features built into a vehicle all affect its capabilities. As vehicle design and safety technology become more sophisticated, it would be impossible in a book of this size to cover the range of variations in, for example, four-wheel drive, transmission systems, adaptive suspension and active safety features. You should always get to know your vehicle's characteristics and adapt your driving to them, and have a good grasp of the manufacturer's guidance for every vehicle that you drive.

What *Roadcraft* does not include

Roadcraft assumes that you're thoroughly familiar with the current edition of the *Highway Code* and is intended to be used in conjunction with that publication.

Certain techniques that require a high level of instruction to ensure their safety, such as those used in pursuit driving and other specialist situations, aren't included. Your instructor will introduce you to these when appropriate.

Using *Roadcraft* for self-study

These are the features that will help you to get the most out of *Roadcraft*, whether you're studying independently or using it as part of formal instruction:

- The main learning points are listed at the start of each chapter. These lists will help you choose the chapters or sections that you need to concentrate on.
- The self-assessment questions in the text are designed to help you develop your awareness of the human factors (for example, personality, mood, stress) that could affect your driving safety, and help you to manage them. These and the practical questions will enable you to transfer the advice in *Roadcraft* to your everyday driving.
- Illustrations and diagrams are used to explain complex ideas. Read them along with the text as they often expand on this or provide a different level of information. Bear in mind that all illustrations are only a guide to the real world – don't rely on them alone.
- Important points are highlighted in coloured boxes.
- The learning points are repeated at the end of each chapter to help you check your understanding.

Working through the chapters

Chapters 1, 2 and 3 are the foundations on which later chapters build so you should ideally read these in order first. If you're using *Roadcraft* as part of a driving course, your instructor may suggest you study certain sections of the book in a different order.

Personal risks, practice and self-assessment

Just reading *Roadcraft* won't make you a better driver. Awareness of your personal risks, practice and self-assessment are an essential part of developing competence. What matters is not how well you can recall what's in this book but how well you can apply what you've learnt to your driving.

Aim to develop your awareness of the human factors that can affect your driving behaviour even before you get into a vehicle. Your personality, state of mind, attitudes to other road users, stress and operational distractions can all affect your performance. In order to achieve the highest levels of driving competence and safety, *Roadcraft* encourages you to develop your self-assessment skills so that you learn to recognise and safely manage the human factors that can put you at risk.

Many of the practical competences explained here are fairly simple in themselves. A sophisticated driving ability comes from applying them consistently. All competences depend on judgement and this only comes with practice. Aim to apply the techniques in *Roadcraft* systematically so that they become an everyday part of your driving.

You can't absorb all the information in *Roadcraft* in one reading, so we suggest that you read a section, select a technique, practise it, assess your progress, and then refer to *Roadcraft* to refine the technique further.

Using *Roadcraft* for reference

The contents pages at the front of the book list all the main headings and a selective list of the most useful sub-headings. Cross references throughout the book will help you find linked information in other chapters. There's also a comprehensive index on page 303.

Learning is a continual process

Being a good driver means that you never stop learning. *Roadcraft* offers advice on the principles of better driving but can't be a definitive guide to all driving situations and techniques. Vehicles and driving conditions are constantly changing, and your driving competences need to keep pace with this change, otherwise they could become outdated and even dangerous. Aim to constantly self-evaluate and, where necessary, adapt your driving so that you maintain high standards and continually improve your performance. Every time you drive, use the journey as an opportunity to develop your driving ability.

> Is your hazard perception as good as you think it is? See page 62.

- Vehicle safety technology and equipment have advanced at such a rapid pace that they can give drivers a false sense of security, leading them to take more risks. Driving a vehicle that has many more safety features than the one you learned in can lead you to take risks that you would not have taken before.

This is why critical and honest self-awareness is so important. It will help you to keep your actual driving ability and your perceived ability in balance.

Self-assessment will help you continually improve

People who develop a high level of ability in any field have better than average self-assessment skills. They're continually reviewing their performance, analysing their mistakes, and working out how they can improve.

People who aren't very good at assessing themselves find it difficult to develop a higher level of competence as they fail to reflect on what they can do to improve.

Aim for a cycle of continuous improvement in your driving competence.

 Self-assessment is only possible through reflective practice. Monitor your actions as they are actually happening, and review your performance after a drive. Ask yourself:

- What's my aim?
- What went well and why?
- What went less well and why?
- How could I do better next time?
- Have I been honest with myself?

Be honest

The first thing you should focus on when you review a drive is your own safety and that of other road users. Being honest with yourself about what didn't go so well is vital if you want to continue to improve. For example, you might look back on a drive to consider:

- how you controlled the vehicle
- how you managed traffic situations, and anticipated and planned for hazards
- what aspects of the journey you found challenging
- what personal characteristics affected your driving behaviour.

See Appendix 4, Goals for Driver Education, page 296.

Reviewing things that went well and analysing why you handled them well is also important. It will help you to transfer your competence in one particular situation to other situations. This will broaden your ability to make accurate decisions and judgements.

But in the end, you'll only become a better driver if you understand your own vulnerability, know the limits of your driving capabilities and recognise the human factors that affect your safety. Studying *Roadcraft* and practising continually to develop your driving ability will increase your satisfaction, enjoyment and safety on the road.

✅ Check your understanding

You should now be able to apply learning from this chapter in your driver training so that you can:

- [ ] explain the competences required for police driving
- [ ] identify the human factors that may increase your vulnerability as a driver
- [ ] explain the Goals for Driver Education and how these can help you manage risks and assess your own driving
- [ ] show that you give priority to safety at all times
- [ ] show that you can recognise and manage the human factors that may affect your decision-making and driving performance
- [ ] show that you can honestly and critically assess your own driving behaviour to achieve continuous improvement.

Chapter 1

Becoming a better driver

Learning outcomes

The learning in this chapter, along with driver training, should enable you to:

- explain the competences required for police driving
- identify the human factors that may increase your vulnerability as a driver
- explain the Goals for Driver Education and how these can help you manage risks and assess your own driving
- show that you give priority to safety at all times
- show that you can recognise and manage the human factors that may affect your decision-making and driving performance
- show that you can honestly and critically assess your own driving behaviour to achieve continuous improvement.

Becoming a better driver

This chapter is about how you can become a better driver. Driving should be a safe, satisfying and rewarding task. This chapter focuses on the personal qualities that are essential for safe and competent driving. Understanding your personal risks and knowing how to increase your safety will lay the foundations for a long, enjoyable and rewarding driving career.

Across the UK and the European Union, driver training at all levels now encourages learners to consider the effects of human factors – personality, attitudes, state of mind and emotions – on their driving abilities. Research shows that all these factors strongly influence how safe you are on the road.

This is because your personal characteristics affect how you approach technical skills, use your vehicle, respond to traffic conditions and to other road users, and deal with the demands of a particular journey and the job of driving. This chapter introduces the main European Goals for Driver Education and explains how these can support your awareness of personal risks and your self-assessment abilities.

See Appendix 4, page 296.

Your ability to honestly self-assess your own driving performance accurately and learn from experience is the most important skill of all. Without this, you can't become a better driver.

 As self-assessment is so important, each chapter in *Roadcraft* includes questions to help you check your understanding of police driving competences and assess your own driving behaviour. Questions are highlighted like this in a coloured panel with a self-assessment symbol.

What makes a good driver?

The qualities of a safe and competent driver are:

- critical and honest self-awareness and understanding of your personal characteristics, attitudes and behaviour, which are necessary for safe driving
- taking action to keep identified risks to a minimum
- awareness of your own limitations and those of the vehicle and the road
- awareness of the risks inherent in particular road and traffic situations
- concentration and good observation
- continuously matching the vehicle's direction and speed to the changing conditions
- skilful use of vehicle controls.

Police and other emergency services drivers should be exemplary drivers. Your attitude towards your driving is noticed by members of the public and influences other drivers. Always be aware that you're seen as a role model and can influence the behaviour of other drivers for the better. If other drivers see you with a courteous attitude and an obvious concern for safety, they're more likely to behave in the same way.

The hierarchy of road users

Drivers of larger or less vulnerable vehicles are expected to allow for those who are more vulnerable, such as pedestrians and cyclists; this is known as the 'hierarchy of road users'. By extension, drivers of emergency vehicles are expected to take account of others when responding to emergencies. You should always be aware of the potential presence of more vulnerable road users, and be ready to take account of that vulnerability. However, it would be unwise to assume that you will be given the same consideration by others; you should always be prepared for the potential actions of others not to conform to this principle.

Competences for police drivers

> **Competence** is the ability to do the job – the knowledge, skills and behaviour required for police driving

There are three core competences that are the foundation of all driving. Police and other emergency services drivers need to develop these competences to the highest possible standards:

- the knowledge and skills to drive safely
- an understanding of factors that increase your risk of a collision
- the ability to accurately assess your driving behaviour.

See Appendix 4, Goals for Driver Education, page 296.

As an emergency services driver, your working life is characterised by the number and variety of different tasks that you must carry out, often within a single shift. A police driver's day that starts with a routine patrol might end up at the scene of a multi-vehicle collision on the motorway, or in a fast pursuit. Whatever the driving task, you're expected to maintain the highest possible standard of driving and to complete the task in hand calmly and efficiently.

As well as the core competences above, there are task-specific competences that are particularly important for the operational police driver. These are:

- multi-tasking – being able to carry out complex driving tasks effectively, at the same time as monitoring incoming information from various sources (see page 13)
- alertness – being vigilant and remaining focused so as to spot potential hazards early and leave nothing to chance
- attention distribution – sharing your attention across all aspects of a driving task
- situational awareness – using your senses to build and maintain an accurate mental picture of the operational environment
- anticipation – using your observational skills and driving experience to spot actual and potential hazards and predict how the situation is likely to unfold

- planning – planning precisely and making rapid and accurate decisions throughout the task
- making judgements – judging situations accurately and taking safe and appropriate action.

See Chapter 5, page 97, Making observation links, for more on alertness.

See Chapter 4, Information, observation and anticipation, for more on alertness, anticipation and planning.

> **Situational awareness** is essential for everyone on the road, but it's particularly expected of police and other emergency services drivers and riders.
>
> This involves gathering, interpreting and using any relevant information to make sense of what's going on around you and what's likely to happen next, so that you can make intelligent decisions and stay in control.

Developing these multiple and complex abilities begins with training but is a process of continuous improvement. It needs constant practice and accurate self-assessment throughout your professional driving career.

How good is your situational awareness?

Your vulnerability as a driver

Most drivers think they're both safer and more skilful than the average driver – but we can't all be right. Driving safety is not an add-on extra – it must be built into the way you drive, on every journey without exception.

What are the commonest causes of collisions?

The commonest recorded causes of collisions in the UK are:

- **Driver error or reaction** – this is a factor in nearly 3 out of 4 of all collisions. The commonest errors are:

  > failure to look properly
  > failure to judge the other person's path or speed
  > loss of control.

- **Action based on poor judgement** – this contributes to around 1 in 6 collisions. The main factors are:

  > travelling too fast for the conditions
  > exceeding the speed limit
  > following too close
  > sudden braking.

- **Being careless, reckless or in a hurry** contributes to over 1 in 6 collisions.

> Nearly half of the drivers involved in a daylight collision with a motorcyclist fail to look properly and don't see the rider before the crash. (This is often referred to as SMIDSY, which means 'Sorry, mate, I didn't see you'.)

> Even a small mistake at the wrong speed can result in loss of control.
>
> An inappropriate speed could be 20 mph in a narrow street crowded with pedestrians moving in and out of the road ...
>
> ... or 60 mph on a straight open road if you are tired and your attention is split between several tasks.

Who is most likely to be involved in a collision?

Young drivers, especially young male drivers, are at higher risk of crashing than older drivers:

- Fewer than 1 in 10 full licence holders are aged 16–24, but they account for around 1 in 7 of all reported collisions on Britain's roads and over 1 in 6 collisions in which someone is killed or seriously injured.
- Young drivers are more likely than average to be involved in a collision as a result of failure to look properly, careless or reckless driving, loss of control of the vehicle or travelling too fast for the conditions.

People who drive at work are more likely to be involved in a collision than those who don't:

- Over a quarter of all road traffic incidents involve someone who's driving as part of their work.

If you fall into both of these categories – driving at work and being a young driver – this increases your vulnerability.

As a police driver, your work may put you on the road when drivers may take greater risks, for example on weekend evenings.

In addition, for police and other emergency services drivers, driving in an operational environment involves multi-tasking. This can distract attention from the driving task.

Critical learning from experience

To become a better driver, the first step is to recognise the resistance in ourselves to accepting responsibility. The second step is to accept every near miss and collision as a learning opportunity to assess how you can avoid the same mistake in future.

The habit of driving too close to the vehicle in front, or tailgating, shows why we tend not to recognise or change risky behaviour. This is one of the commonest causes of vehicle collisions. As risky actions like this don't always end in a collision, they quickly become bad habits, which increase the chances that one day the driver will be involved in a collision.

Most drivers involved in a collision don't accept that they contributed to it. If you think that you didn't cause a collision, you'll also think that you have nothing to learn from it, and so your driving behaviour won't change.

Tailgating is so common that many drivers see no risk in it. But a common cause of rear-end shunts is when the vehicle in front brakes sharply and the vehicle behind can't stop in time.

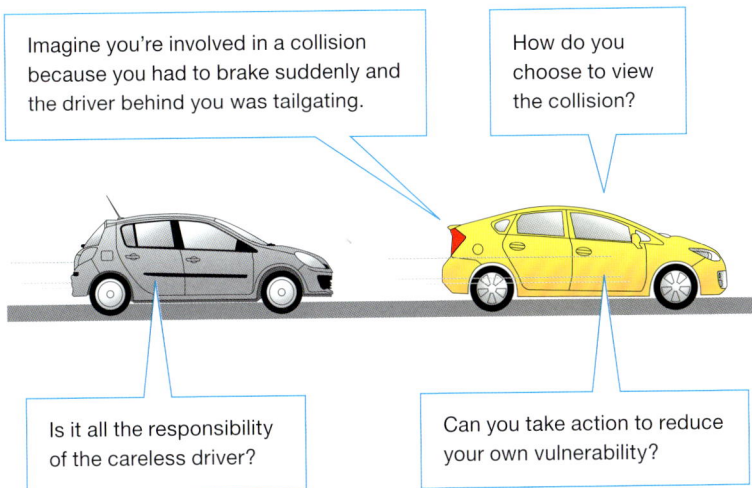

You can choose to reduce your chances of this type of collision. If the driver behind is too close, you can decide to increase your own following distance. This allows you and the driver behind more time to brake. Why did you have to brake suddenly? Using good observation to anticipate hazards should help you to avoid sudden braking – this will also reduce your risk from a tailgating driver.

See Chapter 4, Information, observation and anticipation.

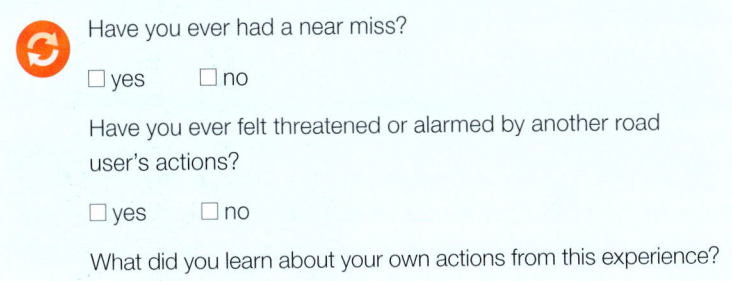

Develop awareness of your personal vulnerability

To develop your awareness of risks and your ability to honestly assess your own driving, it can be helpful to think about the driving task in terms of four different levels. It's useful to think about these separately at the start of the learning process but the goal of learning and practice is to integrate them.

Four levels of the driving task

The four levels set out in the European Goals for Driver Education (GDE) are:

- human factors that affect your driving
- the purpose and context of your journey
- traffic situations
- vehicle and vehicle control.

See Appendix 4, Goals for Driver Education, page 296.

When you first learned to drive, you started with the basic skills of vehicle control. With practice, you gradually combined smaller skill elements until they became automatic. Once you had mastered the basic controls and manoeuvring skills, you were able to concentrate on traffic situations, learning to anticipate and respond to hazards. Eventually you built up and integrated these complex skills and competences until you were able to drive safely in traffic and plan and make journeys independently.

But the most important point about the learning process is that we're not a blank canvas when we learn to drive. We bring to the task our personality, our life experiences, our beliefs about the world and our own attitudes to driving based on what we've seen as pedestrians or passengers. These factors all have a strong influence on how we learn to drive, how we make decisions on the road and our chances of being involved in a collision.

Let's consider the four levels in more depth:

- **Human factors** – your personal characteristics can increase or reduce your risk of a collision compared to other drivers. Your attitude to your own vulnerability and to other road users, and your emotions, mood and levels of tiredness or stress all affect your driving behaviour. Learn to recognise personal tendencies that increase your risk and find ways to manage them.

See Appendix 1, I AM SAFE checklist, page 290, to make sure you are fit to drive.

- **The journey** – each journey you make has a purpose and involves decisions and judgements: what preparation is needed, which route is best, what distractions there are and how to minimise them. The ability to deal with operational distractions is vital for police and other emergency services drivers. Assess the risks of the journey and your own fitness to drive. Take account of these in the way you manage each journey.

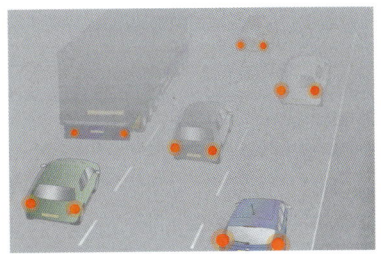

If there is heavy fog, ice or snow, ask yourself: 'Is my journey really necessary?'

- **The traffic** – training will increase your hazard perception skills and your ability to negotiate your way safely through traffic. It will develop your competence at scanning the road and anticipating hazards, and increase your awareness of the risks that drivers face in traffic. Situational awareness is essential for all drivers. Allow your senses to provide you with information and help you maintain an accurate picture of your environment.

- **The vehicle** – a vital part of knowing your own limitations as a driver is knowing exactly what the vehicle you're driving can and cannot do. Take time to familiarise yourself with a vehicle before you drive it. Check the vehicle is fit to drive. Check its condition (for example, lights, tyre tread depth, brakes), its capabilities, its safety features, and how to use the controls correctly. Make the mental adjustments necessary if you regularly drive another vehicle.

See Chapter 2, Advanced driver-assistance systems, for more information about vehicle safety features.

See Appendix 2, POWDER checklist, page 292, to make sure your vehicle is fit to drive.

The table below shows how you can use these four levels of the GDE matrix to consider your personal risks and assess your driving in a structured way.

	Potential risks	Possible self-assessment questions
Human factors	Personal tendencies, motives or attitudes that might affect your driving. Risks might include a risk-taking or impulsive personality, operational stress, competitiveness, overconfidence in driving ability, justifying risk-taking for a noble cause, or distraction caused by deeper stresses such as family or financial problems.	How easy is it to detach yourself from wider problems or stresses when you get into a vehicle? Do you tend to react to or disengage from other road users' aggressive behaviour? Do you know how operational stress affects your driving?
Journey	Risks could include an unfamiliar route, time pressure, peer pressure, distraction due to multi-tasking, 'red mist' or fatigue.	Are you fit to drive? What can you do to reduce the risk of general distractions? Of distractions from operational tasks?
Traffic	Maintain a high level of alertness in traffic, scanning the road so you can anticipate what's likely to happen next. Risks could include loss of concentration, failure to look properly or weather conditions.	What are the traffic, road and weather conditions? How should you adjust your driving for the conditions?
Vehicle	Always drive within your vehicle's capabilities. An unfamiliar vehicle increases your risk.	Is the vehicle fit to drive? Are the seat and steering wheel adjusted for best position and comfort? Do you know how its safety features behave?

Human factor risks for emergency services drivers

Police and other emergency services drivers have to deal with demanding and difficult situations in the course of their work. Certain human factors linked to the nature of the job can put you at risk:

- distraction due to multi-tasking and in-vehicle technology
- driving stress
- operational stressors
- time pressure and the purpose of the journey
- 'noble cause' risk-taking
- 'red mist'.

Distraction due to multi-tasking

Operational driving requires emergency services drivers to deal with multiple tasks. The demands on your attention from radios and other technologies, the operational tasks and even passengers can be intrusive. Be aware that your vulnerability increases if you fail to focus on the primary task of driving safely. Even minor distractions can severely impair your ability to anticipate hazards.

Where possible, ask a passenger to operate in-vehicle technology. In some circumstances, you may need to override technologies such as lane-assist systems to avoid distraction.

Driving stress

All drivers are vulnerable to driving stress, especially emergency services drivers who regularly deal with difficult and hazardous situations. During a demanding or difficult drive where brain processing is already stretched to the limit, operational stressors can overload the system and impair your decisions and judgement. Training aims to increase your information-processing and problem-solving effectiveness. This gives you more time to think and complete the driving task efficiently, which helps reduce the effects of driving stress.

Deeper stresses can also affect your driving. For example, a driver may be dealing with heavy demands in their personal life. Family problems, financial difficulties or even a new baby can increase chronic stress and fatigue, and impair concentration and driving performance.

We each respond differently, so what you find stressful may not be stressful for a colleague, and vice versa. Learn to recognise your personal stressors – the things that you believe could impair your driving.

Operational stressors

Emergency services drivers are also exposed to several types of operational stress:

- the anticipatory stress of facing a difficult or demanding task (for example, anxiety about what you'll find on arrival at an incident)
- the 'adrenaline rush' arising from a sudden event such as an emergency call-out: a degree of arousal enhances performance but, beyond this optimum level, alertness and concentration tend to fall away
- stress related to aspects of the task – difficult traffic or weather conditions, navigation problems, lack of advance detail about an incident, time pressure and the length of time you spend exposed to risk
- the stress of being in a situation in which you or others may be exposed to extreme hazards
- stress arising from repeated exposure to distressing incidents in the past; aspects of a current situation may 'prompt' recall of distressing memories and the effect may impair current decision-making and judgement
- preoccupation with a previous error of judgement
- stress from other work factors: working long shifts or night shifts, peer pressure or difficult working relationships can affect driving performance.

Under pressure, in difficult and demanding conditions, stress and tiredness can cause the release of powerful negative feelings:

- impatience – through a desire to get to the incident quickly
- intolerance – a belief that the importance of the task automatically gives the police driver priority over other road users
- impulsiveness – rushing decisions because time is short
- anger or frustration – for example, at other road users getting in your way
- personalisation – getting into personal conflict with another road user.

Learn to recognise when these reactions are affecting your judgement. You can then make a conscious decision to disengage from them.

There's more about dealing with tiredness in Chapter 4, Information, observation and anticipation.

Practical steps to combat stress

Be aware that stress is cumulative. Research shows that repeated exposure to stress can increase the chances of a collision and, in more severe cases, susceptibility to stress-related illness. Look after your health – getting regular exercise and learning to relax can help reduce chronic stress.

- Adjust the seat and steering wheel so that you are not physically tense or uncomfortable.
- Use the techniques you learn in training and practise them continually – well-learned techniques are less likely to break down under stressful conditions. This is an advantage of using the system of car control (Chapter 3).
- Maintain a calm professional approach to your driving – especially in an emergency situation.
- Learn techniques to help you focus on your driving and switch off other problems when you get into your vehicle.
- After a journey, reflect on any stressful experiences or errors of judgement, but don't dwell on them.

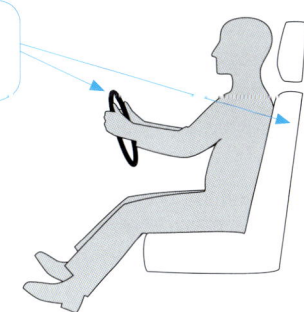

Time pressure and the purpose of your journey

Police and other emergency services drivers are trained to respond to urgent calls without taking undue risks. But it's a fact that drivers who feel their journey is urgent, because of organisational time pressure or the purpose of the journey, tend to respond less safely to hazards and take more risks. A sense of urgency doesn't give the right to take risks.

> No emergency is so great that it justifies the possibility of injuring or killing someone. It is better to arrive later than not at all.
>
> A sense of urgency doesn't give you the right to take risks or to use a lack of proportionality in judgements.

'Noble cause' risk-taking

Never justify risk-taking by telling yourself that the risk is for a noble cause – to help someone else, or to catch a person suspected of a crime.

If you're tempted to take risks in an emergency, **STOP**. Think about the consequences for yourself and other people if you crash and fail to arrive. You will be of no help to the people in need. If you injure yourself or someone else on the way, you will have turned an emergency into two emergencies and a possible tragedy. And you will have to live with the consequences of what you've done.

'Red mist'

'Red mist' is a colloquial term used to describe the state of mind of drivers who become determined to achieve some objective on the journey – catching the vehicle in front, or getting to an incident in the shortest possible time. Fixed attention on a particular goal (sometimes referred to as 'target fixation') can lead to blindness to other potential hazards, such as pedestrians or other vehicles at intersections. This means a driver is at best less able and at worst no longer capable of realistically assessing driving risks.

The key to preventing 'red mist' is to concentrate on the driving task in hand rather than on the incident. You'll need to develop your own strategy for achieving this, but there are some steps you can take:

- Don't get into a personality conflict with another road user.
- Be dispassionate and concentrate on your driving – use neutral, non-aggressive language to describe other road users (to yourself and others).
- Don't try and imagine what you'll find at the incident – assess the situation when you get there.
- Concentrate on driving – talking yourself through the hazards you identify can help you to focus on the driving task and keep negative emotions under control.

'Red mist' means your attention is not on your driving but on some specific goal; you've become emotionally and physiologically caught up in the incident.

How you learn

You'll find it easier to improve your driving ability and safety if you understand how you learn and apply new competences. The basic requirements are training, practice, feedback and experience.

Training, practice and feedback

Roadcraft training mirrors the process by which you learned the basic driving skills to pass your test. At first, manoeuvres such as changing gear or turning round in the road demand all your attention. But when you've mastered the basic controls and skills, you can give more of your attention to the road and traffic conditions. You'll improve your ability to anticipate and respond to hazards, and learn to use the system of car control and other routines so that you can respond rapidly, safely and flexibly to the demands of police driving.

Driver training can accelerate your learning, enabling you to develop your critical awareness and competences that you might otherwise never possess. It can draw your attention to risky driving behaviour and to parts of a task or ways of doing things that you were unaware of. But practice is the only way in which new competences become integrated, automatic and readily available when you need them. Practice will steadily develop your core driving competences at all levels.

See Appendix 4, Goals for Driver Education, page 296.

To develop these competences to a high standard, you also need continuous feedback on the effects of your actions. At first you'll need feedback from your instructor, but from the outset you should critically review all your actions. You'll be expected to continuously assess your own driving behaviour and performance. Your aim is to develop your own internal feedback – your ability to question, honestly self-assess and modify your actions – whenever you drive.

Overconfidence after training

Overconfidence in the period after training is a risk you should be aware of. Don't underestimate the amount of practice that's required to develop your driving competence to the highest possible standard. You'll encounter many new traffic and operational situations as an emergency services driver and lack of experience in dealing with these situations means that you're vulnerable.

Overconfidence can take you into situations you can't handle and will increase your risk of a collision. Drivers can overestimate their abilities in various ways:

- With increased training comes the feeling that the task of driving is automatic and relatively easy, but the operational demands of the job mean greater demands on your attention from radios, etc. This can lead to attention overload, making you less likely to notice hazards and more likely to crash.
- Less experienced drivers tend to believe their hazard perception is better than it actually is, when measured objectively.

Chapter 2
Advanced driver-assistance systems

Learning outcomes

The learning in this chapter, along with driver training, should enable you to:

- explain the purpose of advanced driver-assistance systems (ADAS)
- explain in general terms how ADAS work on a vehicle
- explain how ADAS help the driver
- identify the types of ADAS technologies that may apply to your vehicle.

What are ADAS?

Advanced driver-assistance systems (ADAS) are technologies that assist you with driving. The various features can help you avoid collisions by alerting you to potential dangers and, in some cases, intervening to take evasive action.

How do ADAS work?

Vehicles with ADAS fitted use cameras, radar and other sensors that combine to monitor your surroundings. When the system perceives a danger, it may send you a visual or audio signal, or even a vibration through the steering wheel or seat. In some cases, it may intervene and take control of the vehicle. The system may also make adjustments to maximise your vehicle's stability.

You can think of ADAS as your vehicle's senses; they help your vehicle detect things around it, whether they're other vehicles, pedestrians or obstacles like potholes or rubbish bins. Sensors can quickly spot objects around your vehicle and figure out where they are, how fast they're moving, and in which direction. This may help your vehicle react faster than you could, especially in complex traffic situations.

The systems can also provide information in poor driving conditions. Whether it's raining, foggy or dark outside, these sensors don't get tired or distracted, giving your vehicle the ability to gather information even in low-visibility situations, which can help you spot a hidden obstacle that might be difficult to see on your own.

ADAS do, however, have limitations. They may struggle in extreme weather conditions or give off false alarms. They may not anticipate unpredictable behaviours, such as a child darting onto the road or another driver making an erratic move. ADAS features might feel intrusive, but they are designed to assist drivers, not to take over or reduce the need for focused attention.

Why do ADAS matter?

ADAS matter because, as the technology becomes increasingly commonplace, you can expect them to be a feature of your toolkit as a driver. Many vehicles are already fitted with them, and the number and types of features are expanding. Additionally, these systems are increasingly being developed to interact with each other to further enhance the range of tools available to you as a driver.

The kind of help these systems can give you includes:

- putting safety first – by tracking the movements of other vehicles, people and objects around your vehicle, the sensors can alert you to potential dangers before you even notice them; this could be as simple as warning you about a car in your blind spot, or braking automatically if someone steps into the road
- driver-assistance functions – the technology acts like a co-pilot; for example, keeping your vehicle centred in your lane or guiding you into a parking spot
- heightened awareness – the system can tell the difference between something small, like a bike, and something bigger, like a car or lorry; this extra awareness helps your vehicle react better in a variety of driving scenarios.

Think of ADAS as a co-pilot, not a replacement

Imagine ADAS as a helpful co-pilot; they give you extra information and assistance, like monitoring your blind spots or helping with parking.

Don't assume they can make judgement calls or replace the need for a fully attentive driver.

Maintain a proactive approach to driving to be better equipped to handle any situation, whether ADAS work flawlessly or encounter a limitation.

ADAS features at a glance

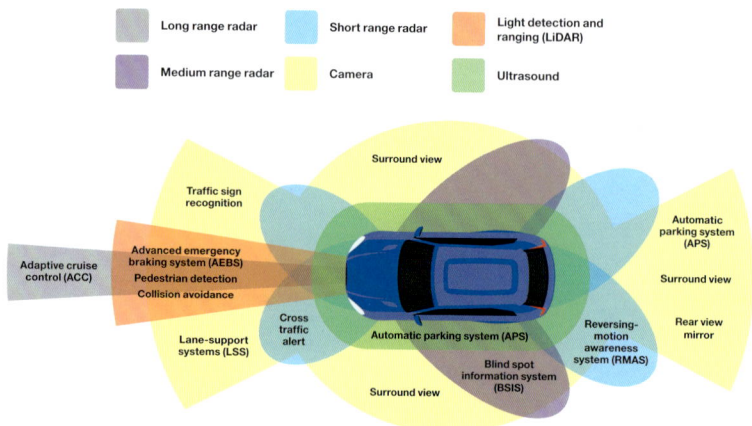

Diagram showing examples of ADAS

This table summarises many of the ADAS features and how they can help you. They are explained in more detail on the pages following this table. However, be sure to refer to your vehicle's handbook.

Remember that ADAS are evolving technologies and the list will continue to grow.

Feature	How it helps you
Adaptive cruise control (ACC)	Intelligently controls your cruise speed by monitoring the traffic ahead of you.
Adaptive front-lighting system (AFS)	Automatically turns the headlight beams depending on the direction you steer and other factors.
Adaptive light control (ALC)	Adjusts the headlight beam according to oncoming traffic and the vehicles in front.
Advanced/autonomous emergency braking system (AEBS)	Warns you and automatically brakes if a frontal collision is imminent.

Automatic parking system (APS)	Detects a suitable parking space and manoeuvres the vehicle into it with minimal input from the driver.
Blind spot information system (BSIS)	Uses sensors to let you know there is another vehicle in your blind spot.
Drowsiness and attention warning (DAW)	Monitors your behaviour and checks for signs of possible distraction or fatigue.
Electronic stability programmes (ESP)	Helps improve stability and directional control by adjusting power and braking inputs, with various levels of sophistication.
Emergency brake assist (EBA)	Helps avoid a collision by automatically adding pressure when the driver brakes but does not apply enough pressure.
Emergency stop signal (ESS)	Activates your vehicle's brake lights or rear indicators to flash at a high frequency.
Hands-off detection (HOD)	Designed to keep your hands on the steering wheel.
Hill-start assist (HSA)	Helps prevent your vehicle rolling backwards when starting on an incline.
Intelligent speed assistance/intelligent speed adaption (ISA)	Helps you stay below the speed limit.
Lane-support systems (LSS)	Helps you maintain proper lane discipline, to reduce the likelihood of lane-departure collisions.
Moving-off information system (MOIS)	Alerts the driver to pedestrians or cyclists within the blind spot in front of a large vehicle.
Reversing-motion awareness system (RMAS)	Helps prevent collisions when reversing via ways such as warnings, braking and steering.
Tyre-pressure monitoring system (TPMS)	Alerts to you a change in tyre pressure.
Unresponsive-driver intervention	May take control of the vehicle if the driver stops responding to the road or loses control due to drowsiness, distraction or a medical emergency.
Vehicle-to-everything (V2X)	Allows vehicles to share information with their surroundings.

ADAS features in more detail

The following is a description of many of the constantly evolving ADAS features. While they are listed as separate systems here, remember that they may communicate and work with each other in various driving situations.

There will be differences from manufacturer to manufacturer and vehicle to vehicle in how each feature behaves, and how much autonomy each feature provides. There may also be differences in the terminology used. Refer to your vehicle's handbook for more information.

Adaptive cruise control

Adaptive cruise control (ACC) is a development of earlier cruise control systems. It automatically adjusts the selected speed in relation to vehicles in front and maintains a constant following distance.

ACC has other names such as active cruise control, radar cruise control, autonomous cruise control and intelligent cruise control.

See Chapter 8, page 150, Controlling your vehicle's stability.

Adaptive front-lighting system

The adaptive front-lighting system (AFS) automatically adjusts the direction and intensity of your vehicle's headlights based on factors such as the direction you are steering and your speed, as well as weather conditions and road curvature. In some vehicles, additional cornering lights installed in the front corners of the vehicle may be activated in response to you steering or using your indicators.

Adaptive light control

Adaptive light control (ALC) can reduce the likelihood of other drivers being dazzled by your headlights by automatically adjusting the headlight beam according to oncoming traffic and the vehicles you are travelling behind.

Advanced/autonomous emergency braking system

The advanced/autonomous emergency braking system (AEBS) senses when a collision is imminent (for example, with a vehicle ahead or with a pedestrian or cyclist crossing the road) and automatically brakes if you take no action.

You should be aware that AEBS may only operate at low speed. Consult your vehicle's manual.

Automatic parking system

The automatic parking system (APS) helps manoeuvre your vehicle into a parking spot with minimal input from you. It can assist you with various parking situations, depending on the system's capabilities. It may, however, struggle in poorly marked spaces, on uneven terrain or in adverse weather conditions.

Blind spot information system

The blind spot information system (BSIS) aims to let you know there are other road users like cyclists, motorcycles and cars in your blind spot. The alerts may be visual, audible or vibrational.

You should note that BSIS:

- should not be used in place of using your mirrors, or looking over your shoulder before changing lanes
- may not work properly in severe weather conditions
- is not designed to detect parked vehicles, pedestrians, animals or infrastructure

Drowsiness and attention warning

Drowsiness and attention warning (DAW) systems monitor your behaviour, gaze direction and blink frequency to check for signs of possible distraction or fatigue, alerting you if necessary. The DAW system examines, for example, how long you've been on the road, your driving patterns, or the time of day; if you're driving erratically, swerving or taking longer to react, it might be a sign that you're tired or distracted.

If the system detects signs of drowsiness or distraction, it will sound a warning, usually a beeping sound or visual alert on your dashboard. Some systems also recommend that you take a break, giving you a reminder to stay refreshed and focused.

Electronic stability programmes

Electronic stability programmes (ESP) are active safety systems that incorporate anti-lock braking and traction control systems, which are designed to help improve stability and directional control. ESP are becoming more sophisticated and are likely to incorporate more variables as the technology develops.

See Chapter 8, page 154, Electronic stability programmes.

Emergency brake assist

Emergency brake assist (EBA) increases braking pressure in an emergency situation.

See Chapter 6, page 131, Emergency brake assist.

Emergency stop signal

Emergency stop signal (ESS) is a safety feature that activates your vehicle's brake lights and/or rear indicators to flash at a high frequency if you brake hard, or brake suddenly at a higher speed, or if ABS or EBA is activated.

You should be prepared to act if ever you notice this on another vehicle.

Hands-off detection

Hands-off detection (HOD) uses a steering wheel sensor to detect if you have at least one hand on the wheel, and signals you if not.

Hill-start assist

Hill-start assist (HSA), also known as hill hold or hill control, helps prevent vehicles rolling backwards when starting on an incline. After you release the brake pedal, it maintains brake pressure for a few moments, allowing you time to accelerate without rolling back.

Intelligent speed assistance

Intelligent speed assistance (ISA) helps you manage your speed by notifying you of the current speed limit. It uses a camera and satellite navigation to detect speed signs and track local limits. Some systems prevent the vehicle driving at a higher speed than the limit, unless overridden.

Lane-support systems

Lane-support systems (LSS) (also known as lane departure warning) help to keep you safely in your lane. If your vehicle drifts relative to the road's lane markings, the system signals you to get your attention. The point where the system starts operating can vary from vehicle to vehicle.

LSS rely on the visibility of lane markings, so may not work in poor weather, on faded or obstructed markings, or in areas without defined lanes.

Moving-off information system

Intended mainly for larger vehicles, the moving-off information system (MOIS) alerts the driver to the presence of pedestrians or cyclists within the blind spot in front of the vehicle when the vehicle is stationary, moving off from rest, or travelling straight ahead at low speeds.

Reversing-motion awareness system

The reversing-motion awareness system (RMAS) uses cameras, sensors and alarms to provide information about obstacles or people behind the vehicle. They are activated when the driver selects reverse gear.

In confined spaces, consider using another person as a guide (or 'banksman') when carrying out forward and reverse manoeuvres.

See Chapter 7, page 144, Reversing in a confined space, and page 146, Manoeuvring with a guide.

Tyre-pressure monitoring system

The tyre-pressure monitoring system (TPMS) helps you keep track of the air pressure in your tyres. If the TPMS warning appears, use a tyre-pressure gauge to measure the tyre indicated and adjust the air pressure to the appropriate level.

> Even with TPMS, check the condition of your tyres and your tyre pressure regularly.

See Chapter 6, page 103, The tyre grip trade-off.

Unresponsive-driver intervention

An unresponsive-driver intervention system helps when the driver stops responding to the road or loses control due to drowsiness, distraction or a medical emergency. This system is designed to prevent collisions by taking over the vehicle if necessary.

The system uses a driver-monitoring system (DMS) to check if the driver is paying attention. It looks for signs like hands not being on the steering wheel, no steering inputs for a long time, or eyes closed or not looking at the road (in some systems).

If the driver doesn't respond to warnings (like beeping or vibrating alerts), the system assumes that the driver is unresponsive and so may:

- turn on hazard lights to alert nearby vehicles
- gradually reduce speed to bring the vehicle to a stop
- park the vehicle in its lane or a safe spot on the side of the road
- contact emergency services or use the vehicle's connectivity features to alert someone.

Vehicle-to-everything

Vehicle-to-everything (V2X) is a technology that can give vehicles the ability to communicate with the world around them. It can be used, for example, to communicate with traffic lights, to operate bus priority systems or to take account of approaching emergency vehicles.

Autonomous vehicles

A vehicle equipped with autonomous driving (AD) is one with a system that allows the vehicle to drive independently of the driver and may behave differently in some circumstances to a non-autonomous vehicle.

For more information, see **www.gov.uk/transport/self-driving-vehicles**

Check your understanding

You should now be able to apply learning from this chapter in your driver training so that you can:

- [ ] explain the purpose of advanced driver-assistance systems (ADAS)
- [ ] explain in general terms how ADAS work on a vehicle
- [ ] explain how ADAS help the driver
- [ ] identify the types of ADAS technologies that may apply to your vehicle.

Chapter 3

The system of car control

Learning outcomes

The learning in this chapter, along with driver training, should enable you to:

- explain the system of car control
- demonstrate how to apply the system to any hazards.

The need for a system of car control

This chapter explains the system of car control used in police driver training. It outlines the competences that will enhance your ability to master a wide range of traffic situations.

Driver error is a feature of nearly all collisions on the road. The system of car control aims to increase your safety by providing a systematic approach to hazards. It's a decision-making process that enables you to efficiently assess and act on information that is continuously changing as you drive. Using the system gives you more time to react, which is vital in complex and demanding driving situations.

If you use the system consistently with the information-processing, observation and anticipation skills discussed in Chapter 4, it will help you anticipate dangers caused by other road users and avoid collisions. Your progress will be steady and unobtrusive – the sign of a safe and competent driver.

Integrating a range of competences

As described in Chapter 1, driving to police standards requires more than just the ability to control your vehicle. It's essential to develop honest self-assessment of your own capabilities, understanding of traffic situations and 'situational awareness' – your ability to read the road. Many hazards that drivers meet are unpredictable. The system gives you a methodical way of processing information, and applying observation and anticipation so that you recognise and negotiate hazards safely.

See Chapter 1, Becoming a better driver.

Human factors/ the purpose of the journey

Take into account personal factors and attitudes and the goals of the journey that might influence your driving behaviour.

- Are you aware of your own driving abilities and limitations?

The traffic situation

Scan the environment, recognise, anticipate and prioritise hazards, and form an achievable driving plan.

- What are the prevailing weather and road conditions?
- How are other road users likely to behave?

Vehicle control

Translate intentions and thoughts into physical action – manoeuvre your vehicle accurately and smoothly.

- Are you familiar with the capabilities of your vehicle?

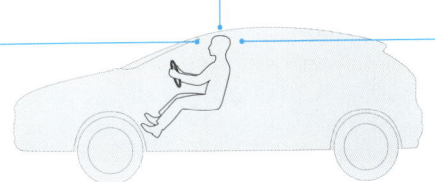

What is the system of car control?

The system of car control increases your safety in a constantly changing driving environment by giving you time to react to hazards.

> A hazard is anything that is an actual or potential danger.

See Chapter 4, page 59, What is a hazard?

The system of car control is a way of approaching and negotiating hazards that is methodical, safe and leaves nothing to chance. It involves careful observation, early anticipation and planning, and a systematic use of the controls to maintain your vehicle's stability in all situations.

Driving hazards fluctuate: they come singly and in clusters, they overlap and change all the time. The system takes account of this continual flux as:

- it has a centrally flexible element – you, the driver
- it draws together all levels of driving competence into a logical sequence of actions to help you deal with hazards and respond to new ones safely and efficiently.

How the system works

The system of car control consists of processing information and four phases – **position**, **speed**, **gear** and **acceleration**. Each phase develops out of the one before.

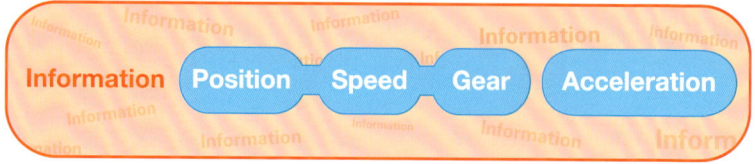

 Processing information is central to the system – it runs through and feeds into all the phases. Start by asking yourself:

- What information do I need to gather about the road conditions, the behaviour of other road users, and actual and potential dangers?
- What do other road users need to know about my intentions?

Then work through each of the phases in turn. As road conditions change, you'll need to process new information and this will mean re-entering the system at an appropriate point, then continuing through it in sequence. If a new hazard arises, re-apply the system and consider all the phases in sequence.

The importance of information

Your ability to process complex information is essential to becoming a better driver.

Processing information introduces the system and continues throughout. Remember **TUG** – **t**ake, **u**se and **g**ive information.

See Chapter 4, page 54, Processing complex information.

You need to:

- take and use information to plan your driving
- give information whenever other road users could benefit from it.

| Take | Use | Give |

Information

Develop your competence at assessing the continuous flow of information. This competence underpins the entire system and enables you to adapt it to changes in road circumstances.

See Chapter 9, Driver's signals.

Mirrors and signals

Whenever you consider changing position or speed, always check first what is happening to the front, sides and behind you. You must check your mirrors at this point.

Give a signal whenever it could benefit another road user. Sound your horn when you think another road user could benefit but remember its purpose is to tell other people you are there – not to rebuke them.

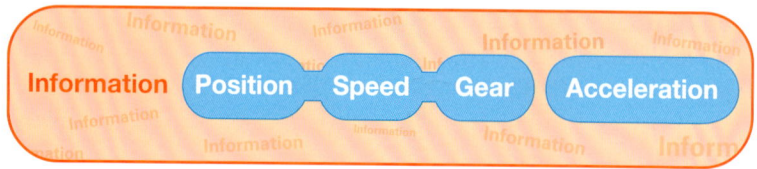

The system of car control

The system of car control is set out in detail here. Use this information in conjunction with the other chapters in *Roadcraft* for a complete understanding of the system. When and how you read each chapter depends on your own study plan. If you're using *Roadcraft* as part of a course, ask your instructor for advice.

Information

Processing information runs throughout all phases of the system.

Take information

Look all round you. Scan to the front and sides, including your blind spots. Use your mirrors at appropriate points in the system.

Obtain information through your other senses as well as your eyes. Sounds such as a horn or siren can warn you of other road users. Smells such as diesel or a bonfire can alert you to hazards such as spills or smoke.

See Chapter 4, Information, observation and anticipation.

Use information

Use information to plan how to deal with the hazards you identify. Use the system to decide on your next action. If new hazards arise, consider whether to rerun the system from an earlier phase.

See Chapter 4, page 60, Planning.

Give information

Give a signal if it could help other road users, including pedestrians and cyclists. Use indicators, the horn or flash your lights. For maximum benefit, give your warning signal in good time. You may also need to signal to override lane-changing technology.

Be aware that the position of your vehicle gives valuable information to other road users.

See Chapter 9, Driver's signals.

Position

Position yourself so that you can negotiate the hazard(s) safely and smoothly.

See Chapter 10, Positioning.

Take account of the size of your vehicle and other road users, including pedestrians, cyclists and children.

Speed

Adjust your speed as necessary. Use the accelerator or brake to give you the correct speed to complete the manoeuvre safely. Make good use of acceleration sense.

See Chapter 6, page 109, Acceleration sense.

Use your anticipation skills so that you make all adjustments in speed smoothly and steadily.

Gear

Once you have the correct speed for the circumstances, engage the appropriate gear for that speed.

See Chapter 6, page 113, Using the gears.

Brake/gear overlap can be used in specific circumstances. It must always be part of a planned approach. Please turn to page 49 for a full discussion of this point.

Acceleration

Apply the correct degree of acceleration to negotiate and leave the hazard safely.

Taking account of your speed, the presence of other road users, and the road and traffic conditions ahead, choose an appropriate point to accelerate safely and smoothly away from the hazard. Adjust acceleration to the circumstances.

See Chapter 6, page 105, Using the accelerator.

Continuously assessing information runs through every phase of the system.

Use the system flexibly

The system works if you use it intelligently and proactively and adapt it to circumstances as they arise:

- Consider all phases of the system on the approach to every hazard, but you may not need to use every phase in a particular situation.
- Take, use and give information throughout to constantly re-assess your plans.
- Be ready to return to an earlier phase of the system as new hazards arise.

With practice, the system will become second nature and form a sound basis for developing the finer points of your driving skill. It will help you process information, make decisions and plan your approach to hazards so that you're able to avoid, or give yourself plenty of time to react to, potential dangers.

See Chapter 4, page 54, Processing complex information.

Applying the system of car control

When you begin using the system, it may help to name each phase out loud as you enter it. After you practise using the system, review your performance:

- Do you take, use and give information throughout all phases? If not, what can you do to improve?
- What can you do to ensure you consider each phase systematically?
- Do you think about all aspects of each phase?

Where you've identified problems in using the system, work through them one by one, solving the first before you go on to the next.

Also, think about human factors that might create difficulties in using the system, such as work pressure, stress or tiredness. If you're distracted or preoccupied, consider giving a running commentary to help you to focus on working through the system as you approach each hazard.

We now look at how you can apply the system to four common hazards: a left-hand turn, a right-hand turn, a roundabout, and a potential hazard – in this case, children on the pavement. Before you look at these examples, make sure you know the *Highway Code* advice on road junctions and roundabouts.

Applying the system to a left-hand turn

Information

Take information and identify hazards. What can you see in the junction? What's the current traffic flow? What hazards are visible or anticipated? Use your mirrors throughout. Scan to the front, sides and rear, and check your blind spot to know the position of other road users and anticipate their intentions. Give a signal at any point where this could help other road users, including pedestrians and cyclists.

Know what is going on all around you, and let other road users know what you intend to do. You must take, use and give information before you change speed or direction.

Position

Consider the size of your vehicle and the presence of pedestrians. Adapt to the road and traffic conditions. In a larger vehicle, take a central position on your side of the road or, if necessary, consider positioning further to the right. In a smaller vehicle, consider a position towards the left of the road.

Acceleration

Depress the accelerator to maintain road speed round the corner. Choose the appropriate point to accelerate safely and smoothly away from the hazard, paying attention to the amount of acceleration, the nature of the road and road surface, traffic conditions ahead, and the position and movement of other road users.

See Chapter 6, page 105, Using the accelerator.

Gear

Once you have the correct speed for the circumstances, engage the appropriate gear for that speed.

See Chapter 6, page 113, Using the gears.

See page 50 for further discussion of braking and gear changing on a left-hand turn.

Speed

Adjust your speed to the conditions. Use the accelerator or brake to give you the correct speed to complete the turn. Use acceleration sense. Generally a left turn is slower than a right because the turning arc is tighter.

Chapter 3 – The system of car control 45

Applying the system to a right-hand turn

Information

Take information and identify hazards. How far ahead is the junction? What can you see in the junction? Use your mirrors throughout. Look to the front, sides and rear, and check your blind spot to know the position of other road users and anticipate their intentions. Give a signal at any point where this could help other road users, including pedestrians and cyclists.

Acceleration

Depress the accelerator to maintain road speed round the corner.

Choose the appropriate point to accelerate safely and smoothly away from the hazard, paying attention to the amount of acceleration, the nature of the road and road surface, traffic conditions ahead, and the position and movement of other road users.

Gear

Once you have the correct speed for the circumstances, engage the appropriate gear for that speed.

Position

Alter your position to make the turn in good time. The usual position would be towards the centre of the road, but think about:

- the size of your vehicle
- the width of the road
- lane markings
- hazards in the road
- the speed, size and position of other vehicles
- the flow of traffic behind you
- getting a good view
- making your intentions clear to other road users.

Speed

Adjust your speed to the conditions. Use the accelerator or brake to give you the correct speed to complete the turn. Use acceleration sense.

See Chapter 6, page 109, Acceleration sense.

Applying the system to a roundabout

Information

Take information and identify hazards. Use your mirrors throughout. Scan to the front, sides and rear, and check your blind spot to know the position of other road users and anticipate their intentions.

Decide early which exit to take and in which lane to approach the roundabout.

Give a signal when it could help other road users.

Take an early view of traffic on the roundabout and traffic approaching it from other entrances.

As you approach the roundabout, be prepared to stop but look for your opportunity to go.

Acceleration

Choose an appropriate gap in the traffic to accelerate safely and smoothly onto the roundabout without disrupting traffic already using it. When you are on the roundabout, deal with any new hazards using the appropriate phases of the system.

Gear

Choose the appropriate gear to move forward onto the roundabout. This will depend on your speed and the traffic conditions.

Speed

Adjust your speed to the conditions. Use the accelerator or brake to give the correct speed to approach the roundabout. Use acceleration sense.

Plan to stop, but look to go.

Position

Your approach position will depend on your intended exit and the number of approach lanes.

Re-applying the system to leave the roundabout

Information

As you leave the roundabout, re-apply the system. Plan the appropriate lane for your exit. If you need to move into the left-hand lane, check that your nearside road space is clear. Use your nearside mirror and check your blind spot. Signal left if it could benefit other road users.

Exit position

If there is more than one exit lane, choose the most appropriate, taking into account the position of other exiting vehicles. Move over in plenty of time for your exit.

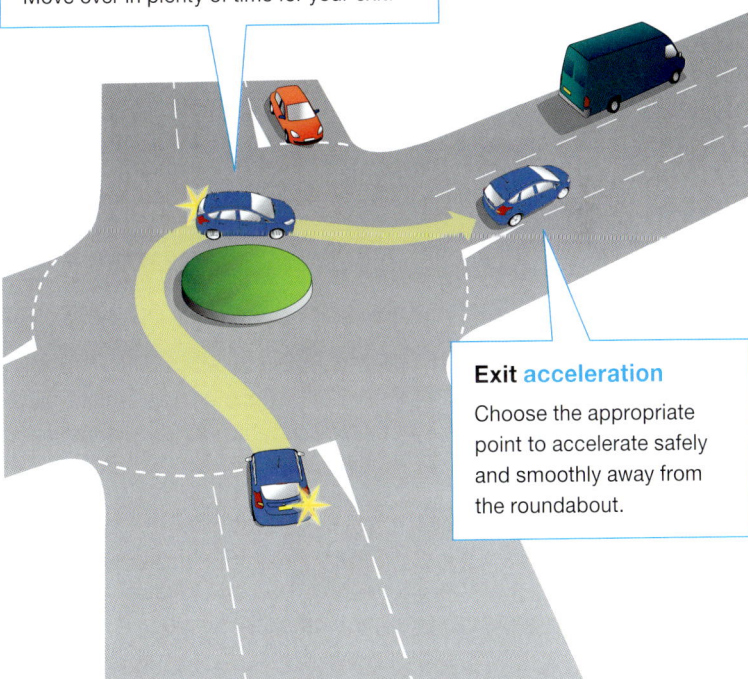

Exit acceleration

Choose the appropriate point to accelerate safely and smoothly away from the roundabout.

Applying the system to a potential hazard

Information

Use your mirrors throughout. Look to the front and sides to know the position of other road users and anticipate their intentions. Give a signal at any point where this could help other road users, including pedestrians and cyclists.

Acceleration

Accelerate safely and smoothly away once you have passed the hazard.

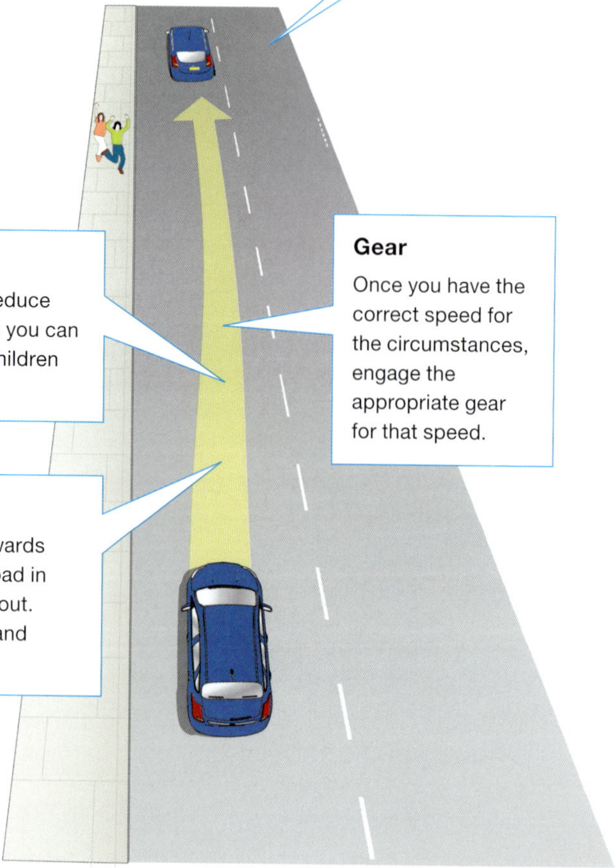

Speed

Use the brake to reduce your speed so that you can stop safely if the children step into the road.

Gear

Once you have the correct speed for the circumstances, engage the appropriate gear for that speed.

Position

Take a position towards the centre of the road in case a child steps out. Adapt to the road and traffic conditions.

Overlapping braking and gear changing

The individual phases of the system of car control are usually applied separately. The principle is that brakes are to **slow**, gears are to **go**.

In some circumstances, it may be helpful to overlap braking with the gear change by braking normally but changing the gear towards the end of braking.

> If you use this technique, it must be part of a planned approach to a hazard. *Begin applying the system at the same time and in the same place as you would normally.* The system isn't compressed.

When drivers first learn the system of car control, they separate braking and gear changing and try not to overlap. With tight turns, the problem with this approach is that if you brake some distance before the turn to avoid an overlap, you can confuse other drivers, with unexpected results. Drivers following you may think you are stopping and be tempted to overtake. Approaching drivers preparing to turn into the same junction may think you've slowed to leave space for them to turn ahead of you.

Situations where brake/gear overlap would be appropriate:

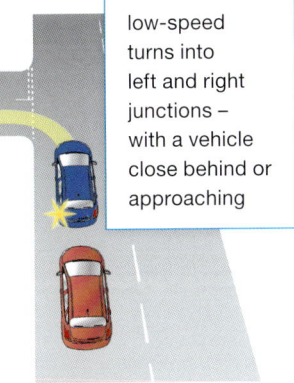

low-speed turns into left and right junctions – with a vehicle close behind or approaching

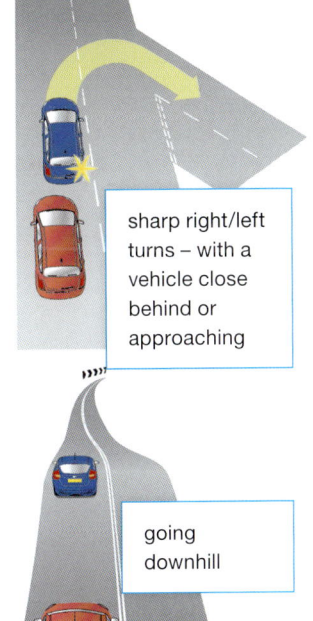

sharp right/left turns – with a vehicle close behind or approaching

going downhill

Brake/gear overlap – an example

Here's an example of using brake/gear overlap as a planned approach to a hazard, in order to maintain the correct speed.

If you turn left into a side road that's part of the way down a hill, the vehicle will start to accelerate when you take your foot off the brake. Instead, apply the system as normal up to and including the speed phase.

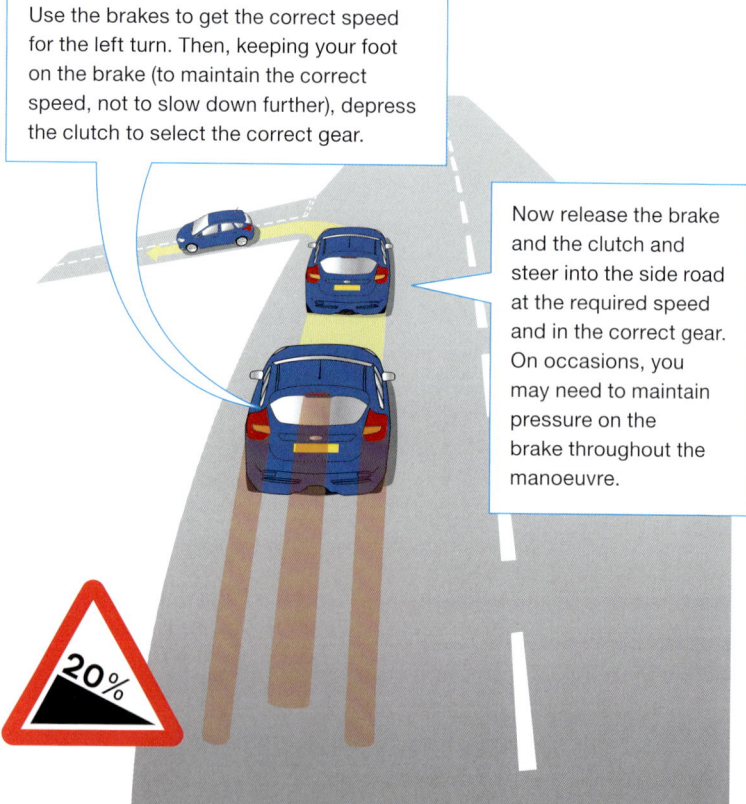

Use the brakes to get the correct speed for the left turn. Then, keeping your foot on the brake (to maintain the correct speed, not to slow down further), depress the clutch to select the correct gear.

Now release the brake and the clutch and steer into the side road at the required speed and in the correct gear. On occasions, you may need to maintain pressure on the brake throughout the manoeuvre.

Incorrect use of brake/gear overlap

Brake/gear overlap has had a bad reputation because it's frequently misused by drivers who approach a hazard too quickly:

- Overlap that isn't properly planned results in late, excessive braking and rushed gear changes.
- Braking late and rushing a gear change can destabilise your vehicle at exactly the point where you need greatest stability to negotiate the hazard.

But applied carefully in certain circumstances, brake/gear overlap takes less time.

Check your understanding

You should now be able to apply learning from this chapter in your driver training so that you can:

☐ explain the system of car control
☐ demonstrate how to apply the system to any hazards.

Chapter 4

Information, observation and anticipation

Learning outcomes

The learning in this chapter, along with driver training, should enable you to:

- explain how your brain processes information and how you can improve your ability to process complex information when driving
- explain the three main types of hazard you will meet on the road
- show how to use the information you gather from observation to plan your driving actions
- demonstrate good observation and anticipation skills
- identify human and physiological factors that can affect observation and anticipation, and show how you manage these.

Processing complex information

To develop your driving to police operational standards, you'll need to expand your ability to process complex information. Practice will help you to do this.

The diagram below is a simple model that explains how your brain processes the information that you receive through your senses when you drive. Your brain uses this information and past experience to understand the situation and decide what to do. It then continually monitors and, if necessary, adjusts the action as you carry it out:

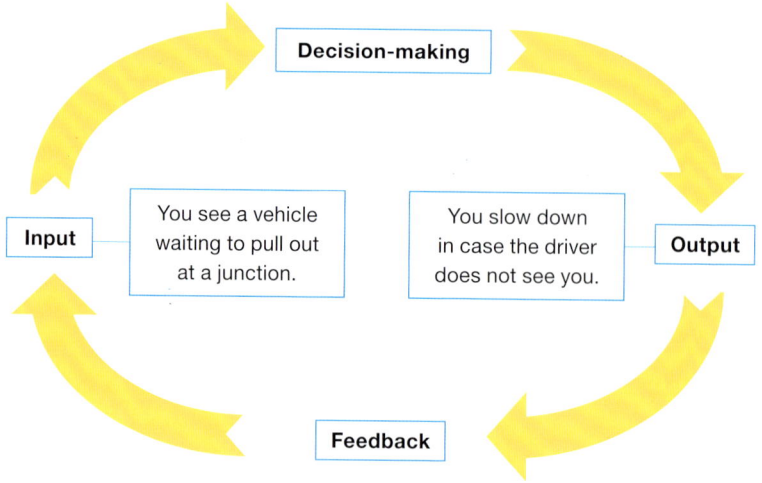

Input

Vision is the most important sense for driving but you should learn to use all your senses to build up the fullest possible picture of yourself, your surroundings and your situation. Your brain uses your observations – and information from your previous knowledge and experience that's stored in your long-term memory – to build up a detailed mental map or 'picture' of your situation.

Decision-making

Your brain compares this mental picture with situations from your experience, identifies what actions you took in the past and chooses a plan of action for the current situation.

Your brain assesses the suitability of the proposed plan by comparing it with actions that you've carried out safely in similar circumstances before. You use several types of judgement:

- anticipating how events are likely to unfold
- assessing the proposed plan for risk, noting hazards and grading them based on previous experience
- assessing your space, position, speed and gear.

Output

Take action – make an appropriate response.

Feedback

As you put your plan into action, your brain takes in new information and continuously checks it so that you can modify your actions at any time. Developing this ability to a high standard takes experience, practice, alertness and full concentration.

> The ability to judge a situation, grade risks and anticipate how things are likely to unfold is essential to safe driving, especially at high speeds.

Improving your information processing

The highly demanding nature of emergency services driving means that the brain's information-processing capacity can become overstretched, reducing driving performance and compromising safety. When information-processing capacity is stretched, it can lead to:

- increased reaction time
- errors of perception

- a decreased focus of attention
- issues with memory storage.

If you understand these, you can take steps to improve your information-processing ability.

Reaction time

Your reaction time is the time between gathering new information about a hazard and responding to it.

Reaction time = decision time + response time

Decision time is the time between observing the hazard and deciding what to do.

Response time is the time to start the physical response.

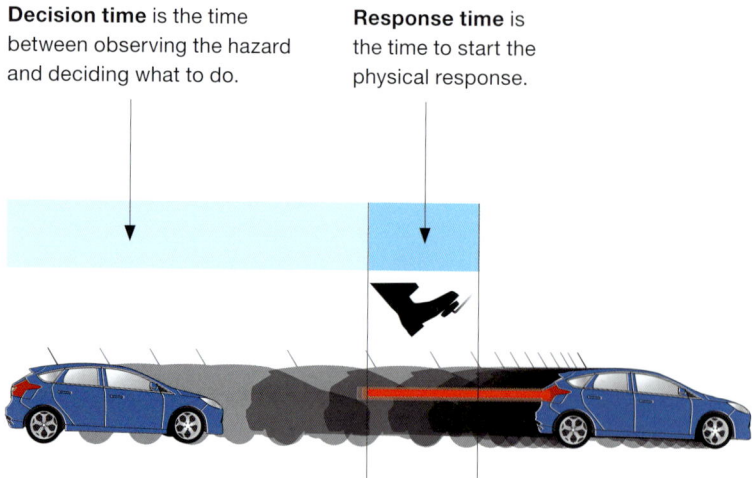

Most drivers have a similar response time but **they vary greatly in the amount of time they need to decide what to do**.

As situations become more complicated, you need more decision time and so your overall reaction time is also longer. As an emergency services driver, you may be dealing with situations requiring many complex decisions and judgements – often under pressure and at high speed – where a delayed reaction can have catastrophic results. The system of car control gives you a structured method for rapid decision-making. This reduces decision time and gives you more overall time to react in complex situations.

If you're using a radio, be aware that your reaction time for spotting hazards will be longer because of the greater demands on your attention. Take steps to reduce these demands wherever possible if you are also facing a particularly challenging driving situation.

Errors of perception

In demanding situations like high-speed driving, it's sometimes possible to misinterpret the information that you receive through your senses.

Common errors of perception are:

- **Errors of judgement** – for example, less experienced drivers often perceive a bend as being less sharp than it actually is so they negotiate it too quickly and risk loss of control or a collision.

  See Chapter 11, Cornering.

- **Errors of hazard perception** – drivers using a radio make perceptual errors such as looking directly at hazards but not seeing them because their attention is directed elsewhere.

- **Habit and expectancy** – when you drive regularly on familiar roads, habit can prevent you from spotting a hazard that you don't expect, such as a vehicle emerging from a disused garage forecourt.

- **Regression effects** – drivers who switch vehicles regularly can, when under a lot of pressure, revert to previously learned routines – for example, confusing the position of the controls. Do a pre-driving check to make sure you know where all the controls and technology devices are on an unfamiliar vehicle.

  See Appendix 2, Is your vehicle fit to drive?, page 291.

Focus of attention

Emergency services drivers have to process information from several different sources through different senses at the same time: road conditions, radio traffic, navigation, the mobile data terminal, the nature of the operation, and so on. Processing complex information can affect your perception and slow your reaction times. Distractions such as passengers or the radio may divert attention from more important information.

While training and practice can help you learn to filter complex information and concentrate on the priorities, it will not make you immune to distraction. Part of driving safely is having an understanding of how in-vehicle distractions can compromise safety, and taking steps to mitigate this wherever possible.

Memory storage

The brain can't always deal with all the information it receives. In complex and demanding situations, your brain may fail to process adequately the information your senses are bringing in. This means that the information may not pass into your long-term memory, so that you cannot recall it later.

Tips to improve information processing

- Regularly practise driving techniques and manoeuvres so that you can do them accurately and efficiently.
- Sharpen your observation and perception, and develop your situational awareness.
- Use the system of car control whenever you drive so that you make decisions methodically and quickly (Chapter 3).
- Learn to hold on to important pieces of information until you need them by repeating them, relating them to things you know well, or using other memory techniques.
- Try to avoid distraction so that you're focusing your full attention on the task in hand.

Why observation and anticipation are essential for better driving

The ability to process complex information will give you more time to anticipate hazards accurately when under pressure. An important goal of police driver training is to develop sophisticated anticipation skills.

Anticipation is the ability to identify hazards at the earliest possible opportunity.

Looking well ahead and anticipating potential hazards reduces fuel consumption by cutting down on unnecessary acceleration and braking.

See Appendix 3, Fuel-efficient driving, page 295.

What is a hazard?

A hazard is anything that is an actual or potential danger. It's useful to think in terms of three types of hazard:

- physical features (for example, junctions, bends, road surface)
- the position or movement of other road users (for example, drivers, cyclists, pedestrians)
- weather conditions (for example, icy road, poor visibility).

A hazard may be immediate and obvious, such as a car approaching you on the wrong side of the road. Or it might be something less obvious but just as dangerous – for example, a blind bend could conceal an obstacle in your path. Failing to recognise hazardous situations is a major cause of collisions.

Observation is a key component of anticipation. Careful observation allows you to spot hazards and give yourself extra time to think, anticipate and react. You can then deal with unfolding hazards before they develop into dangerous situations.

Sight is the most important sense for observation when driving. But also make full use of your other senses, such as:

> hearing (horn sounds, children)

> smell (e.g. new-mown grass could mean slow-moving grass-cutting machinery)

> physical sensations such as vibration (e.g. juddering from road surface irregularities).

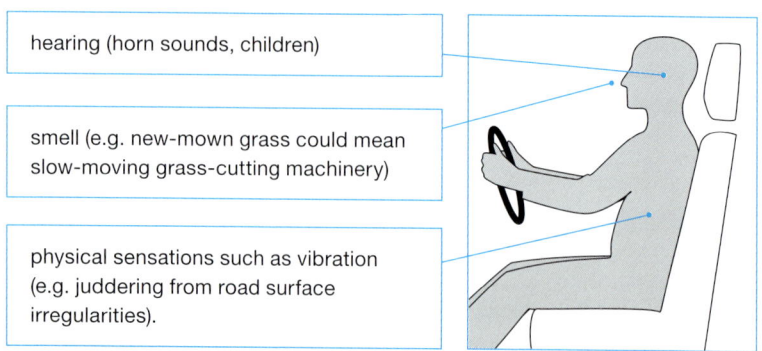

Good anticipation involves more than just good observation. It means 'reading' the road and extracting the fullest meaning from your observations. Remember that distraction can affect observation and hazard perception, making the anticipation of hazards much harder.

Planning

Safer driving depends on systematically using the information you gather from observation to plan your driving actions:

- anticipate hazards
- prioritise
- decide what to do.

Generally, things don't just happen; there's usually enough time to anticipate how a hazard might unfold. Good planning depends on early observation and early anticipation of risk.

The purpose of the plan is to put you:

- in the correct position
- at the correct speed
- with the correct gear engaged
- at the correct time

to negotiate hazards safely and efficiently.

As soon as conditions change, a new driving plan is required; effective planning is a continual process of forming and re-forming plans.

The diagram shows how the key stages of planning encourage you to interpret and act on your observations.

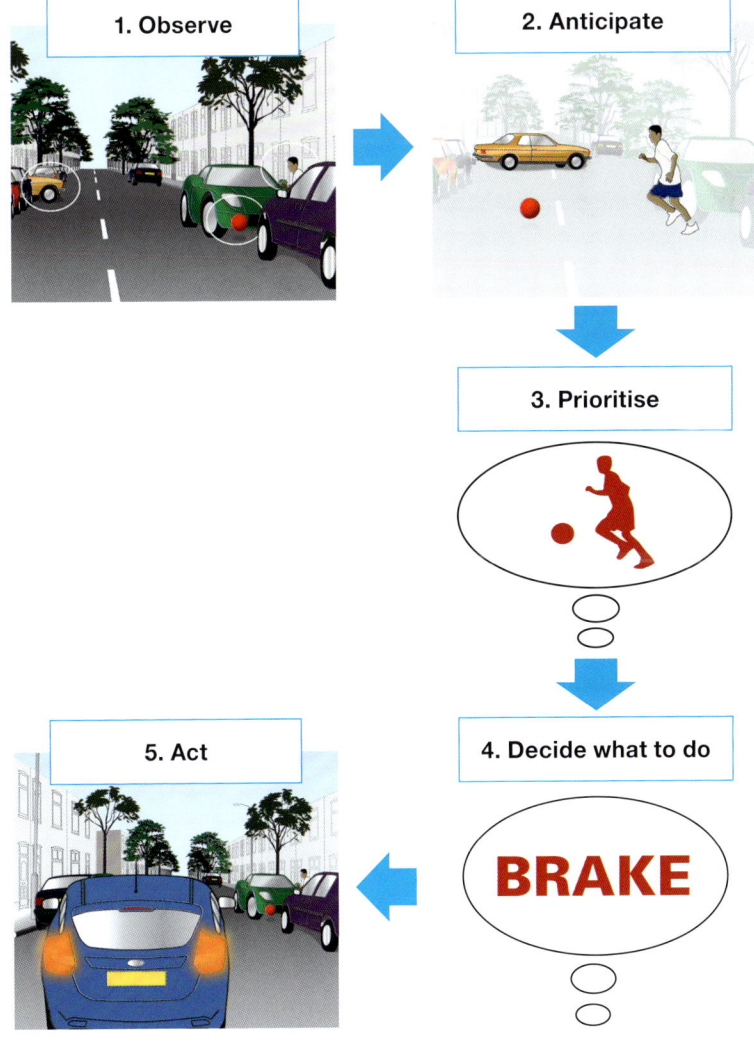

Anticipate hazards

You can develop your ability to anticipate hazards through specific training in hazard perception. But you can also learn to anticipate through experience, if you honestly assess your own performance and that of other road users each time you drive.

Young, inexperienced drivers tend to react very quickly to simple hazards but react more slowly to complex traffic hazards. This is because they lack experience of the kinds of hazardous events that can lead to a collision. As they're not aware of the risks, they fail to anticipate them. Trained drivers spot the early signs of possible trouble and anticipate what might happen, so they react early and appropriately. They're constantly monitoring risks at a subconscious level so that they're ready to respond quickly if the situation develops.

Observation and anticipation reinforce each other. On a familiar route, for example, you may know from experience where there are likely to be hazards, even if your view of the road is blocked by vehicles. Anticipating hazards means that you search the road for visual clues. From this careful observation, you gather new visual clues that increase your ability to anticipate.

You can develop your competence at anticipating the actions of other drivers by carefully observing their progress and behaviour, and their head, hand and eye movements. Even careful drivers can make mistakes, so learning to anticipate other road users' intentions can give you and them an extra safety margin.

> Anticipating hazards gives you extra time. The more time you have to react to a hazard, the more likely it is that you can deal with it safely.

A useful technique to help develop your anticipation is to do a running commentary in your head as you drive. Describe what hazards you can observe and how you plan to deal with them. Remember to observe other drivers as well as their vehicles.

Ask yourself 'What if …?' when you observe a hazard.

For example:

'What if that driver waiting at the junction pulled out without looking?'

'What if there's a parked vehicle just round this bend?'

With practice you should find that you observe more hazards, earlier and in more detail, and gain more time to react.

Prioritise hazards

Where there are multiple hazards, deal with them in order of importance. The level of danger associated with particular hazards varies with:

- the hazard itself
- how close it is to you
- road layout
- whether the hazard is stationary or moving
- how fast you're approaching it.

The greater the danger, the higher the priority, but be ready to re-adjust your priorities as the situation develops.

Practise applying the three stages of planning during every journey until you do it automatically, even when you're driving under pressure.

Decide what to do

The purpose of your plan is to decide on and adopt a course of action that ensures the safety of yourself and other road users at all times, taking account of:

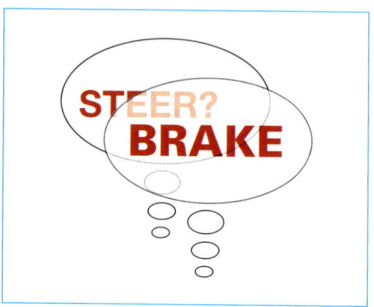

- what you can see
- what you can't see
- what you might reasonably expect to happen
- which hazards represent the greatest risk
- what to do if things turn out differently from expected (contingency plans).

If you plan your driving, you should be able to make decisions in a methodical way at any point and without hesitation.

While you're driving, you should be continuously anticipating, prioritising hazards and deciding what to do. At first, you might find it difficult to consciously work through these three stages all the time but, with practice, this will become second nature and prove a quick and reliable guide to action.

Forward planning beyond the next hazard

Dealing with the hazard immediately ahead is only the start to the process of managing hazards effectively, particularly when travelling in urgent situations. Look beyond the next hazard and consider what other hazards you can see. It's no help to identify the first bend as a relatively minor hazard in isolation if the result is that you're travelling too fast for the hazard beyond it. Similarly, an opportunity to overtake may appear to be available, but if you adopt the speed necessary to overtake safely, it may mean you're travelling too fast for the approaching bend beyond it. The process of identifying and prioritising hazards is an ongoing one. Continually make adjustments in your planning to allow for how an upcoming hazard may affect how you deal with a closer one. Be prepared to re-visit the system of car control if priorities change.

Planning through a series of hazards – sometimes effectively treating them as one complex hazard – can help you make progress, as well as prevent unsafe driving. Quickly observing the road ahead from the furthest you can see back towards where you are now, rather than working away from yourself towards the horizon, can help with this. Use as much information as you can gather to help you plan effectively.

Improving your observation

Observation and anticipation depend both on visual skills – how you use your eyes to observe the environment – and on mental skills, such as information processing and concentration. These vital skills are interlinked.

Scanning the environment

Our ability to handle information about the environment is limited so we tend to cope with this by concentrating on one part of it at a time. But drivers who rapidly scan the whole environment looking for different kinds of hazards have a much lower risk of incident than drivers who concentrate on one area.

Imagine your field of view as a picture – you can see the whole picture but you can only concentrate on one part of it at a time. This is why you need to develop the habit of scanning repeatedly and regularly.

When you use a radio, you largely focus your visual attention on one point – usually directly ahead – and fail to look across the scene to peripheral areas.

If you concentrate your vision on a small area, you are less aware of the whole picture.

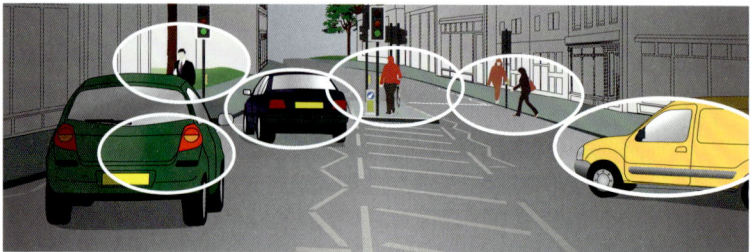

> Continually scan different areas of the environment in turn so that you build up a whole picture.
>
> Routine scanning enables you to process information, spot hazards and monitor the situation as it changes.

Learn to use your eyes in a scanning motion that sweeps the whole environment – the far distance, the middle distance, the foreground, the sides and rear – to build up a picture of what's happening all around you, as far as you can see, in every direction.

Scanning is a continuous process. When a new view opens out in front of you, quickly scan the new scene. By scanning the whole of the environment, you'll know where the areas of risk are. Check and re-check these risk areas in your visual sweeps. Avoid fixing on particular risk areas because this stops you placing them in the broader context. Use all your mirrors, and consider a shoulder check when it's not safe to rely on your mirrors alone – for example, to check any blind spot when reversing, moving off from the kerb, joining a motorway or leaving a roundabout.

Make use of all the visual clues available, including information given by hazard warning signs. Use these to help you prioritise hazards.

Looking but not seeing

What we see largely depends on what we expect to see. Have you ever had a near miss because you looked but failed to see a cyclist or motorcycle? We saw in Chapter 1 that mistakes of this type are common because drivers tend to see larger objects such as cars or lorries but can miss road users such as cyclists or motorcyclists. Further away, a cycle or motorcycle is a small point in your overall field of vision and it remains a relatively small object until it gets quite close.

When we concentrate we don't just look at a particular part of a scene, we look for particular types of objects in that scene. We more easily detect and react to objects that we expect to see. Cycles or motorcycles represent a small proportion of vehicles on the road so are much less common than cars or lorries, for example. Drivers build their expectations on what they commonly see and this affects how they process visual information. This is why drivers sometimes fail to see a cyclist or motorcyclist until it's too late.

Don't relax your concentration when driving in familiar situations or you may not see the unexpected hazard. Give as much attention to observation and anticipation on routes you use every day as on journeys you're making for the first time. Also, take extra care when manoeuvring in familiar places at low speeds, such as when parking your vehicle at the end of a shift.

See also Chapter 7, Manoeuvring at low speeds.

When you scan, look out for solo road users.
If you are not expecting them, they can become 'invisible' to you.

Peripheral vision

Peripheral vision is the area of eyesight surrounding the central area of sharply defined vision. The eye's receptors in this area are different from the central receptors and are particularly good at sensing movement.

Peripheral vision:

- gives you your sense of speed and your position on the road
- registers the movement of other road users
- acts as a cue for central vision, warning of areas to examine more closely.

Learn to react to your peripheral vision as well as your central vision.

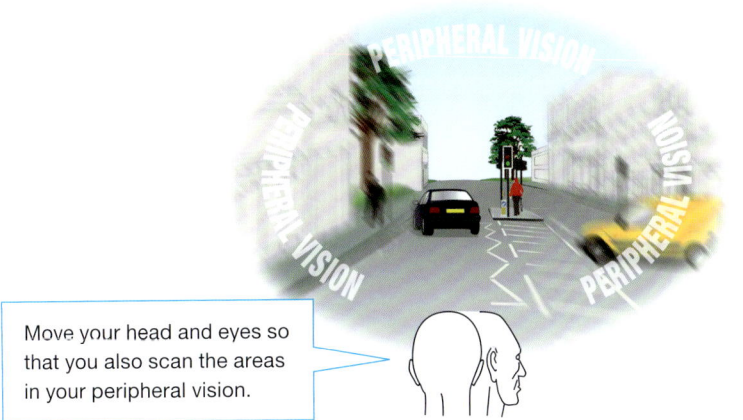

Move your head and eyes so that you also scan the areas in your peripheral vision.

Zones of visibility

The road around you is made up of different zones of visibility. In some areas, you'll have a good view and, in others, you'll only be able to see what's directly in front of you – for example, at junctions in towns or in winding country lanes.

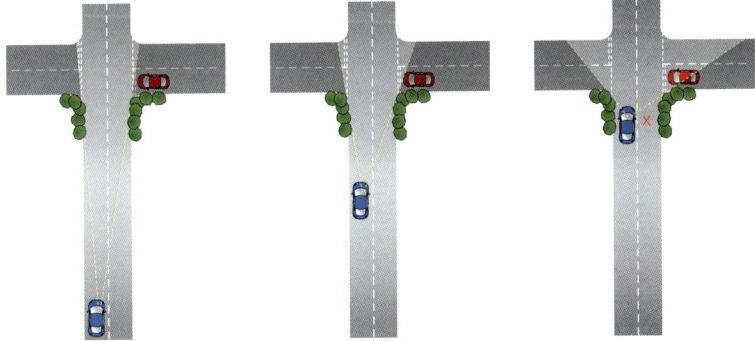

The driver is approaching a crossroads where the view is restricted. For most of the approach, the view improves very little and the driver needs to approach the hazard with great care. From point X, the view into the crossroads improves rapidly so the driver can see the position and behaviour of other road users. The driver now has enough information to decide what to do.

On the approach to a hazard where the view is restricted, position your vehicle to get the best view that is consistent with safety. It's often possible to assess the severity of a bend or gradient using lateral information such as the position of trees, hedges or lamp posts.

On the approach to a hazard where the view is restricted, use every opportunity to get more information about the road ahead:

open spaces and breaks in hedges, fences and walls on the approach to a blind junction

a curving row of trees or lamp posts

reflections in shop windows

the angle of approaching headlights

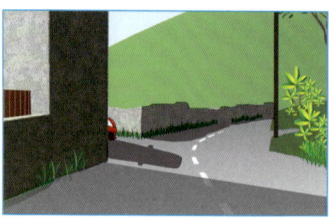

the shadow of an approaching vehicle.

Next time you drive along a familiar route, look for additional sources of information. Look for glimpses of wider views and information from lights and shadows.

Your choice of speed

Speed affects your perception and judgement, so your choice of speed has a major impact on your ability to anticipate hazards.

Adjust your speed to how well you can see, the complexity of the situation and the distance it will take you to stop.

At 70 mph, you would typically need to allow a safe stopping distance of about 100 metres (328 feet). This is the distance between motorway marker posts.

How speed affects observation and anticipation

The faster you go, the further ahead you need to look. This is because as you drive faster, the nearest point at which you can accurately focus moves away from you. Foreground detail becomes blurred and observation becomes more difficult because you have to process a lot more information in less time. The only way to cope with this is to scan further ahead, beyond the point where your eyes naturally come to rest, to give yourself more time to assess, plan and react.

At higher speeds, you'll travel further before you can react to what you've seen and you need to build this into your safe stopping distance.

> Remember the safe stopping distance rule:
>
> **Always drive so you can stop safely within the distance you can see to be clear on your own side of the road.**

When you're driving at high speed, remember the following:

- Driving at higher speed requires a high level of attention and judgement, which you can't sustain if you're tired. Plan regular rest periods to help you to stay alert and get some fresh air. Rest for longer when tired.

  See page 77, Practical steps to combat tiredness.

- Your ability to take in foreground detail decreases with speed and increases as you slow down. In areas of high traffic density, such as town centres, you must slow down so that you're able to take in as much foreground information as possible.
- Statutory speed limits set the maximum permissible speed, but this isn't the same thing as a safe speed. The safe speed for a particular stretch of road depends on the conditions at the time. It's your responsibility to select a speed appropriate for the conditions so that you maximise your ability to observe and anticipate hazards.

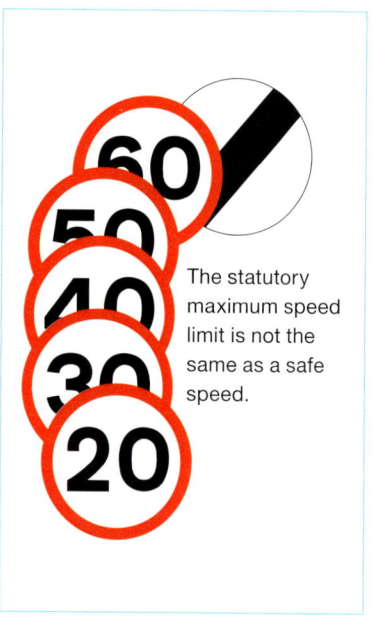

The statutory maximum speed limit is not the same as a safe speed.

 Know your limits and keep within the speed at which you feel safe and comfortable – resist the pressures that might encourage you to drive faster.

Speed and safety

A central aim of *Roadcraft* is to equip you with the attitude and practical abilities to use speed safely. For this, you need to understand how speed affects your perception and judgement and to always stay within the limits of your competence.

Accurate assessment of your own driving competence is essential. If you don't choose a safe speed for the circumstances, you won't have enough time to anticipate hazards.

Your safety and that of other road users depends on your ability to accurately assess what is a safe speed. This depends on:

- your driving capability
- your awareness of human factors, such as tiredness, stress or peer pressure, which may affect your capability on any given journey
- your vehicle's capabilities
- the road and weather conditions.

> At 30 mph a minor misjudgement might be corrected but at 70 mph the same mistake could be disastrous.

Underestimating speed

Some common errors of perception are described earlier in this chapter. It's easy to underestimate the speed at which you're driving. This is because your perception of speed depends on several factors:

- the difference in detail perceived by your forward and side vision
- engine, road and wind noise
- the evenness of the ride
- your idea of 'normal' speed
- the road – its width and whether it's enclosed or open
- your height off the ground.

Underestimating your speed means you'll have less time to observe and anticipate hazards. Your speed perception can be distorted in many situations:

- When you come off a motorway or other fast road onto a road where speeds below 30 or 40 mph are appropriate, you'll feel as if you're travelling much more slowly than you really are. Allow time for normal speed perception to return.
- Low visibility can distort your perception of speed (for example, in fog, sleet, heavy rain and darkness), so you find yourself driving faster than you realise.

- If you drive a vehicle that's smoother, quieter or more powerful than your usual vehicle, you may not realise how fast you're travelling because you use road noise, engine noise and vibration, as well as sight and balance, to assess your speed.
- On wide open roads, speeds will seem slower than on narrow or winding roads.

Always keep a check on your speedometer. Take particular care when you leave a motorway or fast road, especially at roundabouts.

Assess yourself honestly – do you always keep to the safe stopping distance rule at higher speeds? The next time you make a journey involving higher speeds, monitor whether you can always stop within the distance you can see to be clear on your own side of the road.

Keep your distance

The closer you are to the vehicle in front the less you'll be able to see beyond it, especially if it's a van or lorry. In slow-moving traffic, it's better to drop back slightly so that you can see what's happening two or three vehicles in front.

See also Chapter 10, page 181, Following position.

You particularly need a good view of the road ahead on motorways and other fast-moving roads. Your view will depend on the curvature and gradient of the carriageway, the lane that you're in, the size and position of other vehicles and the height of your own vehicle. Allowing for these, keep back far enough from the vehicle in front to maintain a safe following distance. Do not sit in the blind spot of other vehicles.

Have you ever had a near miss or collision from driving too close:

- on a fast-moving road?
- in slow-moving traffic?

How did you react to this experience? Did it change the way you drive?

Always check that no one is sitting in your blind spot before you change lanes. Make sure you know where the offside and nearside blind spots are on any vehicle that you drive. If you're not sure, get a colleague to help you work this out before you make a journey.

See Chapter 13, page 251, Overtaking.

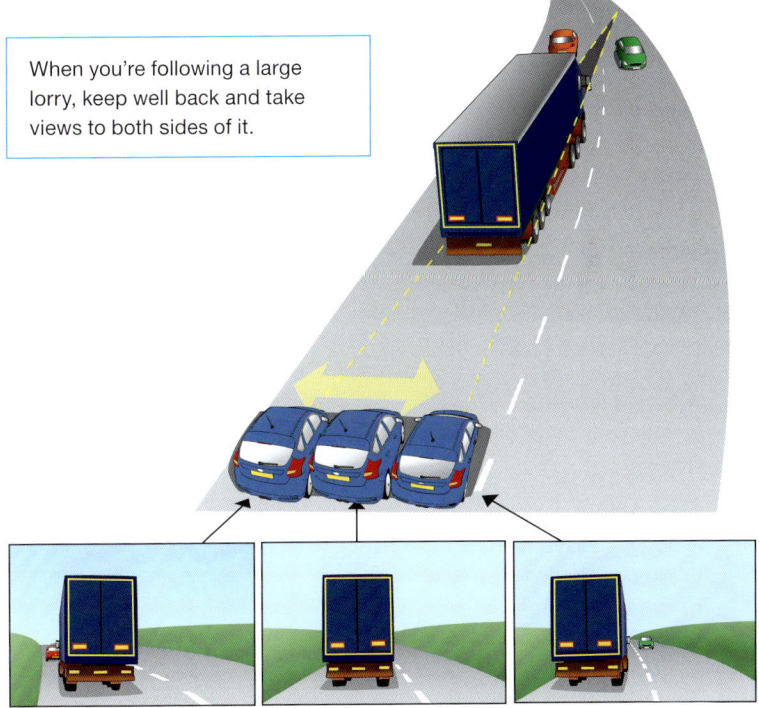

When you're following a large lorry, keep well back and take views to both sides of it.

Human factors that affect observation and anticipation

Safe driving is about more than handling your vehicle and the immediate traffic situation. We look at human factors that can affect police drivers in Chapter 1.

Here we look at factors that can affect alertness, observation and anticipation.

Alertness

To anticipate hazards we need to remain alert – ready to identify and respond to constantly changing driving conditions. Alertness determines the amount of information your brain can process. It depends on many things but tends to decrease with time spent on routine tasks. Most driving is routine and places few demands on your abilities. A low level of stimulation makes it easy to lose concentration, so you need to take active steps to stay alert, especially on long journeys on motorways or rural roads.

Tiredness

Alertness is reduced if you drive at times when you would normally be asleep, if you haven't had enough sleep, or your sleep has been disturbed. It also varies with the time of day:

- Your reactions tend to be slightly slower in the morning than in the early evening.
- There's a dip in alertness after the midday meal.
- The greatest risk of tiredness-related collisions is between the hours of 11.00 pm and 6.00 am.

The risk of tiredness also increases with:

- Irregular work and shift patterns, which disrupt the body's biorhythms or 'biological clock'. This equips your body to perform most tasks by day. At night, many brain functions are normally damped down to allow recuperation and renewal of the body's reserves.
- Disturbed sleep patterns, which can reduce the brain's ability to process information during complex driving tasks.
- The total time spent at work and not just the time spent at the wheel. If you're tired from other duties before you start a journey, you're much more at risk from tiredness during the journey. Tiredness is a particular problem for emergency services and other professional drivers because the demands of the job may mean that they have to drive at the margins of their safety limit.
- Driving for long periods of time in monotonous conditions, such as:
  - in low-density traffic
  - in fog
  - at night
  - on a motorway.
- Driving for longer than about four hours, whatever the conditions.

It's estimated that up to 1 in 4 fatal collisions are caused by drivers who have fallen asleep at the wheel and that 1 in 5 collisions on major roads are caused by tiredness.

Practical steps to combat tiredness

The demands of the job and shift work mean that emergency services drivers have to learn to deal with tiredness. Watch out for the warning signs such as blinking, yawning or loss of concentration and take steps to manage tiredness well before it becomes dangerous:

- Adjust your seat so that your driving position is comfortable. Bad posture causes muscular tiredness, which in turn causes mental tiredness. This can be a problem during emergency driving when some drivers become physically tense. If you can, try to relax your posture during emergency driving.

- Make sure that you have enough ventilation to stay alert. Use the air conditioning if it helps.
- Take regular breaks – once every two hours is recommended. Don't wait until you feel drowsy. Most people need a rest break of at least 15 minutes to restore alertness.
- Be aware that if you have several caffeine drinks over a long period, each dose of caffeine will have less effect.
- On long journeys plan a series of rest breaks, but recognise that each successive break will give less recovery than the one before.
- Physical exercise helps you recover from fatigue – a brisk 10-minute walk can energise you.

> If you know you're tired, allow yourself a greater safety margin – slow down and be aware that you need more time to react.

Drivers over 45 are more at risk of and recover less quickly from tiredness than younger drivers. If you regularly start your shift feeling tired, or suffer from disturbed sleep, think about how to manage these problems as they will affect your driving.

Other physiological factors

Other things that may affect your concentration and reaction times are:

- minor illness (colds and other viral infections, hay fever, post-viral states)
- medications (especially those causing drowsiness)
- residual blood alcohol
- low blood sugar arising from hunger
- cyclical mood swings caused by hormone changes (this applies to men as well as women)
- life stress such as bereavement.

Be aware that any of these are likely to affect your concentration and alertness. Take account of them, slow down and allow yourself a greater safety margin.

As your ability to anticipate hazards increases, your driving will become smoother and your fuel consumption will decrease.

See Appendix 3, Fuel-efficient driving, page 295.

 Anticipating hazards

Think about the last time you misjudged a hazard. Did this happen because you failed to observe the hazard? Or did you see the potential hazard but fail to anticipate what would happen next?

Did any human factors affect your ability to observe and anticipate? For example, tiredness, time pressure or lapse of concentration?

What can you learn from the situation to improve your anticipation of hazards in future?

Check your understanding

You should now be able to apply learning from this chapter in your driver training so that you can:

- [ ] explain how your brain processes information and how you can improve your ability to process complex information when driving
- [ ] explain the three main types of hazard you will meet on the road
- [ ] show how to use the information you gather from observation to plan your driving actions
- [ ] show improved observation and anticipation skills
- [ ] explain human and physiological factors that can affect observation and anticipation, and show how you manage these.

Chapter 5

Anticipating hazards in the driving environment

Learning outcomes

The learning in this chapter, along with driver training, should enable you to:

- demonstrate awareness of hazards that you may meet at night, in poor weather conditions and on the road surface
- take appropriate steps to reduce or avoid potential dangers from these hazards
- show that you make full use of road signs and markings, your own local road knowledge and observation links to anticipate hazards.

Night driving

It's harder to see in anything less than full daylight and so your vision gives you less information. For example, pedestrians are harder to see unless there's significant backlighting. This section gives advice on what you can do to make the best of what you can see at night.

You

As the light fades, there's less contrast, colours fade and edges become indistinct. Your body naturally wants to slow down as night draws on and you're more likely to grow tired.

Night driving puts extra strain on your eyes. Even a slight eyesight irregularity can cause stress and tiredness. If you find you're unexpectedly tired from driving, especially at night, get your eyes tested as soon as possible.

Your vehicle

Make sure that all windows, mirrors, and the lenses of lights and indicators are clean to give yourself the best possible visibility. The slightest film of moisture, grease or dirt on windows or mirrors will break up light and increase glare, making it harder to see what's going on. Check your lights are correctly aligned and adjusted for the vehicle load. The bulbs should all work and the switching equipment should function properly. Are your windscreen washers, wipers and demisters all working properly?

See Appendix 2, Is your vehicle fit to drive?, page 291.

Your lights

On unlit roads put your headlights on main beam and only dip them for other road users.

Use dipped headlights:

- in built-up areas with street lights
- in situations when dipped headlights are more effective than the main beam – for example, when going round a left-hand bend or at a hump bridge
- in heavy rain, snow and fog, when these reflect glare from your headlights on full beam.

Dip your headlights to avoid dazzling oncoming drivers, the driver in front or other road users. When you overtake another vehicle, return to full beam when you're parallel with it.

Only use fog lights when visibility is 100 metres (328 feet) or less.

> Always drive so that you can stop safely within the distance you can see to be clear on your own side of the road. At night, this is the area lit by your headlights unless there's full street lighting. Even in the best conditions your ability to assess the speed and position of oncoming vehicles is reduced at night, so allow an extra safety margin.

If you use a satnav at night, make sure it's positioned so that it doesn't obstruct your vision in the dark, and its screen doesn't dazzle you. Use the aural prompts whenever possible.

Following other vehicles at night

When you follow another vehicle, dip your headlights and leave a large enough gap so that your lights don't dazzle the driver in front. When you overtake, move out early with your headlights still dipped. If you need to warn the other driver that you're there, flash your lights instead of using the horn. Return to full beam when you're alongside the other vehicle. If you're being overtaken, dip your headlights when the overtaking vehicle draws alongside you and keep them dipped until you can raise them without dazzling the other driver.

Information from other vehicles' lights

You can get a great deal of useful information from the front and rear lights of other vehicles; for example, the sweep of the headlights of vehicles ahead approaching a bend can indicate the sharpness of the bend, and the brake lights of vehicles in front can give you an early warning to reduce speed.

Intelligent use of information given by lights can help your driving.

Dazzle

Headlights shining directly into your eyes may dazzle you. This can happen on sharp right-hand bends and steep inclines, and when the lights of oncoming vehicles are undipped or badly adjusted. The intensity of the light bleaches the retinas of your eyes so that you can see nothing for some moments.

To avoid dazzle, look towards the nearside edge of the road. This enables you to keep your road position but doesn't tell you what's happening in the road ahead, so reduce your speed. If you're dazzled, slow down or stop if necessary until you can see properly again.

Reflective studs and markings

Reflective studs and markings are a good source of information about road layout at night. To get the most out of them you need to be familiar with the *Highway Code*. Roadside marker posts reflect your headlights and show you the direction of a curve before you can see where the actual road goes.

Reflective studs or 'cat's eyes' indicate the type of white line along the centre of the road. Generally, the more white paint there is in the line, the greater the number of cat's eyes. They're particularly helpful when it's raining at night and the glare of headlights makes it difficult to see.

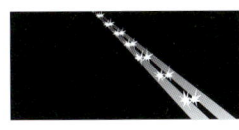

Centre lines:
one cat's eye every other gap.

Hazard lines:
one cat's eye every gap.

Double white lines:
twice as many cat's eyes as hazard lines.

Other ways to improve observation at night

- Keep your speed down when you leave brightly lit areas to allow time for your eyes to adjust to the lower level of lighting.
- Any light inside the vehicle that reflects off the windows will distract you and reduce your ability to see. Interior lights, torches and satnav screens can cause reflections, so limit their use.
- Some glasses with tinted or photochromatic lenses may be unsuitable for night driving, so check with your optician.

When you drive at night, think about how to adapt your driving to take account of these factors:

- Your physiological and mental responses to night-time conditions. For each journey, ask yourself whether you're fully physically and mentally alert for night-time driving.
- The condition of your vehicle. Is it properly equipped and prepared for night driving?
- Information in the environment. How do you adapt your observation and anticipation when you make a journey in darkness?

Weather conditions

You must take responsibility for how you deal with weather conditions. Bad weather is blamed for causing collisions when the cause may well be driver error, leading to driving inappropriately for the conditions. Careful observation, good anticipation, the correct speed and adequate braking distances are crucial for safe driving in difficult weather conditions.

In extreme weather conditions, ask yourself: 'Is my journey really necessary?'

The weather affects how far you can see, and your vehicle's road-holding, so it's central to your observation, anticipation and driving plan. When weather conditions reduce visibility, reduce your speed and regularly check your actual speed on the speedometer. You should always be able to stop within the distance you can see to be clear on your own side of the road. If it's foggy, follow the *Highway Code* advice on driving in fog.

Examples of weather conditions that reduce visibility are:

- fog and mist
- heavy rain
- snow and sleet
- bright sunshine, especially when it's low in the sky.

For more on dealing with these weather conditions, see Chapter 13, page 258, Bad weather conditions on fast-moving roads.

Using lights in bad weather

Choose your lights according to the circumstances.

- Switch on your dipped headlights when visibility is poor in daylight or fading light. Use dipped headlights in fog or heavy rain in daylight, because sidelights are virtually invisible.
- As a general rule, use your dipped headlights whenever your wipers are in constant use.
- When there's fog or falling snow at night, fog lights often give a better view than dipped headlights. Use them if visibility is 100 metres (328 feet) or less.
- Switch off your fog lights when you leave the fog so you don't dazzle other drivers.
- Don't use your main headlight beam when you're behind another vehicle in fog – it may dazzle the driver and will cast a shadow of the vehicle on the fog ahead, disrupting the driver's view.
- The brightness of rear fog lights can mask the brake lights – allow more distance between you and the car in front and aim to brake gently yourself.

Using auxiliary controls and instruments in bad weather

Make full use of your washers and wipers to keep your windscreen and rear window as clear as possible. When there's a possibility of freezing fog, put freeze-resistant screen wash in the screen wash reservoir. In fog, rain or snow, regularly check your speedometer for your actual speed. Low visibility distorts your perception of speed so you can't rely on your eyes to judge speed accurately.

Observing when visibility is low

When visibility is low, keep to a slow steady pace and use the edge of the carriageway, hazard lines and cat's eyes as a guide, especially when approaching a road junction or corner. Staring into featureless mist tires the eyes very quickly. Focus instead on what you can see: the vehicle in front, the edge of the road or the road ahead. But avoid fixing your focus on the tail lights of the vehicle in front because they'll tend to draw you towards it and you could collide if the vehicle stops suddenly. Be ready to use your horn to tell other road users you're there.

Always be prepared for a sudden stop in the traffic ahead. Don't follow closely, and only overtake other traffic when you can see that it's absolutely safe to do so. This is seldom possible in fog on a two-way road. At junctions when visibility is low, wind down your window and listen for other vehicles, and consider using your horn.

Micro climates

Look out for evidence of micro climates. These can cause frost and wet patches to linger in some areas after they've disappeared elsewhere. Ice can linger in landscape features such as valley bottoms, shaded hillsides and shaded slopes, or large areas of shadow cast by trees or buildings, and result in sudden loss of traction. Bridge surfaces are often colder than the surrounding roads because they're exposed on all sides, and can be icy when their approach roads are not. Patchy fog is particularly dangerous and is a common cause of multiple collisions.

Ice and wetness can linger in areas of shadow.

Road surface

 Have you ever failed to spot a problem on the road surface that affected your tyre grip or vehicle handling?

The type and condition of the road surface affects tyre grip and vehicle-handling characteristics. Driving control depends on tyre grip for steering, acceleration and braking. Even the best tyres on a high-performance vehicle can lose traction on a poor road surface. Most drivers don't pay enough attention to this.

Always look well ahead to identify changes in the road surface, and adjust the strength of your braking, acceleration and steering to retain adequate road-holding.

Always observe the camber of the road on a curve or bend.

| Surfaces that slope downwards to the inside of the curve help cornering. | Surfaces that slope upwards to the inside of the curve make cornering more difficult. |

See Chapter 11, page 194, Camber and superelevation.

The surfaces of most roads are good for road-holding when they're clean and dry. Snow, frost, ice, rain, oil, moist muddy patches, wet leaves, dry loose dust or gravel can cause tyres to lose grip, making skids more likely. Rain may produce a slippery road surface, especially after a long dry spell. At hazards such as roundabouts or junctions, tyre deposits and diesel spillage may make the surface slippery at exactly the point where effective steering, braking and acceleration are needed to negotiate the hazard safely.

Road surface irregularities

Look out for irregularities, such as potholes, projecting manhole covers, sunken gullies and bits of debris, which can damage the tyres and suspension. If you can alter your road position in plenty of time to avoid them without endangering other traffic, do so; if not, slow down to reduce shock and maintain stability as you pass over them.

Chapter 5 – Anticipating hazards in the driving environment

Surfacing materials	Grip characteristics	Problems
Tarmac or asphalt	Tarmac or asphalt surfaces give a good grip when they're dressed with stones or chips.	In time, they become polished and lose some of their skid-resistant properties.
Anti-skid surface	High-grip anti-skid surfaces are designed to give extra grip on the approach to fixed hazards such as roundabouts, traffic lights and zebra crossings.	When newly laid, loose gravel on the surface can reduce grip; patches can become polished over time.
Concrete	Concrete road surfaces often have roughened ribs, which give a good skid-resistant surface.	Some hold water, which freezes in cold weather and creates a slippery surface that isn't easily seen.
Cobbles **Brick paving** or **pavers** on roads in home zones **Road paint**	Low grip when wet.	Rain increases the likelihood of skidding.
Metal hazards on the road surface such as tram lines, temporary metal sheeting, inspection covers	Poor grip when dusty or wet.	Rain increases the likelihood of skidding.

The road surface in winter

In winter, the ice or frost covering on road surfaces isn't always uniform. Isolated patches remain iced up when other parts have thawed out, and certain slopes are especially susceptible to this. Be on the lookout for ice or frost patches, which you can detect by their appearance, by the behaviour of other vehicles and by the sudden absence of tyre noise: tyres travelling on ice make virtually no noise. Adjust your driving early to avoid skidding.

See Chapter 8, Maintaining vehicle stability.

Driving through water

Driving at speed through water can sharply deflect the front wheels and cause you to lose control.

See Chapter 8, page 162, Aquaplaning.

Take extra care at night, when it's difficult to distinguish between a wet road surface and flood water. Flood water can gather quickly where the road dips and at the sides of the road in poorly drained low-lying areas. Dips often occur under bridges.

Slow down as you approach a flooded area. Avoid driving through water wherever possible. When you have to drive through water, drive through the shallowest part but look out for hidden obstacles or subsidence.

If the road is entirely submerged, stop the vehicle in a safe place and cautiously find out how deep the water is. The depth of water that you can safely drive through depends on how high your vehicle stands off the ground and where the electrical components, engine, air intake and exhaust pipe are positioned. For example, submerging a hot catalytic converter could cause damage.

Refer to the manufacturer's handbook for specific advice for your vehicle.

If you decide to drive on, follow the steps below:

- **In a vehicle with a manual gearbox** – engage first gear and keep the engine running at just above idle speed (just enough to prevent stalling). In older vehicles, driving at higher revs could prevent water being drawn into the exhaust system. In many newer vehicles, the air intake is positioned below the front bumper so avoid higher revs as this would cause water to be sucked into the engine causing extensive damage.
- **In a vehicle with automatic transmission** – refer to the manufacturer's handbook for specific advice as this varies from one automatic system to another.

Whichever type of vehicle you are driving:

- Drive through the water at a slow even speed (a slow walking pace).
- Grip the steering wheel more tightly to maintain direction as you drive through the water.
- When you leave the water, continue driving slowly and apply the foot brake lightly until the brakes grip. Repeat this again after a short while until you're confident that your brakes are working normally.

If just one wheel enters a deep puddle (usually the nearside wheel), that wheel will slow rapidly causing the vehicle to veer in that direction. If you can't avoid the puddle, prepare by tightening your grip on the steering wheel and holding it straight until clear.

Road signs and markings

Road signs and markings warn of approaching hazards and give instructions and information about road use. Use your observation skills to read the road and link the signs to the hazards ahead, especially at night.

> On road signs, the furthest hazard is shown at the bottom and the nearest at the top.
>
> Use your own observations to link the signs to the road layout ahead. Observe all hazards from the distance to the foreground, and prioritise their importance.

Look for changes in the white lines in the centre of the road. A change from centre lines to hazard lines may help you to anticipate an unseen hazard.

Road markings	Explanation
	The centre line on a single carriageway road.
	The line that separates traffic travelling in the same direction on a single or dual carriageway road.
	This is a hazard warning line. It may be accompanied by an upright sign that specifies the type of hazard, such as a bend in the road. The marking is also used on the approach to a junction.
	This is seen at the edge of the carriageway, other than at junctions, exits from private drives and lay-bys. Used on the left-hand side of the road and alongside the central reservation of dual carriageway roads.
	This is seen at the edge of the main carriageway at a junction (particularly where a slip road leaves or joins), at an exit from a private drive or at a lay-by. Also used to divide the main carriageway from a traffic lane that leaves the main carriageway at a junction ahead (lane drop).
	Diagonal white lines (hatched markings) bounded by broken lines may be used in the centre of the road to separate opposing flows of traffic. They're often provided at junctions to protect traffic turning right. They may also be used on the approach to a central traffic island or the start of a dual carriageway. Hatched markings with a single, broken boundary line may be used at the edge of the road or next to the central reservation of a dual carriageway: the diagonal lines always slope towards the direction of travel. You should not enter any hatched area bounded by a broken line unless it's safe to do so.

The text for the table has been adapted from the sixth edition of *Know Your Traffic Signs*. It is reproduced here under the terms of the Open Government Licence.

Make the best possible use of road signs and markings:

- **Observe** – actively search for road signs and markings in your observation scans, and incorporate the information they give you into your driving plan as soon as possible. Many drivers fail to see and make use of them, and so lose valuable information.
- **Understand** – be able to recognise them immediately. You should be familiar with the current editions of the *Highway Code* and *Know your Traffic Signs*.
- **React** – react to a sign or marking by looking ahead to what it refers to and building the information into your driving plan. Where the sign or marking refers to an unseen hazard, anticipate the hazard and adapt your plan accordingly.

Unofficial road signs such as 'Mud on Road', 'Car Boot Sale' and 'Concealed Entrance' can also help you anticipate the road conditions ahead.

When was the last time you looked at road signs in the **most recent** version of the *Highway Code*?

On your next few journeys, check whether you know the meaning of each sign or road marking you meet and match them to the road layout ahead.

Local road knowledge

Increasing your knowledge of the local roads can help your driving, but never take familiar roads for granted. Collisions are disproportionately frequent on familiar roads (the 'close to home' effect). Loss of attention is a major cause of collisions and drivers are least attentive, and more likely to be distracted by secondary tasks, on roads they know well.

Town driving puts heavy demands on your observation, reactions and driving skills, and you need to be alert at all times. At complicated junctions, where it's important to get into the correct lane, local knowledge is useful. But even when you know the layout of main road junctions, one-way streets, roundabouts and other local features, always plan on the basis of what you can actually see – not what usually happens.

Making observation links

Observation links are clues to physical features and the likely behaviour of other road users. Aim to build up your own stock of observation links, which will help you to anticipate road and traffic conditions as you scan the environment.

Below are some examples of observation links.

When you see a cluster of lamp posts, look out for a probable roundabout ahead.

When you see a single lamp post on its own, look out for the exit point of a junction.

When you see no gap in a bank of trees ahead, look out for the road to curve to the left or right.

Some more observation links

When you see …	Look out for …
A railway line beside the road	The road will invariably go over or under it, often with sharp turns.
A row of parked vehicles	Doors opening, vehicles moving off. Pedestrians stepping out from behind vehicles. Small children hidden from view.
A bus at a stop	Pedestrians crossing the road to and from the bus. The bus moving off, possibly at an angle.
Cyclists	An inexperienced cyclist riding erratically. A cyclist looking over their shoulder with the intention of turning right. Strong winds causing wobble. A young cyclist doing something dangerous.
Flashing brake lights	A hazard a driver ahead has responded to by braking hard.

Practise using observation links. What would you look out for if you observed:

- a pedestrian calling a cab?
- a courier van?
- signs for a hypermarket or superstore?
- a motorway slip road?
- signs warning of roadworks and contraflow ahead on a motorway?
- a row of buses in front of a shopping centre?
- new hedge clippings or grass cuttings on a narrow country road?
- a large leisure complex?

Can you think of a recent occasion where you failed to spot the significance of something you observed?

Could you use this experience to improve your anticipation skills?

Check your understanding

You should now be able to apply learning from this chapter in your driver training so that you can:

- [ ] demonstrate awareness of hazards that you may meet at night, in poor weather conditions and on the road surface
- [ ] take appropriate steps to reduce or avoid potential dangers from these hazards
- [ ] show that you make full use of road signs and markings, your own local road knowledge and observation links to anticipate hazards.

Chapter 6

Acceleration, using gears, braking and steering

Learning outcomes

The learning in this chapter, along with driver training, should enable you to:

- explain how acceleration, braking and steering affect tyre grip and vehicle balance
- show that you can control your vehicle accurately in a range of situations
- show good acceleration sense, using the accelerator accurately and smoothly
- show how to use gears accurately, selecting the correct gear in a range of circumstances and for different purposes, in vehicles with manual or automatic gearboxes
- demonstrate an understanding of the acceleration characteristics and transmission modes of electric vehicles
- explain the safe stopping distance
- show how to use the brakes, engine braking or regenerative braking capability to slow the vehicle appropriately and safely in different circumstances
- demonstrate a method of steering for maximum safety and control
- explain the main factors that reduce fuel consumption.

Developing competence at controlling your vehicle

 Driving smoothly reduces both energy use and wear and tear on your vehicle.

See Appendix 3, Fuel-efficient driving, page 295.

The aim of this chapter is to give you complete control over moving, stopping and changing the direction of your vehicle at all times. To achieve this level of competence, you need to:

- accurately assess your current driving behaviour and the scope for improving your vehicle control skills
- understand in detail how the accelerator, gears, brakes and steering controls work and how to make best use of them.

A moving vehicle is most stable when its weight is evenly distributed, its engine is just pulling without increasing road speed, and it's travelling in a straight line.

Your control of the vehicle, and therefore your own and others' safety, depends on the grip between your tyres and the road surface. The patch of tyre in contact with the road on an average car is about the size of a hand.

 All new tyres have a label that tells you about the tyre's wet grip, fuel efficiency and noise performance. Check tyre pressures regularly because under-inflated tyres can affect stability. Low tyre pressures also increase rolling resistance and fuel consumption.

See Appendix 3, Fuel-efficient driving, page 295.

The tyre grip trade-off

There's a limited amount of tyre grip available. The patch of tyre in contact with the road varies with the size of the vehicle and the width of the tyres. On an average car the contact patch is about the same size as a hand. This is shared between accelerating, braking and steering forces. If more tyre grip is used for braking or accelerating, there's less available for steering, and vice versa.

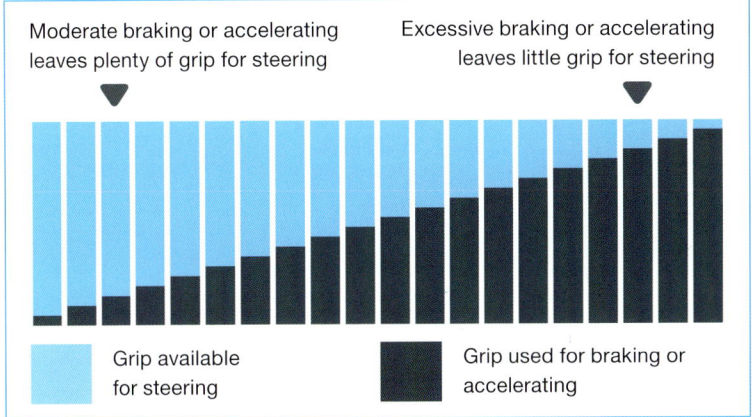

Develop your awareness of tyre grip

Analyse what's happening to your tyre grip as you steer round a corner or bend.

Be aware of the trade-off between accelerating or braking on the one hand and steering on the other.

Do you finish braking before you go into a bend?

Do you avoid accelerating harshly while driving round bends?

Vehicle balance and tyre grip

Tyre grip isn't necessarily the same on each wheel. It varies with the size of the vehicle and the load on the wheel. This affects how the vehicle handles. Braking, steering and accelerating alter the distribution of the load between the wheels and so affect the vehicle's balance.

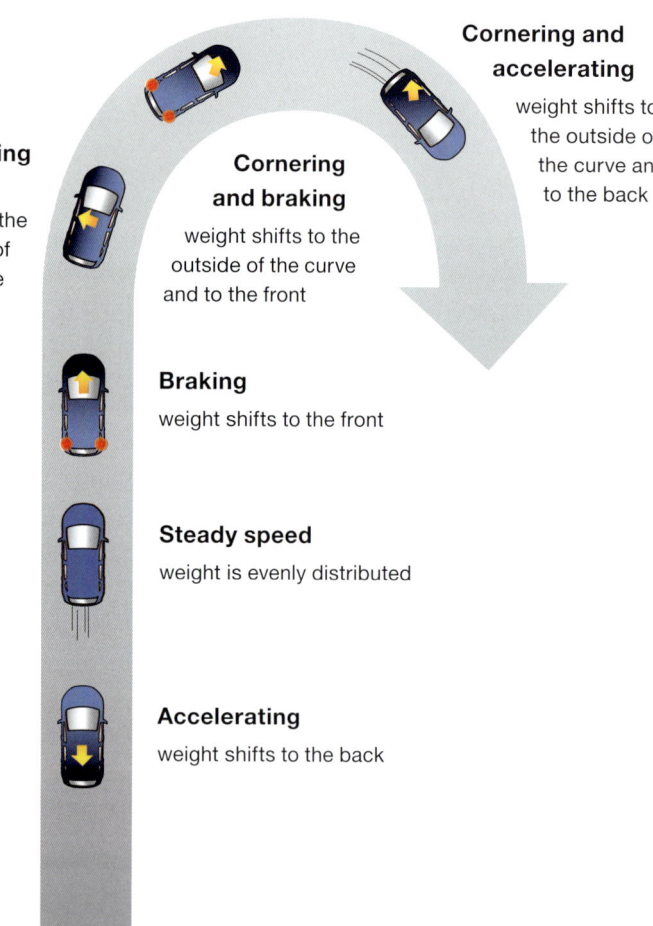

Cornering and accelerating
weight shifts to the outside of the curve and to the back

Cornering
weight shifts to the outside of the curve

Cornering and braking
weight shifts to the outside of the curve and to the front

Braking
weight shifts to the front

Steady speed
weight is evenly distributed

Accelerating
weight shifts to the back

> Braking, steering and accelerating alter the vehicle's balance and tyre grip.

Braking or accelerating as you go round a corner leaves less tyre grip for steering. This reduces your control over the positioning of your vehicle. If there isn't enough tyre grip for steering, you may lose traction. The more slippery the road surface, the earlier this happens. The exact outcome depends on the balance of the vehicle, whether it has front-, rear- or four-wheel drive, and whether it's fitted with safety features such as an electronic stability programme (ESP), traction control system (TCS) or an anti-lock braking system (ABS).

Technology to help keep control of the vehicle

All modern vehicles are now fitted with electronic safety features to help the driver keep control of the vehicle when harsh steering, braking or acceleration might result in a skid. These include ABS, TCS and ESP. The specific technology and how it works varies from one manufacturer to another. This technology is developing fast, with increasing sophistication.

See Chapter 8, page 151, How active safety systems work.

Using the accelerator

Depress the accelerator:

- to *increase* road speed
- to *maintain* road speed; for example, when cornering or going uphill.

Release the accelerator:

- to reduce engine speed and slow the vehicle down.

If you're in the correct gear for your speed, depressing the accelerator will give you a responsive increase in engine speed. If you're in too high a gear, the engine won't respond because the load from the wheels is too great. Changing to a lower gear reduces the load and allows the engine to speed up and move the vehicle faster.

If you release the accelerator pedal, you get the opposite effect – deceleration. The engine speed slows down and cylinder compression slows the vehicle down. The lower the gear, the greater the slowing effect of the engine, or engine braking.

See page 123, Releasing the accelerator – engine braking.

Retarders

Heavy vehicles, including larger emergency vehicles, are fitted with retarders. These are devices which produce additional engine braking to help slow the vehicle. Retarders reduce wear on the brakes and help to maintain a steady speed when continuous braking is required – for example, going down a long hill.

Whenever you fully release the accelerator, the retarder applies braking power to the drive wheels. It may rapidly reduce vehicle speed and so can affect your control of the vehicle. You can control the retarder by careful use of the accelerator. Some retarders may overheat if used over long periods of time, so consider using a lower gear.

There are several types of retarder. Always study the vehicle handbook to understand fully how the retarder operates on each heavy vehicle you drive.

Regenerative braking

Some vehicles, especially those with battery-powered engines (including hybrids), recharge the battery while the vehicle is slowing down. This can affect how the accelerator pedal is used, and you may need to adjust the way you use the accelerator to take account of this. The effect can be very noticeable, slowing the vehicle more and reducing the need to use the brakes. The slowing may be sufficiently pronounced that the rear brake lights come on to warn following drivers that the vehicle is slowing, much as if the brakes were actually being applied.

Familiarise yourself with your vehicle's characteristics. Making good use of this feature can prolong the range of the vehicle, make more efficient use of energy, and provide a smooth journey for yourself and any passengers.

Acceleration and vehicle balance

Acceleration alters the distribution of weight between the wheels of the vehicle. When a vehicle accelerates, the weight is lifted from the front and pushed down on the back wheels. During deceleration the opposite happens. This alters the relative grip of the front and rear tyres.

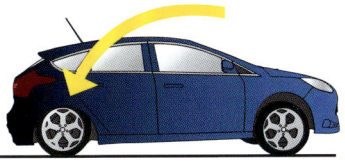

During deceleration

the rear tyres lose grip

the front tyres gain grip

During acceleration

the rear tyres gain grip

the front tyres lose grip

Acceleration and balance on different types of vehicle

The exact effect of acceleration on balance and tyre grip depends on the vehicle's size, power source, driving wheels and construction.

- **Larger vehicles** have less acceleration capability than cars but acceleration, balance and tyre grip will differ markedly depending on whether the vehicle is fully loaded or has no load.

- **Electric/hybrid vehicles** – many electric/hybrid vehicles have brisk acceleration. They may also use regenerative braking, which alters the balance of the vehicle more than just releasing the accelerator would in a car with a petrol or diesel engine. For details, consult your vehicle handbook or the manufacturer.
- **Front-wheel drive vehicles** lose grip or traction on their driving wheels because acceleration transfers weight, and therefore grip, from front to back wheels. This reduces their ability to accelerate. Accelerating too sharply can cause wheel spin. Harsh acceleration or a slippery road surface increases the risk of wheel spin, which can be particularly dangerous when pulling out at a junction. Avoid accelerating sharply, and in slippery conditions depress the accelerator very gently.
- **Rear-wheel drive vehicles** gain extra grip on their driving wheels, which helps acceleration (but harsh acceleration will cause the driving wheels to lose traction). At the same time, the front grip is lightened.
- **Four-wheel drive vehicles** vary in how the power is divided between the front and back wheels, and in the type of central differential they have. This means the effects of acceleration vary according to the model but generally four-wheel drive vehicles have good grip when accelerating. For precise details consult your vehicle handbook or manufacturer.

Developing your competence at using the accelerator

Jerky acceleration is uncomfortable for passengers, puts unnecessary strain on the vehicle, reduces tyre grip and increases fuel consumption. Use accurate and smooth movements to release or depress the accelerator. Remember – ease and squeeze.

Acceleration capability varies widely between vehicles and depends on the fuel or power source, the engine output, its efficiency, the power-to-weight ratio and its load. Take time to get to know the acceleration capability of any vehicle you drive. The safety of many manoeuvres, particularly overtaking, depends on judging it well.

How you use the accelerator affects your own safety and the safety of other road users. Sudden sharp movements of the accelerator reduce tyre grip and jeopardise steering control. The faster you go, the further you'll travel before you can react to a hazard. It will take you longer to stop and, if you collide, the results of the impact will be worse.

Vehicles with regenerative braking systems may also have accelerator controls, which include the braking effect. Be aware of what effect your use of the accelerator control may have.

Acceleration sense

Acceleration sense is the ability to vary vehicle speed in response to changing road or traffic conditions by accurate use of the accelerator, so that you use the brakes less or not at all.

This uses less fuel, causes less wear on the tyres and reduces emissions.

See Appendix 3, Fuel-efficient driving, page 295.

You need acceleration sense in every driving situation: moving off, overtaking, complying with speed limits, following other vehicles and negotiating hazards. Acceleration sense requires observation, anticipation, judgement of speed and distance, driving experience and knowledge of the vehicle's capabilities.

When you come up behind another vehicle, how often do you need to brake to match the speed of the driver in front? If your answer is 'always' or 'nearly always', work at developing your acceleration sense.

Drive along a regular route using acceleration sense rather than braking. Notice how it improves your anticipation and increases the smoothness of the drive.

Acceleration sense helps you avoid unnecessary braking. Common mistakes are:

- accelerating hard away from a junction and then having to brake sharply to slow to the speed of the vehicles in front
- accelerating to move up behind a slower-moving vehicle and then having to brake before overtaking
- accelerating to overtake, then having to brake sharply to move back into a space.

Use of acceleration sense changes a little when driving a vehicle with regenerative braking, but the principles are essentially the same – use the accelerator in a way which avoids the need for sharp reductions in speed. When driving a vehicle with this system you should follow the manufacturer's guidance to understand how to use it to best advantage.

Using the accelerator on bends

A moving vehicle is most stable when its weight is evenly distributed, its engine is just pulling without increasing road speed, and it's travelling in a straight line.

As soon as a vehicle turns into a bend it starts to slow down and lose stability, due to cornering forces. If you keep the same pressure on the accelerator as you go into and round a bend, you'll lose road speed.

For steering control and stability, you need to keep your road speed constant round the bend. Do this by gently depressing the accelerator. Your aim isn't to increase your road speed but to keep it steady.

Practice will help you judge how much to depress the accelerator for a steady speed.

> Use the accelerator to maintain a constant speed round a bend. A constant speed keeps your weight evenly distributed front and rear, and ensures maximum tyre grip.

If you accelerate to *increase* road speed and alter direction at the same time, there may not be enough tyre grip available and you may lose steering control.

When you need to steer and increase speed together, use the accelerator gently. Take extra care when accelerating in slippery conditions or you may cause wheel spin and loss of steering control.

See Chapter 11, page 191, Cornering forces.

Accelerating moves the weight of the vehicle onto the rear wheels and off the front wheels. This reduces the grip of the tyres which are steering the vehicle, so it may understeer. If this happens, don't make the mistake of applying more steering.

As you reduce the amount of steering, start to accelerate but do this gently and smoothly so that you maintain tyre grip. As steering reduces, the tyre grip trade-off allows more grip for acceleration – but beware of accelerating too early. The appropriate point depends on how far you can see, and the conditions on the road surface.

See page 104, Vehicle balance and tyre grip.

Coming out of the bend

Having passed the apex of the bend, your new road view (**B – C**) begins to open rapidly, and is greater than the distance you have travelled (**2 – 3**). If conditions are appropriate, consider gentle acceleration.

Approaching the bend

As you approach the bend, reduce your speed so that you can stop within the distance you can see to be clear on your own side of the road (**1 – A**).

Entering the bend

Your increased road view (**A – B**) is no greater than the distance you have travelled (**1 – 2**) so maintain a constant speed. Increase pressure on the accelerator to maintain but not increase road speed.

Follow the guiding safety principle – you must always be able to stop safely within the distance you can see to be clear on your own side of the road. If that distance shortens, you must slow to match it.

Key points

- **The harder you accelerate, the less tyre grip you have for steering.**
- **Use the accelerator smoothly – jerkiness causes wheel spin and is not fuel efficient.**
- **Use acceleration sense to vary your road speed without unnecessary braking.**
- **For steering control and stability, use the accelerator to maintain a steady speed when you enter a bend.**

Fuel/power source affects acceleration and engine braking

Diesel, petrol, liquefied petroleum gas (LPG) and electric vehicles differ in their acceleration and engine braking characteristics. For example, in electric cars, regenerative braking activates when you ease off the accelerator pedal; it is expected that as electric car technology develops, accelerator-pedal control is also likely to change. (Engine braking is discussed later in this chapter.)

The range of technology built into new vehicles to improve engine performance means that different makes and models with the same type of power source can also have markedly different acceleration or engine braking characteristics. Consult your vehicle handbook for an exact specification and take time to become familiar with the acceleration and engine braking characteristics of any vehicle you drive.

Using the gears

The way you use your gears can make or mar your driving. Correct use of the gears depends on accurately matching the gear to the road speed, and using the clutch and accelerator precisely.

Electric vehicles usually don't have gears and can be driven without the need to deal with gear selection.

Moving off from stationary

From a standing start, accelerate smoothly and gather speed by steadily working up through the gears. You should only use maximum acceleration through the gears if there's a pressing need, and if the road surface and other conditions are safe. Over-accelerating in low gears or remaining in a gear beyond the limits of its best performance damages the engine, uses excessive fuel and results in slower progress. Some engines cut out or misfire if excessively revved.

Accurate use of the gears

Your vehicle can only increase speed if the engine can deliver the power, and it can only do this effectively if you're in the correct gear. Aim to:

- be in the correct gear for every road speed and traffic situation
- make all gear changes smoothly
- engage a chosen gear without going through an intermediate gear first
- know the approximate maximum road speed for each gear
- know the most efficient point at which to change up.

The main effect of the gears is to transform engine revs into usable power.

- In a low gear, the engine is able to rev more freely, which allows the vehicle to accelerate rapidly and to climb slopes.
- In a higher gear, lower revs deliver more speed but less ability to accelerate or to climb slopes.
- Intermediate gears allow progress from one extreme to the other.
- A lower gear also restrains the vehicle's speed when descending a slope.

The greater turning power of low gears also affects tyre grip. The greater the turning power, the more likely that the tyres will lose grip. This is why wheel spin can occur when you accelerate hard in first gear.

It's advisable to use a higher gear when moving slowly in slippery conditions, such as on snow, ice or mud. When moving off from a standstill on ice, use first gear and slip the clutch without accelerating. You'll gain traction and slowly pull forward.

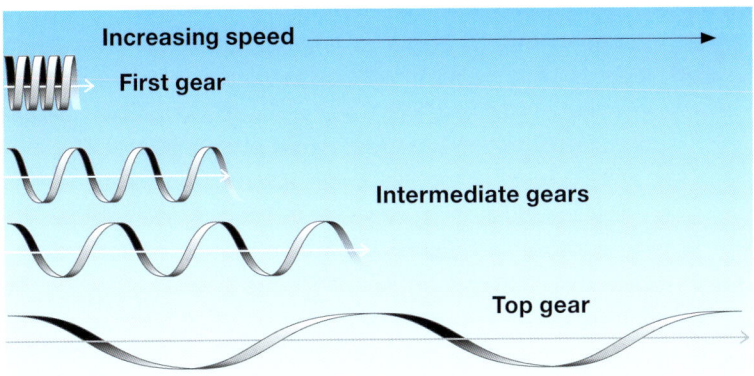

First gear

produces plenty of road wheel turning power but not much speed

Intermediate gears

produce varying combinations of wheel turning power and speed

Top gear

produces plenty of speed but not much wheel turning power

Changing to a lower gear helps when:

- travelling at low speeds
- going uphill
- going downhill, because engine compression slows the descent
- approaching a hazard
- on slippery roads, where you should ease off the accelerator to lose speed gently, so as to avoid skidding.

High gears are good for:

- cruising at speed
- certain slippery conditions where lower gears may cause wheel spin.

The purpose of your journey may influence how you use your gears. For example, on routine journeys your goal is economic progress. For emergency response and pursuit, your goal is to make rapid progress safely.

For economic progress – change up a little earlier. This reduces fuel consumption and carbon emissions. Many new vehicles are now fitted with a gear shift indicator (GSI) on the dashboard, to show you the most fuel-efficient point at which to change gear. Combine this with observation of the road ahead to avoid making unnecessarily frequent gear changes. For example, the GSI may suggest changing up just before you start to climb a steep hill, which would require you to change immediately to a lower gear.

For rapid progress – accelerate up to the engine's peak performance point and then change to a higher gear. Bear in mind the manufacturer's peak engine performance recommendations for your vehicle. This may differ from the maximum revs obtainable from the engine. Do not over-rev the engine.

Key points

- Develop good coordination of hand and foot movements.
- Recognise when to change gear by the sound of the engine.
- Choose the correct gear for the road speed.
- Changing up a little early reduces fuel consumption. Take note of the gear shift indicator if fitted but combine this with observation of the road ahead.
- Brake in good time to slow to the correct road speed as you approach a hazard, and then select the appropriate gear.
- Match engine speed to road speed when you change down.

Are you always in the correct gear?

When you fail to select the appropriate gear, ask yourself why. Are you focusing on other things and not your driving?

Do you ever find yourself changing gear halfway round a corner? Again, ask yourself why this happens, and how you can improve your use of gears.

Don't change gear while cornering. It destabilises the vehicle and requires you to take one hand off the steering wheel.

Vehicle transmission systems

You must be familiar with the transmission system of each vehicle that you drive. You should be competent in using all the features so that you can accurately match the capability of the system to the situation. This may require training because some systems have more features than others, and the operating mechanisms differ across manufacturers.

Vehicles with internal-combustion engines may have a manual or automatic transmission, though increasingly are being fitted with automatic transmissions.

Electric vehicles have neither manual nor automatic transmission systems fitted; an electric motor instantly produces a consistent amount of torque at any revolutions per minute (RPM), and so a conventionally geared transmission isn't required. This contributes to increased vehicle smoothness and reduced noise. Electric vehicles have configurable modes that can be set by the driver that alter performance, efficiency, handling and comfort.

Hybrid vehicles have more than one means of propulsion and so have more than one transmission system. They can have the characteristics of a conventional automatic transmission, powered by an internal combustion engine, and the characteristics of an electric motor, where power is supplied from a battery.

Always consult the vehicle handbook to understand the features of the transmission system of the vehicle you are driving.

Automatic transmission

The gear selector in an automatic vehicle is often in the form of a lever or dial on the floor or on the steering wheel column. Most gear selectors have similar modes:

P – Park

R – Reverse

N – Neutral

D – Drive – automatically selects all forward gears.

Many systems offer additional modes, such as:

S or Sport – This mode changes gear at higher revs than the Drive mode, giving greater acceleration and engine braking. It increases the vehicle's performance but uses more fuel.

Eco or Economy – This mode changes gear at lower revs than Drive mode and is designed for greater fuel efficiency when high performance isn't required.

Manual – Some automatics have a manual control option that you select using a paddle or lever. Manufacturers tend to have their own brand names for this control – for example, Tiptronic, Multitronic and Geartronic.

These features are usually on or next to the gear selector or steering wheel.

Use the mode that best suits your journey and circumstances. For rapid journeys, you might choose a different mode from that for routine tasks, where economy may be more important.

Be ready to change mode if necessary – you don't have to do the whole journey in one mode. But don't fiddle with the gearbox repeatedly. As automatic systems become more sophisticated they need less driver input.

If you choose to use an enhanced mode such as Sport, this will change the engine's performance and will affect the way the vehicle behaves. Always be prepared for the change when you make this choice.

Some systems 'learn', so they adapt to the way you drive the vehicle. Remember this if you change the way you drive during a journey – for example, changing from routine driving to answering an emergency call. The gearbox will take time to adapt to match your change of style.

Using the features of automatic systems

The advice below is general. Exact use of these features varies from one system to another. You must check the manufacturer's advice for each type of automatic vehicle that you drive.

Starting up and moving off – systems vary in what they require you to do before you can start the vehicle. Many systems require you to apply the foot brake in order to start the engine. Some systems allow the engine to be started in P or N, others only in the P position.

Shift lock – this is a security button on the transmission lever that allows you to switch the gear lever to a particular option and lock it; for example, from Park to Drive when you move off, or from Reverse to Park when you've finished your journey.

Kick down – activate kick down by pressing the accelerator firmly to the floor. Some systems require you to do this in a rapid movement. Kick down overrides the current gear selection and will change the gear down to provide an additional burst of acceleration. Always consider carefully before you use kick down, and never use it in a confined situation.

Shorter and longer stops – common advice is to use the foot brake when you need to pause or stop briefly (for example, for traffic lights) but use the parking brake when waiting in traffic or stopping for longer. Most systems advise you not to change to Park unless stopping to park. Check the advice in the vehicle manual as systems vary.

Quitting – when you finish your journey, apply the parking brake and select Park before switching off the engine.

Developing your competence at using automatic systems

Make sure you keep the foot brake depressed when changing between P, R, N and D. Many systems won't let you change modes without doing this. But always use the foot brake when you first engage Drive, or pass through Reverse.

Check that you know what an automatic vehicle will do. When you first drive it, try the kick down mechanism and get the feel of how it behaves, so that you're not surprised by how it acts later.

The system of car control still applies when driving an automatic. It's easy to become lax. Some automatic drivers drift into the habit of losing speed late, entering bends while reducing speed when it would have been better to do so earlier. Make sure there's always time for the car to make a gear change when one will be needed, and that power is applied at the right time to ensure stability.

In some circumstances, a very slight adjustment to the pressure on the accelerator pedal will make a difference to which gear the system chooses. This can be helpful in controlling the balance of the vehicle at times, and to provide a smooth drive. You'll find this easier to achieve if you know the vehicle well.

Vehicles with regenerative battery-charging systems may slow more firmly when the accelerator is being released, so it's essential to learn the amount of foot pressure you need to apply to slow the vehicle to the degree you require.

Some older automatic gearboxes tend to hunt between gears at some speeds and in some circumstances. If you experience this, use the manual override to hold one or other gear, rather than allowing constant changes.

Electric vehicle transmission

The transmission system of an electric vehicle (EV) differs from a manual or automatic transmission in that it does not have a gearbox or clutch.

The instant torque of an electric motor allows for smooth acceleration (and deceleration) without the need for gears.

The driver of an electric vehicle may be able to choose a transmission 'mode' to suit the circumstances. These modes, however, vary between manufacturers.

Most EVs have the following electric-drive modes:

Sport – This mode prioritises performance over energy efficiency.

Eco – This mode prioritises battery conservation and vehicle range over performance.

Drive or Comfort – This mode achieves a balance between Sport and Eco and is a default setting for everyday driving.

When you release the accelerator, the behaviour of each mode is often combined with a level of battery regeneration which in turn affects the rate of deceleration.

Other modes are available that allow customisation; for example, being able to adjust the level of performance when accelerating, or the level of regeneration when decelerating.

Some electric vehicles can be driven using only the accelerator pedal. The rate of deceleration is controlled by the speed at which the accelerator is released; the brake pedal is only ever used to bring the vehicle to complete rest.

Use the mode that best suits your journey and the circumstances. For example, you might choose a different mode for rapid journeys than for routine driving, where range may be more important.

> Be ready to change mode as necessary; you don't have to complete the whole journey in a single mode.
>
> Consider also what you are used to. For example, if after a period of routine driving you choose to use 'Sport' mode, be aware that this affects acceleration and retardation, and you should be prepared for this change.

Developing your competence at using EV transmission

Before you drive an electric vehicle (EV), make sure that you are familiar with the manufacturer's guidelines relating to the operation of the transmission.

Switching an EV 'on', or selecting a drive mode in preparation to move off, requires you to have your foot on the brake pedal. You can, however, select different modes while driving, except for 'reverse', which you can only do when you have come to rest.

Try the various modes to get a 'feel' of how the vehicle performs so that you are not surprised later. For example, in 'Sport' mode, the vehicle may accelerate very quickly.

> Remember:
>
> - The system of car control still applies when driving an electric vehicle.
> - Drive modes and braking/energy recovery may differ in performance and features, and the terms used between vehicle manufacturers. You should always make sure you understand the specific features of your vehicle by referring to the manufacturer's guidelines.

Road conditions

Driving though water – gently brake with your left foot while applying pressure with your right foot, so that you maintain a good level of engine revs to ensure water doesn't flow up the exhaust pipe.

EVs are generally well-protected against water, but you should avoid deep or fast-moving water.

Descending a steep hill – some automatic vehicles have a 'hold' system to maintain a low road speed on a long hill, rather than using the brakes. If your vehicle doesn't do this automatically, use a manual override to hold a lower gear. On a long descent, if you need to brake, try to do so on straighter sections, and only do it occasionally and significantly, not all the time. Hold a lower gear so that you never allow your speed to rise too high.

In an EV, consider setting a higher level of regeneration to maintain a safe road speed. This will charge the vehicle batteries, minimise brake wear and ensure the brakes remain effective if required.

Moving off on snow, ice or wet grass – in some automatics you can manually select a setting for moving off on slippery surfaces, to help avoid wheel spin. In automatics without this setting, try selecting locked position 2 or 3 when moving off or travelling slowly, and use very gentle acceleration. This may give you more grip.

Slowing down and stopping

You need to be able to slow down or stop smoothly and with your vehicle fully under control. Anticipate the need to slow down or stop early and brake progressively. Being able to accurately estimate the required braking distance at different speeds and in different conditions is central to skilful driving. There are two ways of slowing down (decelerating) or stopping:

- releasing or easing off the accelerator
- using the brakes.

Releasing the accelerator – engine braking

When you release the accelerator, the engine slows and through engine compression exerts a slowing force on the wheels. This causes the engine to act as a brake, reducing road speed smoothly and gradually with little wear to the vehicle.

The loss of road speed is greater when you ease off the accelerator in a low gear. This applies equally to automatic gearboxes.

Releasing the accelerator on a larger vehicle fitted with a retarder will activate the retarder. This will apply **additional** braking power.

See page 106, Retarders.

Engine braking allows you to lose speed in conditions where normal braking might lock the wheels – for example, on slippery roads. It's also useful on long descents in hilly country.

Using the brakes

Use the brakes if you need to make more than a gradual adjustment to your road speed, unless you're driving a vehicle with a regenerative braking system. For maximum control, you should keep both hands on the wheel while you brake, and plan to avoid braking on bends and corners. (But note the discussion on brake/gear overlap in Chapter 3.) You can apply pressure to the foot brake to achieve the slightest check or, at the other extreme, until just before the ESP or ABS intervenes. (In an older vehicle without safety devices, you can apply pressure until just before the wheels lock up. Avoid locking the wheels completely because this will cause you to lose steering control.) Remember to make allowances for extra loads or changes in road surface.

> Check the brakes every time you use your vehicle, both before you move off and when the vehicle is moving.

Normal braking (tapered braking)

Braking should normally be progressive and increased steadily. Smooth braking uses less fuel.

See Appendix 3, Fuel-efficient driving, page 295.

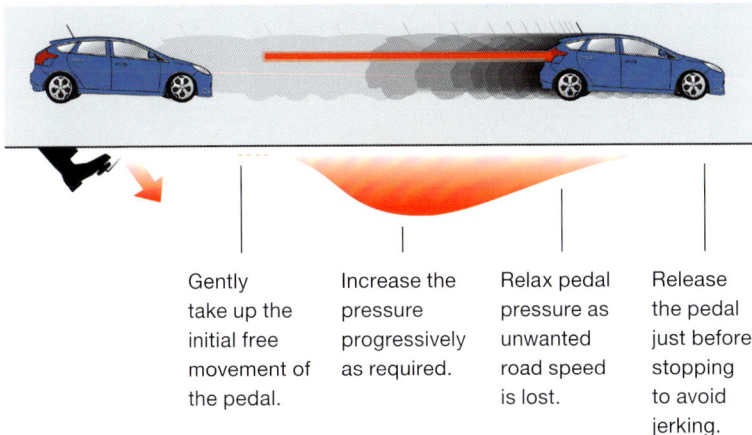

| Gently take up the initial free movement of the pedal. | Increase the pressure progressively as required. | Relax pedal pressure as unwanted road speed is lost. | Release the pedal just before stopping to avoid jerking. |

Braking, tyre grip and balance

Braking moves the weight of the vehicle forward on to the front wheels. This makes the steering heavier and at the same time reduces the grip of the rear tyres. On a bend, this reduces stability and can cause a skid. The harsher the braking, the greater the demand on tyre grip and the less your ability to steer. In slippery conditions, harsh braking almost inevitably results in loss of traction.

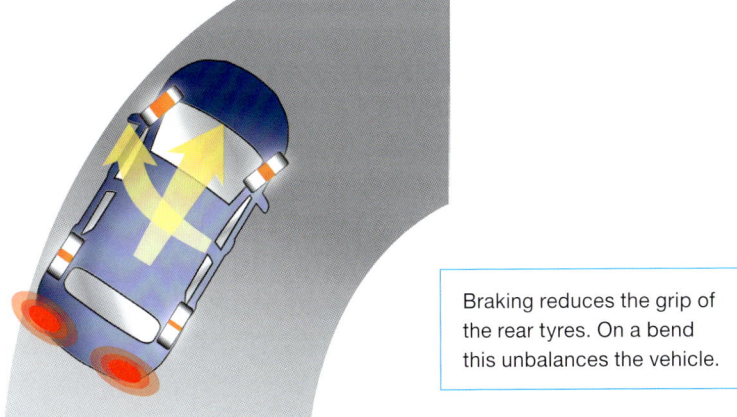

Braking reduces the grip of the rear tyres. On a bend this unbalances the vehicle.

The safe stopping distance rule

The safe stopping distance rule is one of the guiding principles of *Roadcraft*. By relating your speed to the distance within which you can stop, you can adopt a safe speed in any situation.

> Always drive so that you can stop safely within the distance you can see to be clear on your own side of the road.

The importance of observing this rule for your own and other people's safety can't be overstated. It provides a guide to the speed at which you should corner and the distance you should keep from other vehicles in all other traffic conditions. Successfully applying this rule requires skill. You need to be aware of:

- the braking capabilities of your vehicle
- the type and condition of the road surface – in slippery or wet conditions, braking distances increase greatly
- the effects of cornering, braking and vehicle balance on tyre grip.

> In narrow and single-track lanes, allow twice the overall stopping distance that you can see to be clear to allow room for any oncoming vehicle to brake too.

Overall safe stopping distance

To work out the overall safe stopping distance, add thinking distance to braking distance.

Thinking distance + Braking distance = Stopping distance

Thinking distance is the distance travelled in the time between first observing the need for action and acting. This is why attitude, observation, anticipation and information-processing abilities are vital.

> Actual thinking distance varies according to the speed of the vehicle, your physical and mental condition, your attentiveness and whether or not you're expecting something to happen.

It takes much longer to react to unexpected events than to expected ones – you need less thinking time if you're anticipating events and not just reacting to them.

Some common medicines (for example, some antihistamines for hay fever) can make you drowsy and slow your thinking and should be used with care.

Braking distance is the distance needed for braking. Actual braking distance depends on:

- the vehicle's capability, size and weight – larger, heavier vehicles take longer to stop
- the gradient of the road and the condition of the road surface – slippery surfaces greatly increase braking distances.

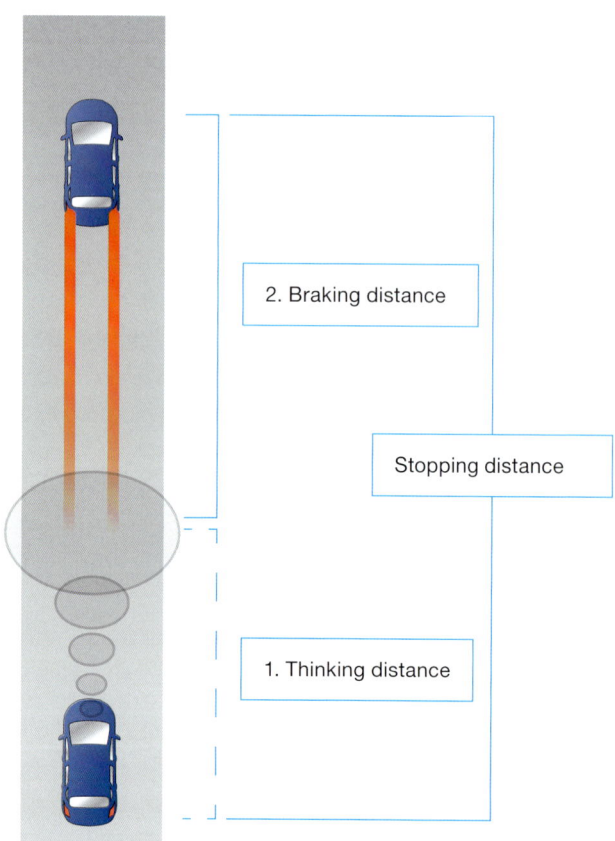

The two-second rule

To keep a safe distance between you and the vehicle in front, leave a gap of at least two seconds. But remember your overall stopping distance depends on your speed and the condition of the road surface.

> An easy way to count two seconds is to say: 'Only a fool breaks the two-second rule'.

You need to allow at least double this distance in wet weather and even more in icy conditions. If the vehicle behind you is too close, drop back further from the vehicle in front. This will allow you to brake more gently in an emergency and may prevent you being rammed from behind.

Note when the vehicle in front passes over a mark or shadow on the road.

Count one second

Count two seconds

If you pass over the mark or shadow on the road before you have counted two seconds, you are too close. Drop back and try the test again.

Braking for corners and bends

Braking affects the balance, stability and cornering ability of vehicles, so you need to plan braking carefully for a corner or bend:

- plan to avoid braking firmly on corners because it increases the demand on tyre grip; if braking is necessary, apply the brakes gently and steadily
- brake in plenty of time

- adjust brake pressure to the condition or grip of the road surface
- on steep winding descents, brake firmly on the straight stretches and gently on the bends – remember to use a low gear at an early stage in the descent.

See Chapter 8, page 151, How active safety systems work.

Braking as you approach a hazard

To apply the system of car control, consider your road speed on the approach to a hazard and slow down if necessary. Always check your mirrors before you reduce speed or change direction. Choose the best road position and then reduce speed safely and smoothly using engine braking, braking or a combination of both.

When and how firmly you apply the brakes, or use regenerative braking capability, depends on your judgement of speed and distance. Consider:

- your initial speed
- the road surface
- weather conditions
- the specific road and traffic conditions.

Sometimes braking may need to be firm but it should never be harsh. Harsh braking usually results from poor observation, anticipation and planning. Aim to lose speed steadily from the first moment until you achieve the correct speed to negotiate the hazard. Timing is crucial: avoid braking so early that you have to re-accelerate to reach the hazard, or so late that you have to brake harshly.

See Chapter 3, page 40, The system of car control.

> Stop-start technology is beneficial as part of fuel-efficient driving, but consider turning it off during emergency response driving.

Emergency braking

The quickest and shortest way to stop on a dry straight road is to brake as hard as you can.

In a vehicle fitted with ABS or emergency brake assist, depress the brake as far and hard as possible and keep it there.

The ABS repeatedly releases the brakes just before the wheels lock up and re-applies them in a pulsing action, so that they never fully lock. ABS only works if you maintain firm pressure on the brake pedal. The advantage of ABS is that it gives you some steering control during emergency braking – see Chapter 8, page 151, How active safety systems work, for a full explanation.

> ABS doesn't always shorten braking distance – it helps steering during harsh braking.

Many vehicles are fitted with ESP, which incorporates ABS. In a vehicle with ESP, depress the brake as far as possible and keep it there until the vehicle has come to a halt.

Emergency brake assist

New vehicles now have emergency brake assist (BA or EBA) as well as ABS. EBA maximises braking pressure in an emergency situation. If you apply the brake with speed and force, EBA will activate and fully apply the brakes until the ABS takes over to prevent the wheels locking up and permit steering. It's important to know what your vehicle is likely to do in this situation, and what may activate the system.

Autonomous emergency braking

Many modern vehicles are fitted with autonomous emergency braking (AEB) in some form. Make sure you understand which system your vehicle is equipped with and what will cause it to operate. You can then avoid making any decision that will trigger the system unexpectedly and understand what has happened should your vehicle's AEB operate when you're not expecting it to.

See Chapter 8, page 152, Anti-lock braking systems.

Using the parking brake

Methods for applying, locking and releasing the parking brake vary, so always check and follow the manufacturer's instructions. For example, many vehicles now have an auto-hold facility. Make sure you're familiar with your vehicle's controls.

In general, only use the parking brake when the vehicle is stationary. New drivers are often taught to use the parking brake every time they come to a standstill on a journey. With experience you can judge whether you need to use it for every short stop.

When stopping at night or in poor visibility, keep your brake lights on to increase the chance of following vehicles seeing you and stopping safely. Once you're both stationary, consider applying the parking brake then releasing the foot brake to reduce glare for the driver behind you. Be aware that auto-hold triggers the brake lights.

Steering

A well-maintained vehicle travelling along a flat, straight road should hold its position with minimal steering. Camber, crossfall or side winds can move the vehicle to one side, but a small steering adjustment will keep the vehicle on a straight course. Usually, you only need to make positive steering adjustments when you alter position or turn the vehicle. Steering characteristics vary between vehicles, so make sure you're familiar with the characteristics of the vehicles you drive.

Steering technique

Police driving schools have developed a range of steering techniques to suit different policing situations. The most widely adopted is the pull–push method, which provides safe and efficient steering in a wide range of circumstances.

Your steering method should be determined by the control, efficiency and comfort you experience throughout the full range of steering movements. This may vary according to:

- the vehicle you're driving (the lightness of its steering, the diameter of the steering wheel, the castor action and the number of turns from lock to lock)
- how you sit in relation to the steering wheel
- your size and shape.

Seat position

Good steering starts with getting your body in the right position in relation to the steering wheel. Adjust the steering wheel position and the position and angle of your seat so that you can reach the controls comfortably. An uncomfortable position will tire you and impair your driving.

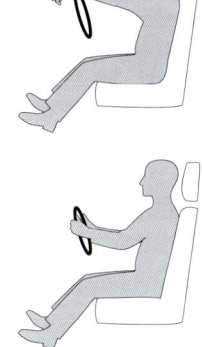

You're likely to be in a good sitting position when:

- both hands are on the steering wheel and your elbows are slightly bent
- you can depress the clutch pedal to its full extent and your knee is still slightly bent.

To set your seat position, extend your arms so that your wrists sit on top of the steering wheel when your arms are straight. Then allow your arms to drop so that your hands are in a comfortable position on the wheel rim – between ten to two and quarter to three, depending on your steering wheel indentations.

How to hold the steering wheel

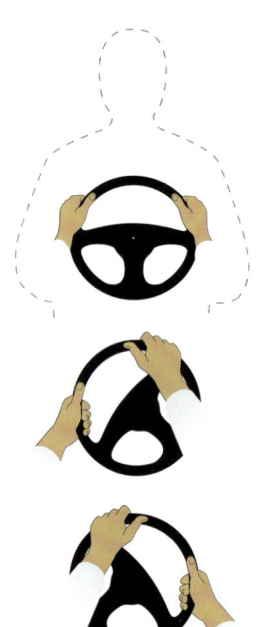

- Hold the wheel so that your palms are on the rim. Extend your thumbs on the rim so that your thumb nails are towards you. (Don't wrap your thumbs round the wheel. If your vehicle hits a kerb, the steering wheel may spin sharply and injure your wrapped round thumbs.)
- Hold the wheel lightly but be ready to tighten your grip if necessary.
- Keep both hands on the wheel while you're driving, unless you need to operate a control.

Make changes in direction smoothly and gradually. Make **small** changes in direction by turning the steering wheel without altering your hand hold. Your hands should not pass the 12 o'clock position.

To make **larger** turns, use the pull–push method described next.

> This standard hold enables you to turn the wheel immediately in either direction and is a feature of most safe and efficient steering techniques.

Pull–push

With the pull–push method neither hand passes the 12 o'clock position. Your hands remain level with each other on the steering wheel except when you move a hand up for the initial pull or when you make small alterations in position. One hand grips and makes the turn, the other slides round its side of the wheel ready to continue the turn. The advantage of pull–push is that it keeps both hands on the wheel and allows an immediate turn in either direction at any point during steering.

The explanation of the pull–push method given below is for a left-hand turn. For a right-hand turn, follow the same method starting with the right hand at 12 o'clock.

Start the turn with a pull and not a push because it gives better control.

Slide the left hand up to a higher position on the wheel, but not past the 12 o'clock point. The starting point will depend on the sharpness of the bend or turn.

Pull the wheel down with the left hand.

As the left hand pulls down, slide the right hand down, allowing the rim to slide through the right hand fingers. Keep the right hand level with the left hand until it nears the bottom of the wheel.

If more turn to the left is necessary, start pushing up with the right hand and at the same time slide the left hand up the wheel, keeping it level with the right.

Repeat these movements until you achieve sufficient turn.

Straighten the vehicle after the turn by feeding the wheel back through the hands with similar but opposite movements to those used for the turn. Don't let the wheel spin back on its own.

When you steer, do you start with a pull rather than a push? If in the past you've tended to start with a push, practise pulling first. Notice how it contributes to the smoothness and control of your steering.

Rotational steering

In exceptional circumstances, for example during skidding or during very slow- or high-speed manoeuvres, this technique may be an option.

Hold the wheel using the standard hold described on page 134. The quarter-to-three position allows the greatest degree of turn without having to reposition a hand.

Most alterations to direction (up to about 120 degrees of steering wheel turn) can be made by turning the wheel while keeping a light but fixed hand hold.

For more acute turns (requiring more than about 120 degrees of steering wheel turn), reposition your lower hand at 12 o'clock and continue smoothly pulling down the wheel.

If you can see that a turn is going to require more than 120 degrees of steering wheel turn, place your leading hand at the top of the wheel before starting the turn.

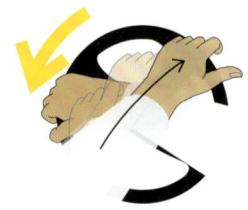

If even more turn is required, place your other hand near the top of the wheel to continue the turning motion.

Straighten the wheel by using a similar series of movements but in the opposite direction. Although the self-centring action of the wheel assists the return, you must keep it under control.

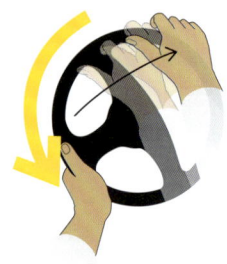

Moving your hands past the 12 o'clock position places your arms across the wheel. Be aware that this increases the risk of injury to hands, arms or face if the steering wheel airbag inflates or explodes in a collision.

Key points

- **Hold the wheel lightly but be ready to tighten your grip when you need maximum steering control.**
- **Keep both hands on the wheel when cornering, braking or driving through deep surface water.**
- **On slippery roads, steer as delicately as possible to maintain tyre grip.**
- **Accurate steering requires good observation, anticipation and planning. If the brakes are applied sharply or if the speed is too high, steering can't be precise.**

Check your understanding

You should now be able to apply learning from this chapter in your driver training so that you can:

- [ ] explain how acceleration, braking and steering affect tyre grip and vehicle balance
- [ ] show that you can control your vehicle accurately in a range of situations
- [ ] show good acceleration sense, using the accelerator accurately and smoothly
- [ ] show how to use gears accurately, selecting the correct gear in a range of circumstances and for different purposes, in vehicles with manual or automatic gearboxes
- [ ] demonstrate an understanding of the acceleration characteristics and transmission modes of electric vehicles
- [ ] explain the safe stopping distance
- [ ] show how to use the brakes, engine braking or regenerative braking capability to slow the vehicle appropriately and safely in different circumstances
- [ ] demonstrate a method of steering for maximum safety and control
- [ ] explain the main factors that reduce fuel consumption.

Chapter 7
Manoeuvring at low speeds

Learning outcomes

The learning in this chapter, along with driver training, should enable you to:

- explain how to use the system of car control to perform low-speed manoeuvres such as parking and turning in a confined space
- show good all-round observation throughout the manoeuvre
- use planning to help you perform low-speed manoeuvres safely and efficiently
- explain the benefits of using a guide
- show how to reverse safely in a limited space
- park your vehicle safely according to the needs of your journey without obstructing other road users.

Developing your competence at low-speed manoeuvring

> Across the UK, one of the most common and costly types of collision happens when drivers are manoeuvring in confined spaces. Even when low-speed collisions don't result in injury, they can cause damage to vehicles, equipment and premises. Most of these collisions can be avoided by taking simple precautions.

People commonly believe that driving at low speed is easy and hazard free – but neither is true. Drivers of larger vehicles may need to perform complicated manoeuvres to turn the vehicle safely, and require more space in which to turn. Low-speed manoeuvring collisions cause a great deal of vehicle damage and high repair costs to fleets.

The majority of vehicle collisions occur when undertaking low-speed manoeuvres in all types of vehicles, so you should always:

- avoid reversing your vehicle unnecessarily
- carry out all manoeuvres at a slow walking speed
- avoid turning in narrow roads with parked vehicles
- consider using junctions in which to turn – or drive to a roundabout.

It takes constant attention to perform low-speed manoeuvres safely and well. You must think through what you're trying to achieve and carry out the manoeuvre with extreme care.

Using the system

Use the system of car control to plan and execute low-speed manoeuvres, just as you would any other driving activity:

- gather information through careful observation throughout the manoeuvre
- give signals if necessary
- plan your route through the manoeuvre.

Consider the best position to take throughout the manoeuvre, not just at the start and end points. Assess where to go forwards and where to reverse, and select the correct speed and gear, so that, if you're not parking, you can accelerate away to best advantage.

Observation

If you can't get a full view, get out of your vehicle and check for hazards. If there's an appropriate person available, ask them to act as a guide to help your observation. If possible, use either someone trained for that role or another driver. If neither of these is available, use someone else rather than attempt the manoeuvre without help.

See page 146, Manoeuvring with a guide.

Good observation is vital for safety. Maintain all-round observation throughout the manoeuvre. Take time to obtain information to give yourself an overall view of what you want to achieve, so that you can plan the best option to do it, especially in tight or awkward situations. Low-speed manoeuvring rarely causes serious injuries but they do happen. Even in a car, it's possible to lose sight of people – especially children – if your observation isn't thorough, especially when reversing. If you do lose sight of someone, STOP!

Don't rely on your mirrors to provide your view to the rear of the vehicle: look behind, through the rear window if the vehicle has one. Make use of all available sources of observation, including reversing cameras as well as mirrors.

When you're reversing, it's still important to look forwards occasionally to check that there's no activity around you that could compromise safety. Be especially aware of low objects such as posts and walls.

Planning

 When you're faced with an awkward manoeuvre, first consider whether it's absolutely necessary. Is there an alternative route that you could use?

If you're planning a complex manoeuvre that involves several movements or shunts, consider other options. Plan an overall path, but be prepared to take more shunts if you need to. Generally one longer shunt is better than several shorter ones – but be aware that this may mean a longer reverse and, therefore, a longer period with limited visibility.

Check to see whether there are any slopes as these can make some parts of the manoeuvre easier or harder to control. Plan to stop and change from forward to reverse, or vice versa, on level areas if possible.

Keep your speed low throughout and think carefully about which way round to do things. Plan to keep awkward features – low bollards, for example – where you can see them throughout the manoeuvre.

Plan your manoeuvre in a way that best supports its purpose. Do you need to unload onto a higher area, or have your vehicle facing a particular direction at the end?

Steering

Manoeuvring in a confined space sometimes requires rapid movements of the steering wheel. The standard pull–push technique generally provides effective steering but, occasionally, other hand holds may give better control, especially when reversing. Don't try to turn the steering wheel while the vehicle is stationary. This damages the tyres and puts excessive strain on the steering linkages.

Reversing hold

Hold the wheel near the top with your right hand and low down with your left hand. If you're driving a car and you find this position difficult, or need to improve your view to the left, it may help to put your left arm on the back of your passenger seat. Look in your mirrors and over your shoulders to get a clear view. If the seat belt restricts your movement, release it but don't forget to put it back on.

Steering in reverse

It's easier to manoeuvre a vehicle when reversing than when going forwards, because the steered wheels are at the back. This may seem counter-intuitive but, once you've achieved competence, it's easier to be precise and to make steering movements at slow speed this way round. (As you increase speed in reverse, it becomes increasingly difficult to steer accurately.)

This means that it's often easier to manage tight turns in reverse, provided you have a good enough view to do so. There's a trade-off between vision and manoeuvrability, particularly for larger vehicles like vans and trucks.

Remember to allow for overhangs. Even a small vehicle will have some overhang from the wheels, and in a tight space this will move differently when steering. The tighter the steering lock, the more pronounced this is.

> Remember to allow for overhangs. Even a small vehicle will have some overhang from the wheels. Be aware this will swing out and could hit another parked vehicle in a tight space. The tighter the steering lock, the more the overhang will swing out.

Reversing in a confined space

Reversing can be difficult, especially in a confined area. The faster it's done, the harder it is to control so always reverse slowly.

Before you reverse:

- Ensure your mirrors are clean and correctly adjusted.

- Scan the area for suitability and any hazards/obstructions. Make sure there's sufficient space for your vehicle. If you're not sure, get out of the vehicle and check.
- Plan to execute the manoeuvre where the space is greatest and visibility is at its best. Ensure that you have an unobstructed view.
- If you can, ask someone to guide you.
- Wind down your side windows to increase awareness and aid communication with your guide.
- Check your mirrors.
- Check the 'blind spots' (the areas you can't see easily in the mirrors).
- Make sure the manoeuvre is legal (for example, it doesn't contravene a 'No entry' sign) and won't obstruct others more than necessary.

While manoeuvring:

- Use all your mirrors and parking aids to help you while reversing but look all round, including to the front. Don't rely on mirrors, reversing cameras or sensors alone.
- If possible, use a guide for both forward and reverse movements.
- Always travel slowly, no faster than a slow walking speed, and ease the clutch if necessary. In automatic vehicles you can check the speed by using the brake.
- Continue to look around you for hazards throughout the whole manoeuvre.
- Be aware that the front of your vehicle will swing out as you turn and could strike nearby objects. Remember to look forward and scan all around for obstructions.
- Stop immediately if you're uncertain of hazards around your vehicle, especially pedestrians. If necessary, stop and get out of your vehicle to check behind.
- If your reversing light fails, use your indicator or brake lights to light the area behind you when it's dark. Be careful not to mislead other road users.

Never rely on a reversing alarm to clear the area behind your vehicle of pedestrians and other road users.

Manoeuvring with a guide

In confined spaces, consider using another person as a guide when carrying out forward and reverse manoeuvres. If necessary – in a large vehicle, for example – use more than one person.

Explain clearly to your guide what manoeuvre you intend to carry out with the vehicle, which direction you intend to travel in and where you want the vehicle to be when you've finished. Use an agreed system of signals/directions, including a signal for stopping.

Your guide will need to stand in a safe position without being in the way. They must be visible to you at all times. If you lose sight of your guide, stop immediately and only move when they are in sight again and have signalled you to proceed.

A guide should wear visible clothing, such as a reflective vest, and ensure that any signals are clearly visible to you. If it's dark, the guide could use a torch to be more visible. Consider whether portable radios or similar communications systems would be helpful.

Parking

Park your vehicle safely. Don't leave it where it may cause inconvenience or danger to others. Ensure that other road users can see your vehicle easily (that is, not just round a bend or over the brow of a hill) and that it's not causing any obstruction. Make sure that you park legally – not on yellow/red lines, etc.

If you park on a hill, apply the hand brake firmly, put the vehicle into a low gear and consider turning your wheels into the kerb. (Bear in mind the run lock fitted to emergency vehicles.)

When you're planning how to park, think about the purpose of your journey. If you need to access the boot for heavy or large items, park facing in the direction that best allows you to do this safely.

Unless your arrival is urgent, it's best to reverse into end-on spaces because:

- the vehicle is more manoeuvrable in reverse mode
- it's safer to drive forwards out of the space than to reverse out
- the vehicle will be available for its next use immediately
- it's slightly more fuel efficient to drive out forwards rather than reverse out.

Take care to respect any signs that tell you to park face in. Buildings could have air intakes at exhaust pipe height, or there may be hidden hazards that cause problems when reversing in.

Next time you complete a low-speed manoeuvre in a confined space, ask yourself the following questions:

- Was the manoeuvre necessary or could I have avoided doing it?
- How could I have improved my good all-round observation throughout the manoeuvre?
- Should I have asked for help with observation to the front and rear? Would this have made the manoeuvre safer?
- Did I adopt a slow walking speed, using the appropriate gear?
- Did I take full advantage of the greater manoeuvrability of the vehicle in reverse?
- Did I accelerate smoothly and safely out of the manoeuvre?
- Was the manoeuvre legal and conducted in a way that caused minimum disruption to other road users?

✅ Check your understanding

You should now be able to apply learning from this chapter in your driver training so that you can:

- [ ] explain how to use the system of car control to perform low-speed manoeuvres such as parking and turning in a confined space
- [ ] show good all-round observation throughout the manoeuvre
- [ ] use planning to help you perform low-speed manoeuvres safely and efficiently
- [ ] explain the benefits of using a guide
- [ ] show how to reverse safely in a limited space
- [ ] park your vehicle safely according to the needs of your journey without obstructing other road users.

Chapter 8
Maintaining vehicle stability

Learning outcomes

The learning in this chapter, along with driver training, should enable you to:

- explain why active safety features can interfere with driver behaviour
- describe the principles of anti-lock braking systems, traction control systems and electronic stability programmes
- explain how to avoid the actions that reduce a vehicle's stability and tyre grip
- identify the causes of skidding and how to minimise the risk.

Controlling your vehicle's stability

A vehicle's stability is reduced when you brake, accelerate or steer because these actions produce forces that alter the vehicle's weight distribution and balance, and reduce tyre grip. A vehicle may skid when one or more of the tyres loses normal grip on the road.

See Chapter 6, page 103, The tyre grip trade-off.

New vehicles are fitted with a growing range of active safety features to increase vehicle stability. There are two types of system:

- drive-assist features that drivers can choose to use, such as adaptive cruise control
- in-built safety features.

This chapter briefly explains the principles of anti-lock braking systems (ABS), traction control systems (TCS) and electronic stability programmes (ESP). (Some manufacturers call this electronic stability control or ESC.)

The principles of each type of system are similar but there are significant differences between manufacturers in how their particular system is activated and how it behaves.

With rapid changes in technology, it's vital that you refer to the manufacturer's handbook to know which safety features are fitted to your vehicle, how to use them and what effect they'll have on the vehicle. Be aware that many police and other emergency service vehicles may have a different specification from standard models.

Safety features are there to protect you so, in non-emergency driving, they should be turned on. However, in some operational circumstances, and in some adverse weather conditions, you may want to consider turning off certain functions.

Attitudes to vehicle safety technology

Research has shown that safety systems can give some drivers a false sense of security, causing them to become over-dependent on these features and take more risks than they would in a vehicle without them.

Safety features can't change the laws of physics – they don't make a vehicle perform better or increase a driver's skill. If you're on the point of losing control of the vehicle, you've misjudged the situation. Safety devices can help you to regain control, but only if you understand the specific feature and know how to use it correctly.

How active safety systems work

Manufacturers are constantly seeking to improve vehicle stability with active safety features that can help safety and stability during braking, acceleration or steering. There are many more, but the active safety systems explained below are:

- anti-lock braking systems (ABS)
- traction control systems (TCS)
- electronic stability programmes (ESP).

If an active safety system is fitted, you'll see an icon light up on the dashboard when you turn on the ignition or start the engine. If more than one device is fitted, they may be displayed separately or combined in a single warning light.

> When the system is activated, vehicles fitted with an active safety system will behave differently from vehicles without.

Skid control in a vehicle fitted with one or more active safety systems will depend on the exact features fitted. Different systems intervene at different points and some models have a deliberately delayed point of intervention.

If you drive different vehicles, you must take note of the manufacturer's advice, and guidance in the driver's vehicle handbook, so that you fully understand how each vehicle is likely to behave in extreme circumstances.

Anti-lock braking systems

Almost all modern vehicles are fitted with ABS. This is an electronic safety device that adds to the conventional hydraulic braking system by giving you some ability to steer during harsh or emergency braking.

The foot brake applies the brakes to all four wheels at once, but ABS controls the braking applied to individual wheels. It works by sensing when a wheel is slowing down and about to lock up. When this happens, ABS releases the brake on that wheel before it locks up fully. It re-applies the brake once the wheel starts to rotate again.

The advantage of ABS is that it allows you to steer the vehicle under full braking power, because it prevents the wheels locking up.

Once you activate ABS, you must maintain maximum pressure on the brake pedal throughout. ABS may reduce or lengthen the stopping distance of the vehicle compared with conventional brakes on different road surfaces but it allows the driver to retain some steering control.

ABS can't increase the grip of the tyres on the road, nor can it fully prevent the possibility of the vehicle skidding.

When the ABS activates, always ask yourself: 'Could I have anticipated the hazard that caused me to brake so hard?'

When ABS is activated, you'll see a warning light on the dashboard and will feel the brake pedal vibrate or judder momentarily as the system modulates the brake line pressures. If you become aware that the ABS is cutting in, you should learn from this and reduce your speed for the rest of the journey. If you feel that you're experiencing brake fade, this may be because the system (combined with electronic stability systems) is managing the braking to avoid the wheels locking up. Steering will affect this. The effects of tyre grip trade-off will still apply and the system has to account for this effect.

Emergency brake assist

New vehicles now have emergency brake assist (EBA) as well as ABS. EBA increases braking pressure in an emergency situation. If you apply the brake with speed and force, EBA will cut in and fully apply the brakes until the ABS takes over to prevent the wheels locking up.

Autonomous emergency braking

Many modern vehicles are also fitted with autonomous emergency braking (AEB) systems. Find out what your vehicle is fitted with and what will cause it to activate.

Traction control systems

When you accelerate, it's possible for the power transmitted to the driving wheels to exceed the amount of available tyre grip. This is more likely when moving off on icy or slippery roads, on a steep hill or accelerating out of a corner. This may cause the driven wheels to spin. Wheel spin reduces both the vehicle's ability to accelerate and its stability.

A traction control system works by controlling excess wheel spin on individual wheels. It applies independent braking to the spinning wheel. Some systems may also limit the wheel-turning power of the engine to increase tyre grip.

TCS allows you to make maximum use of tyre grip, especially on slippery surfaces or where the friction of the road surface is uneven. An example is where one wheel can grip the normal surface but the other slips on ice or snow.

If you activate the TCS, you'll see a warning light on the dashboard.
If traction control activates when you pull away from a standstill, reduce pressure on the accelerator to regain control of the steering. Note that if you switch the system off, the warning light will remain constant to advise you that you no longer have its assistance.

Electronic stability programmes

An ESP is an active safety system which incorporates conventional anti-lock braking and traction control systems. It's designed to help vehicle stability by detecting when the vehicle is driven to the limit of its physical capabilities.

There's more variation between types of ESP than between types of ABS or TCS. Your vehicle's handbook may explain what the manufacturer's system does.

Sensors at each wheel work in combination with a sensor that monitors the rotation and pitch of the vehicle – called a yaw sensor. Another sensor on the steering assembly detects the driver's intended path. If these sensors detect that the vehicle isn't following the intended path, the system intervenes. It applies the brakes to individual wheels in order to correct understeer or oversteer and realign the vehicle. **It's therefore crucial that you steer in the direction you want to go**.

Most systems interact with the engine management system, reducing or increasing the engine power to the driven wheels. Some also interact with the transmission system.

> ESP detects your intended path so it's crucial that you steer in the direction you want to go.
>
> If you drive a vehicle beyond its physical capabilities, ESP doesn't guarantee that the vehicle will remain stable and under control. It can't defy the laws of physics.

Centre of gravity and electric vehicles

An electric vehicle (EV) tends to have a lower centre of gravity compared to an internal combustion engine (ICE) vehicle, due to heavy battery packs, typically mounted low in the chassis. For this reason, be aware that there may be a difference in an EV's handling compared to an ICE.

See Chapter 6, page 120, Electric vehicle transmission.

Key points

- **If you brake too hard, ABS prevents the wheel from locking up.**
- **If you accelerate too harshly, traction control prevents the wheel from spinning excessively.**
- **If you steer too sharply, ESP can help prevent the resulting oversteer or understeer from developing into a skid.**
- **Safety devices aren't a substitute for *Roadcraft* competences.**

If you activate a safety system, work out why you misjudged the situation. Honestly assess your driving behaviour and ask yourself what human factors may have led to the activation.

How could you avoid repeating this mistake in future?

Avoiding skidding

Avoiding a skid by driving safely is far better than having to correct one. Know your own limits and your vehicle's limits for the road, traffic and weather conditions. Often it isn't poor road or weather conditions that cause skids but the driver's response to them. Skidding is caused by excessive speed, coarse steering, harsh acceleration or excessive or sudden braking, or a combination of these. The real cause of a skid may therefore be the driver.

Aim to control your vehicle so that it doesn't skid. This becomes more difficult when road or weather conditions deteriorate. But you can minimise the risk by driving more slowly and using your skills of observation, anticipation and planning.

How does a skid happen?

A skid develops when one tyre or more loses normal grip on the road, causing an involuntary movement of the vehicle. This happens when the grip of tyres on the road becomes less than the force or forces acting on the vehicle.

These forces act on your vehicle whenever you operate the controls – the brake, the accelerator, the clutch or the steering wheel. If you brake or accelerate while steering round a bend or corner, two forces are combined. There's only limited tyre grip available, so if these forces become too powerful they break the grip of the tyres on the road. Remember the tyre grip trade-off. The diagram below shows how each of these forces affects the vehicle's stability and reduces tyre grip.

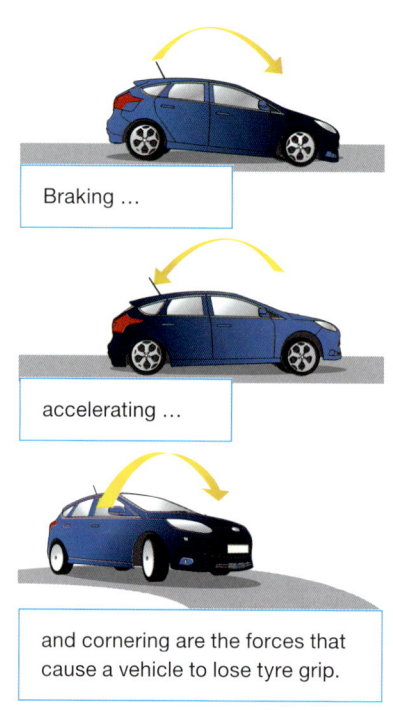

Braking …

accelerating …

and cornering are the forces that cause a vehicle to lose tyre grip.

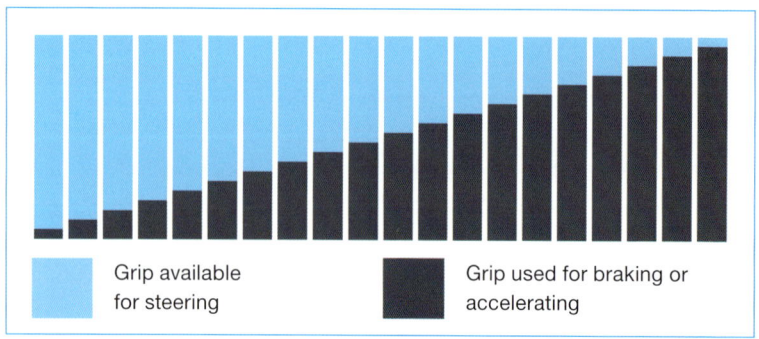

Grip available for steering

Grip used for braking or accelerating

Never drive to the limits of the tyre grip available – always leave a safety margin to allow for the unforeseen.

It takes much less force to break the grip of the tyres on a slippery road surface.

How to minimise the risk of skidding

Check your vehicle

The condition of your vehicle can reduce or increase the risk of skidding:

- check tyre treads and tyre pressure regularly
- check the vehicle's brakes before you drive – defective brakes are especially dangerous on slippery surfaces.

Avoid skidding in the first place – use observation, anticipation and planning to adjust your driving when the road surface may be slippery.

See Appendix 2, Is your vehicle fit to drive?, page 291.

Observe – weather and road conditions to watch for

Skidding is more likely in bad weather conditions and on slippery road surfaces. Watch out for:

- snow, ice, frost, heavy rain
- wet mud, damp leaves or oil, which can create sudden slippery patches on the road surface
- cold spots in shaded areas, under trees, on slopes or hills – watch how other vehicles behave in icy weather
- dry loose dust or gravel
- a shower or rain after a long dry spell – accumulated rubber dust and oil mixed with water can create a very slippery surface
- worn road surfaces that have become polished smooth
- concrete – may hold surface water and become slippery, especially in freezing conditions

- cobbled roads – these become very slippery when wet
- changes in the road surface (for example, on bridges) and how this affects tyre grip.

You're at greater risk from these hazards at corners and junctions because you're more likely to combine braking, accelerating and steering in these situations.

Anticipate and plan – adjust your driving to the road conditions

Use your observation skills – watch out for and assess poor weather and road conditions accurately and adjust your speed accordingly:

- Leave plenty of room for manoeuvres, reduce your speed and increase the distance you allow for stopping to match the road conditions – on a slippery surface, a vehicle can take many times the normal distance to stop.
- Use lower revs in slippery conditions to avoid wheel spin, especially when moving off. Use a higher gear when travelling at low speeds.
- On a slippery surface aim to brake, steer and change gear as smoothly as possible, so that you don't break the tyre grip.
- Use the principles of cornering (see Chapter 11) to negotiate corners carefully in slippery conditions.

Recognising the cause of a skid

If your vehicle loses stability and a skid begins to develop, you need to recognise the cause of the skid. The commonest causes of skidding are:

- driving too fast for the circumstances
- harsh acceleration
- excessive or sudden braking
- coarse steering.

A skid can be caused by these actions individually or in combination.

Speed in itself doesn't cause skidding as a constant speed exerts no change in the vehicle's balance. But at higher speeds, braking or turning places a much higher demand on tyre grip.

> Each skid is unique and every vehicle responds differently. How you apply the principles and techniques outlined in this chapter will depend entirely on the circumstances and on the vehicle you're driving.

Cause: driving too fast for the circumstances

At higher speeds you need more tyre grip to corner or stop. When surface grip is low, altering speed or direction can exceed the available grip, causing a skid. The faster you  go the more likely this becomes. The vehicle's own weight or a change in road surface can reduce the grip of the front or back tyres. Weight in the boot will alter the vehicle's normal balance and tyre grip.

Cause: harsh acceleration

Harsh acceleration can cause the wheels to spin, even at low speeds.

Cause: excessive or sudden braking

In older cars without ABS, excessive braking for the road conditions may cause skidding because the tyres lose their grip.

Cause: coarse steering

A moving vehicle uses least tyre grip when travelling in a straight line. As soon as you start to corner, you place extra demands on the tyre grip. If you steer too sharply for the  speed, you'll cause the vehicle to understeer or oversteer. This may break the tyre grip and the vehicle will then go into a skid. Aim to make your steering as smooth as possible.

In different vehicles, you may need to negotiate the same corner at different speeds.

Understeer and oversteer

Understeer is the tendency of a vehicle to turn less, and oversteer is the tendency of a vehicle to turn more, in response to a given turn of the steering wheel. This can happen even at low speeds.

The tendency to understeer or oversteer is a characteristic of the vehicle itself coupled with the driver using excess speed for the circumstances. Most front-wheel drive vehicles understeer and some rear-wheel drive vehicles oversteer. However, some modern vehicles are designed to compensate for these tendencies. Make sure you know the different steering characteristics of each vehicle you drive and adapt your driving on corners and bends.

In a front-wheel drive car, you'll increase understeer if you:

- enter the bend too fast
- apply too much power in the bend
- steer too sharply.

You can reduce this understeer by reducing power and/or steering. But if you reduce power too much and too suddenly, you may convert the understeer to oversteer ('lift-off oversteer'). This is because weight transfer from the rear to the front increases grip at the front wheels and reduces grip at the rear wheels, allowing the rear to lose traction and slide.

A rear-wheel drive car initially behaves in the same way but, if you apply too much power on a slippery surface, any understeer may convert quite suddenly to oversteer.

Four-wheel drive cars provide better traction all round for acceleration and cornering, but not for braking. When driven to extremes, they behave in a similar way to the front- or rear-wheel drive model from which they're derived.

Understeer – the vehicle runs wide of its intended course

Oversteer – the rear of the vehicle steps out

If you drive an older vehicle that's not fitted with any of the active safety features discussed in this chapter, the action you take to correct a skid will depend on whether the skid is a rear-wheel, front-wheel or four-wheel skid. You need to be able to recognise different types of skid in the early stages so that you can respond appropriately and regain tyre grip as soon as possible. However, vehicles without active safety features are unlikely to be deployed in modern fleets.

Aquaplaning

Aquaplaning is dangerous. It happens when a vehicle on a wet road has water build-up between the front tyres and the road surface. This can lead to increased braking distance, at a minimum, and sometimes a loss of control. It can often be attributed to thin or worn tyre tread.

Wider tyres are more likely to aquaplane. A wide tyre spreads weight over a larger area, allowing it to rise onto the water more easily. Aquaplaning can happen with brand new tyres if the tyre tread grooves aren't able to disperse water quickly enough. Whether you brake or steer, the vehicle won't respond.

The safest solution is to remove pressure from the accelerator, allowing the vehicle to lose speed and the tyres to regain their grip. Don't turn the steering wheel while aquaplaning because the vehicle will lurch whichever way the wheels are pointing when the tyres regain grip.

Take care with weight distribution within the vehicle to avoid increasing the risk of aquaplaning.

Check your understanding

You should now be able to apply learning from this chapter in your driver training so that you can:

☐ explain why active safety features can interfere with driver behaviour

☐ describe the principles of anti-lock braking systems, traction control systems and electronic stability programmes

☐ explain how to avoid the actions that reduce a vehicle's stability and tyre grip

☐ identify the causes of skidding and how to minimise the risk.

Chapter 9
Driver's signals

Learning outcomes

The learning in this chapter, along with driver training, should enable you to:

- demonstrate appropriate use of the full range of signals available to you in different situations
- show appropriate responses to, and caution in interpreting, signals given by others
- show that you make active use of courtesy signals.

Developing your competence at using signals

Using signals may seem to be a basic competence, but many drivers don't use the full range of available signals consistently or to best effect. This chapter will help you improve your competence at using signals.

Giving information to other road users is a key part of information processing in the system of car control.

See Chapter 3, page 39, The importance of information.

See also Chapter 14, Emergency response, for further information about the signals available to emergency services in response situations.

The purpose of signals

Signals inform other road users of your presence or intentions. Don't just consider those road users you can see – also consider road users you can't see and those you may reasonably expect to appear.

Think before you signal. Indiscriminate signalling isn't helpful to anyone.

> Give a signal whenever it could benefit other road users. You may also need to give a signal to override lane-changing technology.

If you decide a signal is necessary, signal clearly and in good time. Always make sure the meaning of your signal is clear. Sometimes a signal is not in itself enough to make your intentions clear and other road users may use your position and speed to interpret what your signals mean. When negotiating a roundabout, for example, your signals may be misinterpreted if you haven't taken up the correct position for your intended exit.

Key points

- Consider the need to give a signal on the approach to every hazard, and before you change direction or speed.
- Give a signal whenever it could benefit other road users.
- Remember that signalling doesn't give you any special right to carry out the actions you indicate.
- Follow the *Highway Code* – check your mirrors before you signal or manoeuvre.

Interpreting signals given by others

You also need to be cautious about how you interpret the signals of other road users. For example, does a vehicle flashing the left-hand indicator mean that the driver intends to:

- park the vehicle, possibly immediately after a left-hand junction?
- turn into a left-hand junction?
- carry straight on, having forgotten to cancel the last signal?

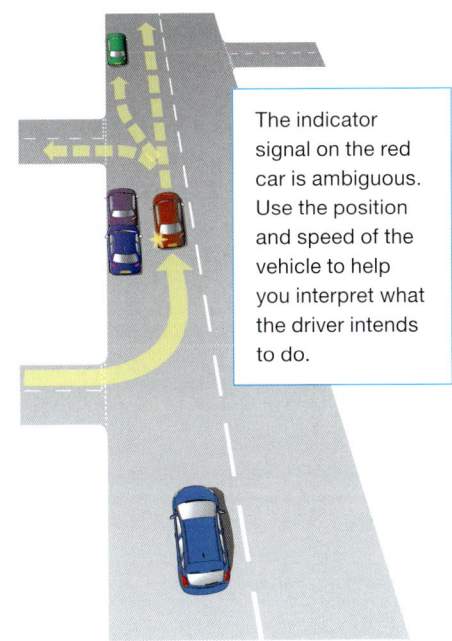

The indicator signal on the red car is ambiguous. Use the position and speed of the vehicle to help you interpret what the driver intends to do.

The range of signals

The signals available to you are:

- indicators
- hazard warning lights
- brake lights
- headlights
- the position of your vehicle
- horn signals
- arm signals
- courtesy signals (for example, raising a hand to thank another driver).

Select the most effective signal for the job. You must give your signal in plenty of time if it's to benefit other road users. Be aware that when you change the speed or position of your vehicle you're also giving information to other road users. Note that heavy goods vehicles (HGVs) initially move to the right in order to turn left.

Using the indicators

The *Highway Code* advises you to give a signal when another road user could benefit. Use observation to anticipate when a signal may be needed. This encourages you to be aware of other road users at all times, especially those behind you. It also reduces unnecessary hand movements and signal clutter.

If in doubt, it's better to signal than not to signal.

The purpose of signals is to warn other road users of your presence and/or your intention and to give you adequate time to achieve its purpose. Signals are informative and do not give right of way.

One signal should not cover two manoeuvres.

Never take an indicator signal as proof of another driver's intention when you're waiting to emerge from a side turning. Look for supporting evidence such as an obvious slowing down or wheels turning before you move out.

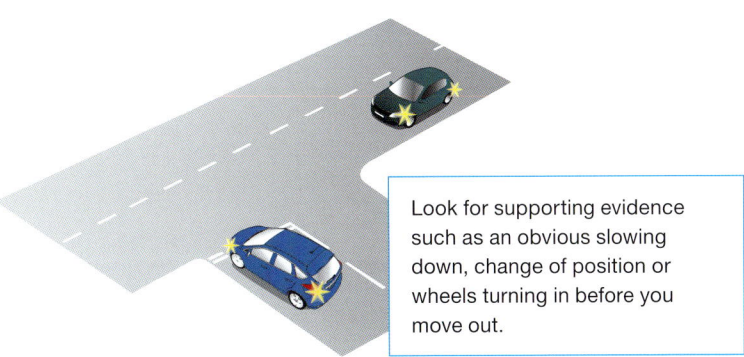

Look for supporting evidence such as an obvious slowing down, change of position or wheels turning in before you move out.

Modern signals are very sensitive. Make sure that your signal stays on throughout the manoeuvre.

Indicator mechanisms don't always self-cancel, especially when a turn is followed by a bend in the same direction. Take care to cancel the indicator manually in such situations – for example, when exiting from a roundabout.

How clear are your signals to other road users?

- Do you always signal when another road user could benefit?
- Do you signal your intentions clearly and in good time?
- Where possible, do you choose a position that helps to make your intentions clear to other road users?

Using hazard warning lights

Consider using hazard lights to alert other drivers to your presence when you've stopped. Don't use hazard lights when moving except on unrestricted multi-lane carriageways and motorways. Here you can use hazard lights briefly to warn the vehicles behind you that there's a hold-up ahead.

Brake lights

Brake lights indicate that you're slowing down or intending to stop. Always check your mirrors before using your brakes unless you're doing an emergency stop.

- Start braking well in advance of an anticipated hazard to alert the driver behind that you mean to slow down or stop, especially if the vehicle behind is too close. Make sure you're giving the information you want to give. Avoid 'dabbing' the brakes as this means you'll constantly be flashing your brake lights.
- If you brake harshly and activate a safety system, the brake lights may pulse and the hazard warning lights may be activated.
- In an electric vehicle, the brake lights may come on as the driver decelerates.
- In larger vehicles with retarders, the brake lights may activate if the driver takes their foot off the accelerator.
- Remember that rear fog lights are brighter than brake lights and may mask them when you're slowing down.

Using the horn

Only use the horn when it's necessary to warn other road users of your presence. If you see that another road user isn't aware of your presence, first choose an appropriate position and speed so that you can stop safely.

Consider using the horn on the approach to hazards where the view is very limited, such as a blind summit or bridge on a single-track road. Never use the horn to challenge or rebuke other road users. Adjust the length of the horn note according to the circumstances.

Electric vehicles are very quiet so you may need to use the horn to make other road users aware of your presence.

As a last resort, it could be beneficial to use the horn:

- to warn another road user who is not aware of you (pedestrians and cyclists – especially children – are most at risk)

- when you approach a hazard where the view is very limited – for example, a blind bend or a steep hump bridge on a single track road

- to warn the occupants of parked vehicles of your presence.

Flashing your headlights

Flash your headlights when the horn would not be heard, and in place of the horn at night. You should flash your headlights for one purpose only: to inform other road users that you're there – not as a signal to come on. **Never assume that another driver flashing their headlights is a signal to proceed**.

Use a headlight flash in daylight:

- when speed makes it likely that the horn would not be heard – for example, on a motorway
- to alert other drivers to your presence when you're approaching from behind.

Use your judgement to decide the duration of the flash and how far in advance you should give it. This is critical and will depend on your speed. The purpose of flashing your headlights is solely to inform the other driver of your presence. It doesn't give you the right to overtake regardless of the circumstances.

During darkness, flash your headlights to inform other road users of your presence, for example:

- on the approach to a hill crest
- when travelling along narrow winding roads.

Don't flash your headlights when they might be misunderstood by road users for whom they're not intended; for example, as a signal to proceed.

Arm signals

If you need to use an arm signal, follow the *Highway Code* advice. Be aware that many drivers may not understand them as they are rarely used.

Using courtesy signals

Courtesy signals encourage cooperative use of the road space and help to promote road safety. Acknowledging the courtesy of other road users encourages good driving and helps foster positive attitudes. Using a courtesy signal to defuse a potential conflict can make a real difference to road safety. Use courtesy signals:

- to thank another driver for letting you go first
- to apologise when you've unintentionally caused inconvenience to another road user.

Use either hand to give a courtesy signal but not at the risk of your steering control. You can signal without removing your hand from the wheel by raising your palm or nodding your head. Or you can ask your passenger to signal for you. But make sure that your courtesy signal can't be mistaken for a 'waving on' signal.

 Do you think you tend to give courtesy signals more or less often than other drivers?

On your next few journeys, make a conscious effort to give and acknowledge courtesy signals.

- How does this affect your own state of mind?
- How does it influence the actions of other drivers?

Responding to other people's signals

Treat with caution any signals other than those given by authorised officials. If someone beckons you to move forward – for example, an arm signal from a cyclist or motorcyclist – always check for yourself whether it's safe to do so. Check that you're familiar with the range of arm signals set out in the *Highway Code*.

If someone beckons you to move forward, always check for yourself whether it is safe to do so.

Check your understanding

You should now be able to apply learning from this chapter in your driver training so that you can:

- [ ] demonstrate appropriate use of the full range of signals available to you in different situations
- [ ] show appropriate responses to, and caution in interpreting, signals given by others
- [ ] show that you make active use of courtesy signals.

Chapter 10
Positioning

Learning outcomes

The learning in this chapter, along with driver training, should enable you to:

- explain how to position your vehicle safely on the approach to hazards
- show how to position your vehicle to get the best view into nearside junctions
- show how to position your vehicle appropriately for following other vehicles, turning and stopping.

Developing competence at positioning your vehicle

For advice on positioning on the motorway, see Chapter 13, Driving on motorways and multi-lane carriageways.

Positioning is a crucial element in the system of car control.

See Chapter 3, page 41, Position.

The ideal road position depends on many things: safety, observation, the size of the vehicle, traffic conditions, road layout, cornering, manoeuvrability, assisting traffic flow and making your intentions clear. Always consider safety before anything else, and never sacrifice safety for any other advantage.

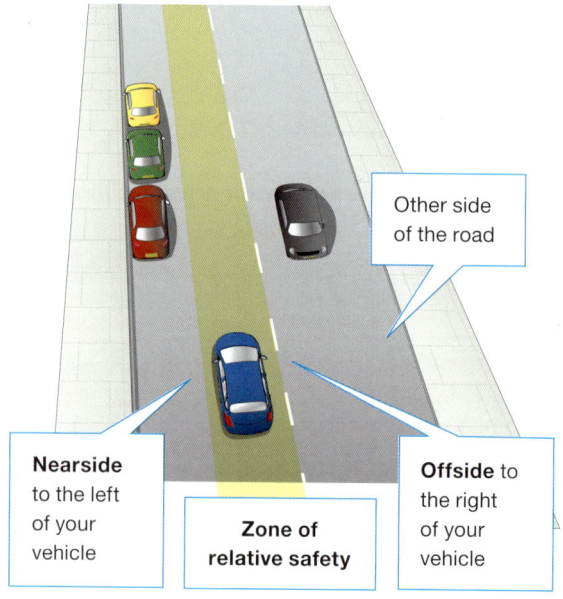

Nearside to the left of your vehicle

Zone of relative safety

Offside to the right of your vehicle

Other side of the road

> Put the car in the best position for you to see and be seen, with due regard to safety.

Positioning for advantage

There are three road positions to consider, as explained in the diagram.

The nearside position

The benefits of this position are:

- it gives early views through right-hand bends
- it allows nearside views past lorries and other large vehicles
- it allows extra space for oncoming vehicles
- it's the best position for left-hand turns when there are no other hazards.

Make sure the nearside road surface is sound and free of drains, debris, dust and grit before using it.

The central position

This is midway between the better part of the nearside edge and the centre line. The benefits of this position are:

- it gives you good margins of safety on both sides
- it allows you to change position to either side.

The offside position

The benefits of this position are:

- it gives early views on the approach to left-hand bends
- it provides increased safety margins away from nearside hazards
- it's generally the best position for right turns.

Anticipate the possibility of large oncoming vehicles straddling the central line on bends and be prepared to move to the left.

Any of these positions should be sacrificed for safety.

When choosing a road position, always take into account the width of the road you're travelling on. Your choice of position will be different on, for example, a narrow or country road without white lines.

> Always prioritise safety over position.

Safety position on the approach to hazards

By carefully choosing your position you can reduce the risk of having a collision. Be aware of hazards on both sides of your vehicle. In urban areas, to the nearside, there's a risk of coming into conflict with cyclists and pedestrians (especially children), and parked vehicles and their occupants. You also need to be aware of other vehicles pulling out from junctions. To the offside, there's a risk of coming into conflict with oncoming vehicles in the centre of the road.

Between the two extremes is a zone that is **relatively** free of hazards, but always adapt your position and speed to the actual circumstances.

The system of car control provides a safe and methodical approach to hazards. Dangers can come from anywhere but you'll generally have less time to react to hazards coming from the nearside. On narrow roads and in one-way systems, you need to pay equal attention to both sides of the road.

Roadside hazards

Common roadside hazards to look out for are:

- pedestrians, especially children, stepping off the footpath
- parked vehicles and their occupants
- cyclists, especially children
- horses

- runners – where there's no footpath
- concealed junctions
- surface water or spray from kerbside puddles.

If you identify hazards on the nearside, take a position closer to the centre of the road. This has two benefits:

- it gives you a better view
- it provides more space in which to take avoiding action if you need to.

If oncoming traffic makes it unsafe to take this position, or if the road is too narrow, reduce your speed. There's an important trade-off between your speed and the clearance around your vehicle. The narrower the gap, the slower the speed. Be prepared to stop if necessary.

Keep as far from rows of parked vehicles as circumstances allow. A good rule of thumb is to leave at least enough space for an opening door to the side of any parked vehicles. If you can't move out, slow down.

 Child pedestrians may not look properly. Get into the habit of asking yourself: 'Could I stop in time if the child ran out?'

If traffic conditions are favourable, they allow a greater safety margin.

The less space you have, the slower you should go.

Cyclists and motorcyclists

When driving in town, be alert to the behaviour of cyclists and motorcyclists, especially if you're driving a large vehicle with limited nearside visibility. Be aware that cyclists and motorcyclists may attempt to overtake on your nearside or filter through narrow gaps in the traffic.

Improving the view into nearside road junctions

Position yourself so that you can see as much of the road ahead as possible and so that other road users can see you. You can improve your view into nearside roads by positioning your vehicle towards the centre of the road. This also makes you more visible to vehicles pulling out from nearside junctions. You must take into account any vehicles on the other side of the road. Take a position that minimises the overall danger from both sides of the road.

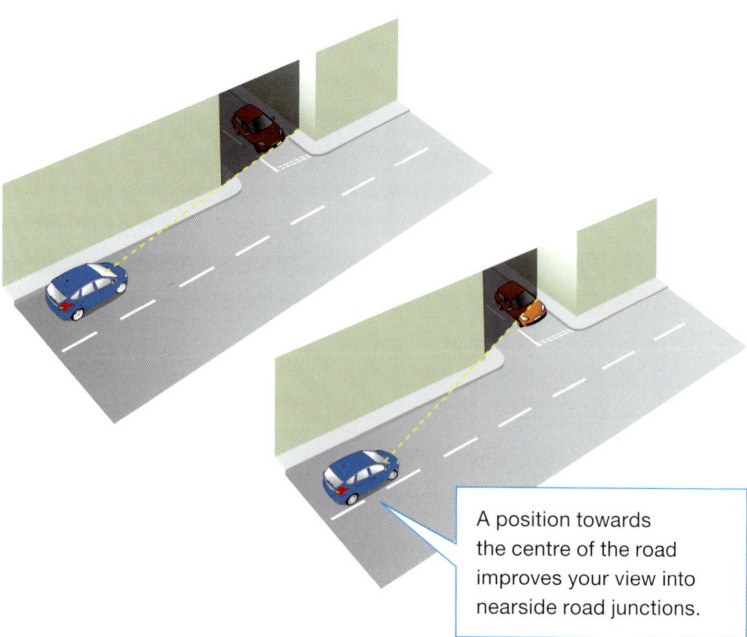

A position towards the centre of the road improves your view into nearside road junctions.

Following position

In a stream of traffic, always keep a safe distance behind the vehicle in front. Follow the two-second rule: leave a gap of at least two seconds between you and the vehicle in front, depending on conditions.

If activated, adaptive cruise control may allow you to adjust your following position.

See Chapter 6, page 128, The two-second rule.

Keeping your distance increases your safety because:

- you have a good view, and can increase it along both sides by slight changes of position – this enables you to be fully aware of what's happening on the road ahead
- you can stop your vehicle safely if the driver in front brakes firmly without warning
- you can extend your braking distance so that the driver behind has more time to react, especially if they're driving too close
- you can see when it's safe to move into the overtaking position
- in wet weather, you get less spray from the vehicle in front.

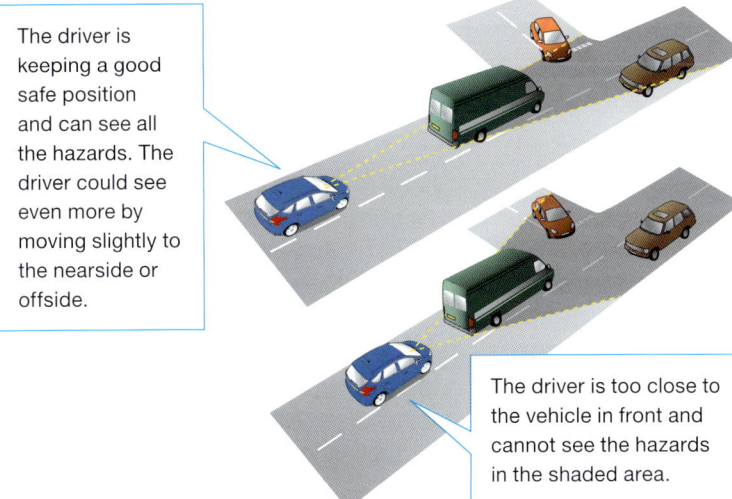

The driver is keeping a good safe position and can see all the hazards. The driver could see even more by moving slightly to the nearside or offside.

The driver is too close to the vehicle in front and cannot see the hazards in the shaded area.

Position on bends

When approaching a bend, position yourself to get the best possible view of the road ahead. Take information on the approach to the bend to help you decide on the best position. This position will be different for right-hand and left-hand bends.

See Chapter 11, page 208, Getting the best view, for further information.

Position for turning

Your position for turning depends on the other traffic, the road width and layout, the size of your vehicle, the position of any obstacles and the effect of these obstacles on traffic behaviour. Take information on the approach to help you decide on the best position. Generally, the best position on the approach to a junction is in the middle of the road for a left turn and towards the centre line for a right turn.

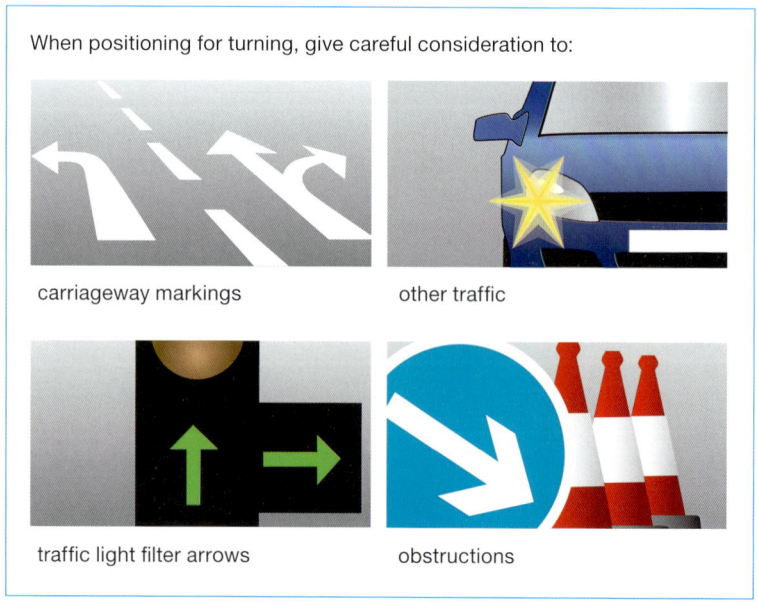

When positioning for turning, give careful consideration to:

- carriageway markings
- other traffic
- traffic light filter arrows
- obstructions

If you intend to turn right and oncoming traffic is encroaching on your side of the road, move back in from the centre line.

If you intend to turn left and the corner has a sharp angle, is obscured, or pedestrians are present, approach the corner from further out than normal. Move further out in good time. Avoid 'swan necking' – approaching close to the nearside and then swinging out to the right just before turning into the junction. This can mislead other drivers about your intentions.

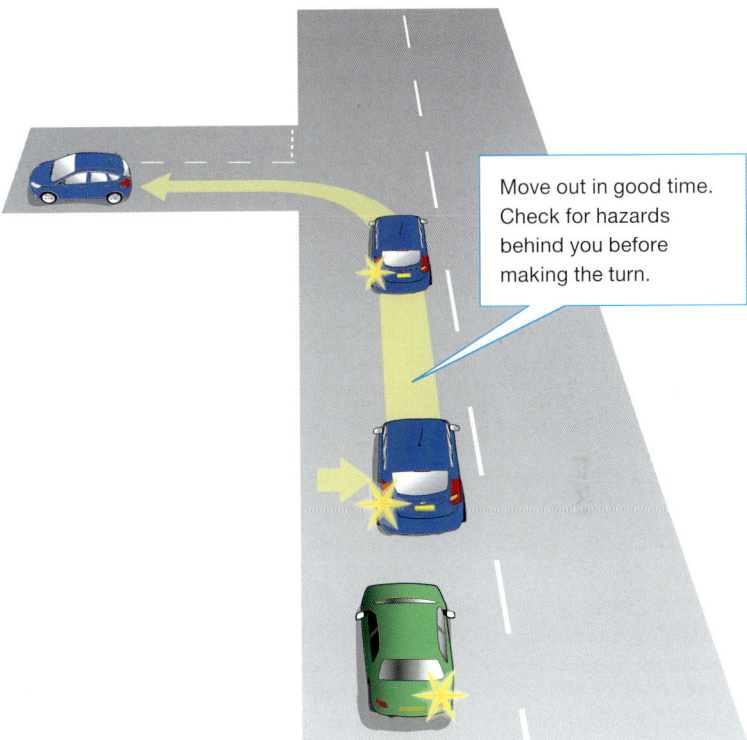

Move out in good time. Check for hazards behind you before making the turn.

Position at crossroads

When turning right at crossroads and the oncoming vehicle is also turning right, there's a choice of two positions. Your choice will depend on the road layout and markings, and the position of the other vehicle:

- pass offside to offside – this gives you a better view
- pass nearside to nearside where traffic conditions, the junction layout or the position of the other vehicle makes offside to offside impractical.

Take extra care on a nearside to nearside pass because your view of the road is blocked by the other vehicle. Look carefully for oncoming traffic.

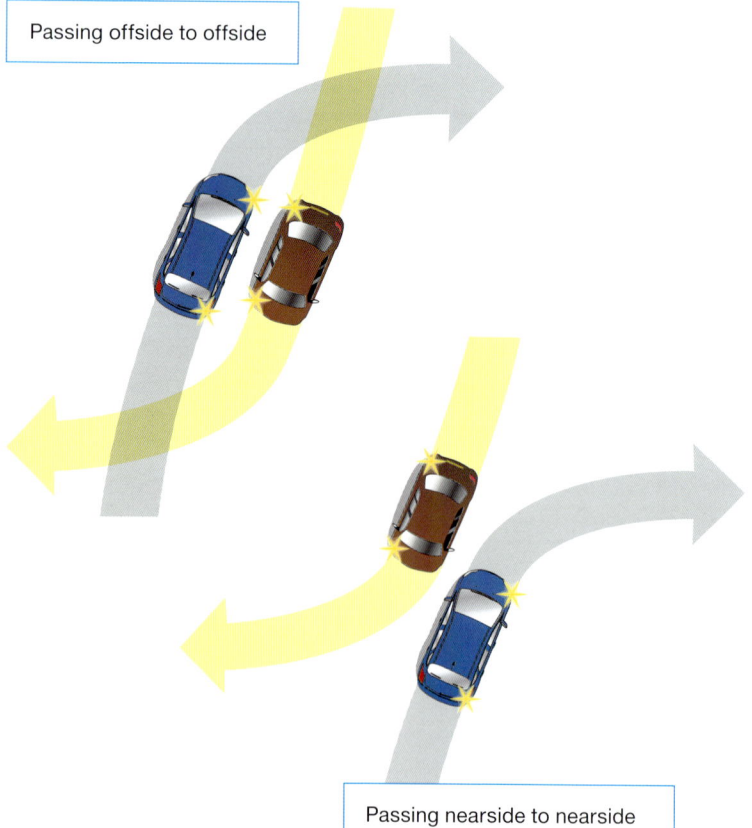

Passing offside to offside

Passing nearside to nearside

Imagine you are in a car turning right in front of the car shown here. Take extra care on a nearside to nearside pass because your view of the road is obstructed by the other vehicle.

Position for stopping behind other vehicles

Before you come to a stop, think about your next move. Position your vehicle so that you can continue with minimum inconvenience to yourself and other road users. You should be able to see the rear tyres of the vehicle in front and some empty tarmac.

> Remember: think 'rubber and road' or 'tyres and tarmac'.

Stopping well short of the vehicle in front gives you several advantages:

- a good view of the road
- room to move around the vehicle ahead if it stalls or breaks down
- if you're hit from behind, the vehicle ahead is less likely to be affected
- the space in front of you is a safe haven for a bike or motorcycle
- if you become aware that a vehicle approaching behind has left braking too late, you can move forward to allow it extra space to stop in
- facing uphill, if the vehicle ahead starts to roll back towards you, you have time to warn the driver.

An example of using your stopping position to increase safety is where there are traffic lights at roadworks close to a bend. Consider stopping before or on the approach to the bend so that drivers who come up behind can see you.

> Leave yourself enough room to pull out and pass the vehicle in front if necessary. You should be able to see the rear tyres of the vehicle in front and some empty tarmac.

Position for approaching the brow of a hill

When approaching the brow of a hill, adopt a nearside position to minimise the risk of colliding with an as yet unseen vehicle approaching on your offside, but also be aware of the possible presence of a pedestrian or cyclist on your nearside just over the brow.

Position at pedestrian crossings and traffic lights

Where the situation allows, consider stopping half a car's length short of pedestrian crossings or traffic lights to provide yourself with a safety margin should your car be shunted from behind.

✅ Check your understanding

You should now be able to apply learning from this chapter in your driver training so that you can:

- [ ] explain how to position your vehicle safely on the approach to hazards
- [ ] show how to position your vehicle to get the best view into nearside junctions
- [ ] show how to position your vehicle appropriately for following other vehicles, turning and stopping.

Chapter 11
Cornering

Learning outcomes

The learning in this chapter, along with driver training, should enable you to:

- explain the principles of safe cornering
- describe the forces involved in cornering and the factors that affect your vehicle's ability to corner
- show how to use the limit point to assess your speed for bends and corners
- show how to plan a corner using cross views
- show how to position your vehicle for the best view when cornering
- show how to use the system of car control for cornering.

Developing your competence at cornering

Cornering – driving a car round a corner, curve or bend – is one of the main driving activities, and it's important to get it right. When you corner, your vehicle loses stability and you place extra demands on the tyre grip available. The faster you go and the tighter the bend, the greater these demands are.

This chapter explains how to apply the system of car control to cornering. We start with some general principles and then look at the forces involved in cornering, the factors affecting your vehicle's ability to corner safely, and how to use the system of car control in conjunction with limit point analysis to corner safely.

See Chapter 3, page 40, The system of car control.

Using the system to corner safely

Cornering is potentially dangerous so you should use the system of car control to help you carry out the manoeuvre safely. Each phase of the system is relevant, but processing information is especially important. Correctly assessing the severity of the bend is essential for safety.

Key principles for safe cornering

- **Make sure that your vehicle is in the correct position on the approach.**
- **Travel at the correct speed for the corner or bend.**
- **Select the correct gear for that speed.**

- **Use the accelerator to maintain a constant speed through the bend.**
- **Be able to stop safely within the distance you can see to be clear on your own side of the road.**

Applying these principles to the variations in bends, visibility, traffic conditions, road surface conditions and other factors calls for good judgement and planning. Before looking in more detail at using the system of car control for cornering, think about the factors that affect a vehicle's ability to corner safely.

Cornering forces

A moving vehicle is most stable when its weight is evenly distributed, its engine is just pulling without increasing road speed, and it's travelling in a straight line. It will continue to travel in a straight line unless you apply some other force to alter its direction. When you steer, the turning force to alter direction comes from the action of the front tyres on the road. You saw in Chapter 6 (page 103) that this force depends on tyre grip. If the front tyre grip is broken, the car will continue in a straight line. On tighter bends, at higher speeds and in heavier vehicles, the demands on tyre grip are greater.

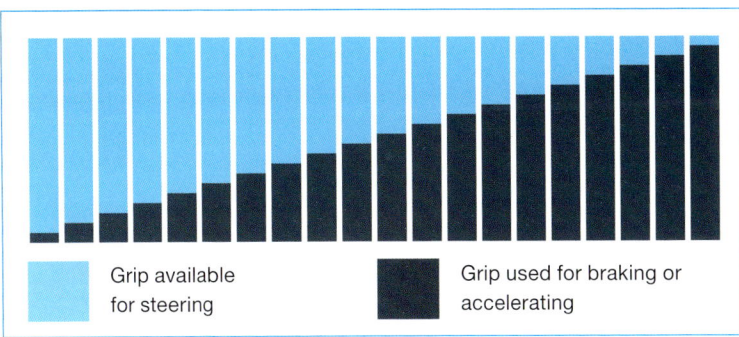

Grip available for steering

Grip used for braking or accelerating

Three forces reduce stability and, ultimately, tyre grip:

- steering
- accelerating
- braking.

The more you brake or accelerate, the less tyre grip you have for steering. The faster you go into a corner or bend, the more you reduce stability and the more tyre grip you need to keep your position.

If one or more of these forces causes loss of tyre grip, the vehicle will continue in a straight line rather than turning. So, in a left-hand bend, as you lose tyre grip, your vehicle drifts to the right of your intended position and, in a right-hand bend, it drifts to the left. The design of the vehicle will reduce or increase this effect.

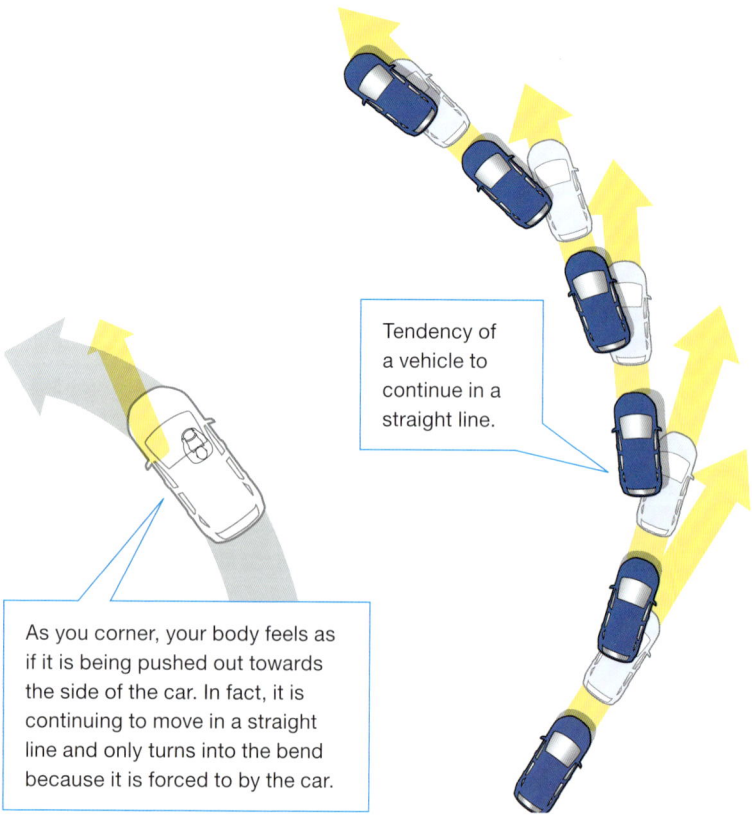

Tendency of a vehicle to continue in a straight line.

As you corner, your body feels as if it is being pushed out towards the side of the car. In fact, it is continuing to move in a straight line and only turns into the bend because it is forced to by the car.

Vehicle characteristics

Roadworthiness

Vehicles vary in their capacity to corner, and they only corner efficiently if they are well maintained. Steering, suspension, shock absorbers, tyres, tyre pressures and the loading of the vehicle all affect its balance and tyre grip when cornering. Position loads evenly so they don't upset the balance of the vehicle.

> Make sure that your vehicle and tyres are in good condition and that you keep your tyre pressures at the recommended levels.

Vehicle specification

The specifications that affect the handling characteristics of a vehicle include:

- the type of drive – front wheel, rear wheel or four wheel
- the fuel or power source
- suspension and damping
- the drive ratio and central differential characteristics on a four-wheel drive vehicle
- active vehicle safety systems
- the type and size of vehicle, whether commercial vehicle or car
- the vehicle's centre of gravity.

Understeer and oversteer

Understeer is the tendency of a vehicle to turn less, and oversteer is the tendency of a vehicle to turn more, in response to a given turn of the steering wheel. The tendency to understeer or oversteer is a characteristic of the vehicle itself and depends mainly on what sort of drive the vehicle has. Make sure you know the different steering characteristics of each vehicle you drive and adapt your driving on corners and bends.

See Chapter 8, page 160, Understeer and oversteer.

Camber and superelevation

Road surfaces usually slope to help drainage. The normal slope falls from the crown of the road to the edges and is called crown camber.

- **On a left-hand bend**, camber increases the effect of your steering because the road slopes down in the direction of the turn.
- **On a right-hand bend**, camber reduces the effect of steering because the road slopes away from the direction of the turn.

This applies if you keep to your own side of the road but if you cross over the crown to the other side of the road, the camber will have the opposite effect on your steering.

In many places, especially at junctions, the slope across the road surface can be at an unexpected angle. Whatever the slope, if it falls in the direction of your turn it will increase the effect of your steering but if it rises in the direction of your turn it will reduce the effect of your steering. Take this into account when deciding your position and speed for a bend.

Superelevation is where the whole width of the road is banked up towards the outside edge of the bend, making the slope favourable for cornering in both directions (similar to banking on a race track).

 Pick out one or two sections of familiar road where cornering is tricky and work out whether unexpected camber is a factor.

Analyse how you took the corner and make an honest assessment of your driving. Did you make the correct decision about the best position and speed to adopt for the bend, for example?

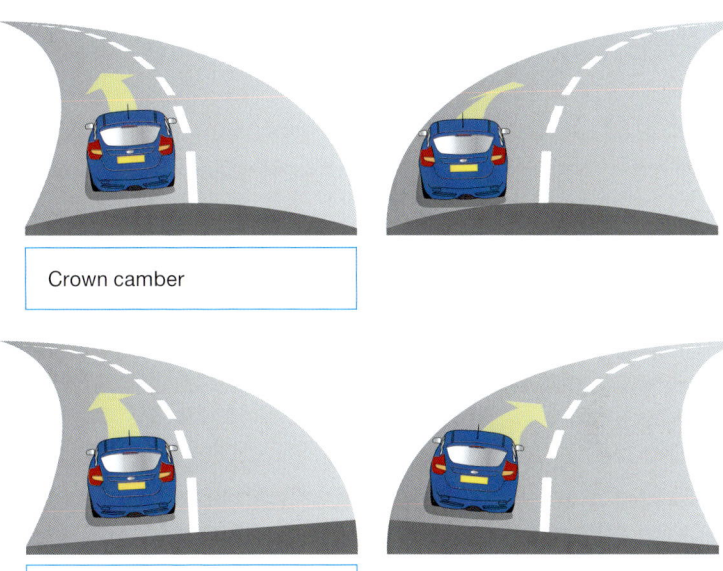

Crown camber

Superelevation

Summary of factors affecting cornering

The factors that determine your vehicle's ability to corner are:

- the specification and condition of your vehicle, including the tyres
- your speed
- the amount of steering you apply
- the amount of acceleration or braking
- the slope across the road surface – camber and superelevation
- the road surface and how the weather has affected its grip.

Assessing the sharpness of a bend

As you approach a bend, seek as much information as possible about the severity of the bend using all the observational clues (for example, weather, road surface, road signs, road markings, the line made by lamp posts and trees, the speed and position of oncoming traffic, the angle of headlights at night) that are available to you. The more information you gather about the bend, the more accurately you'll be able to judge the best position and speed to negotiate it.

See Chapter 4, page 60, Planning.

The limit point

To drive safely you must be able to stop within the distance you can see to be clear on your own side of the road. The limit point is the furthest point to which you have an uninterrupted view of the road surface. This is where the right-hand edge of the road appears to meet the left-hand edge in the distance. The more distant the limit point, the more quickly you can go because you have more space to stop in. The closer the limit point, the slower you must go because you have less space to stop in.

> The limit point gives you a systematic way of judging the correct speed to use through the bend.

For a video explanation of limit points, see the Roadcraft e-learning course.

Watching the limit point enables you to match your speed to the speed at which this point appears to move. If the limit point is moving away from you, and you have a safe stopping distance between you and the limit point, you may accelerate. If the limit point is moving towards you, and your view of the road ahead reduces to below the safe stopping distance, you must decelerate or brake. Even when the bend isn't constant, you can still match your speed to the apparent movement of the limit point, because this will vary with the curvature of the bend. Acceleration sense is useful here.

Using the limit point together with the system helps you:

- adjust your speed so you can stop safely within the distance you can see to be clear on your own side of the road
- decide the correct speed to approach and negotiate the bend
- select the correct gear for the speed
- decide the point at which to start accelerating.

Left-hand bends

On a right-hand bend, you have a view in front of you which includes the scenery (for example, hedges, trees, buildings) just beyond the side of the road, on the outside of the bend. On a left-hand bend, these will seem to be further away because you're looking across the road. This may cause you to misjudge the amount of space available to you and approach the bend at a greater speed than is safe. On a left-hand bend, treat the centre of the road as the right verge.

> On a left-hand bend, you should drive as though the limit point is where the edge of the road meets the central white line (or the centre of the road if there's no white line) so that you can stop safely on your own side of the road.

Using the limit point

Before you look at this diagram, make sure you have read pages 196–7. Read the diagram from the bottom of the page upwards.

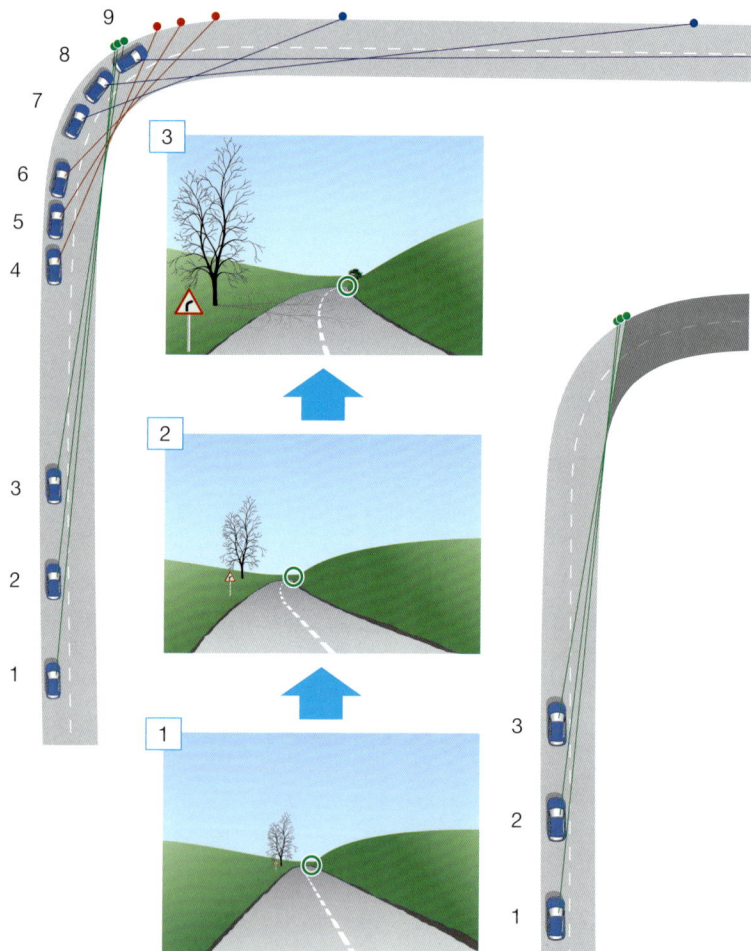

Approaching a right-hand bend

At first the limit point ○ ● appears to remain stationary.

Adjust your speed so you can stop safely within the remaining distance.

As you approach the bend, take information about the sharpness of the bend and carefully assess the appropriate speed for cornering.

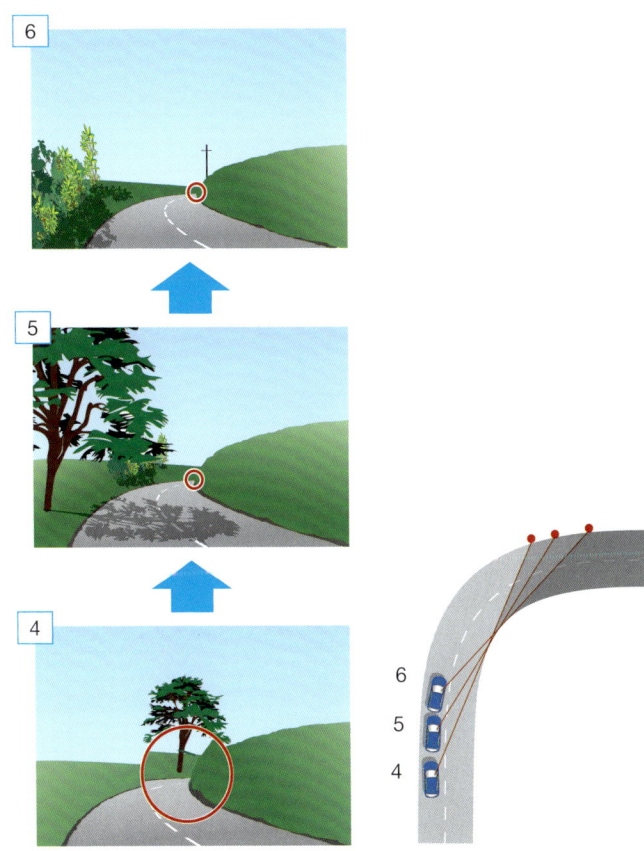

Just before you enter a right-hand bend

Just before you enter the bend the limit point ○ ● begins to move round at a constant speed. Adjust your speed to the speed of this movement.

You now have the correct speed to go round the bend. Select the gear to match this speed before entering the bend. Use the accelerator to maintain a constant speed for maximum stability through the bend.

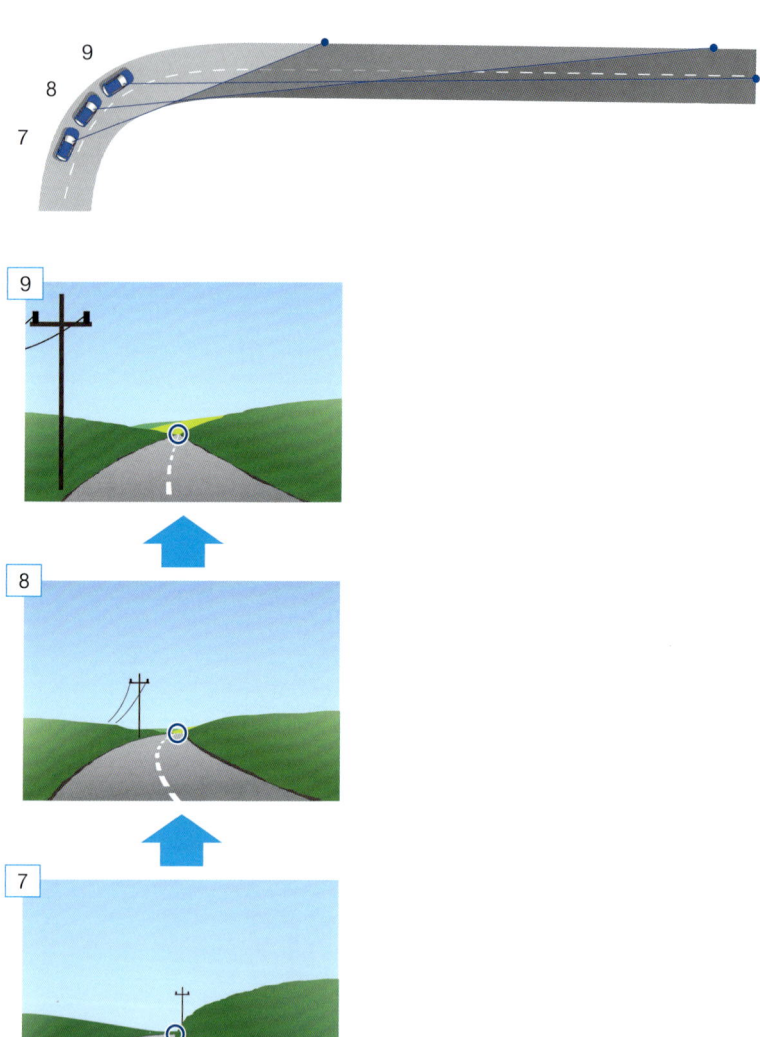

Going through a right-hand bend

As the bend starts to straighten out your view begins to open up, and the limit point ○ ● starts to move away more quickly.

You can then accelerate steadily as you straighten your steering.

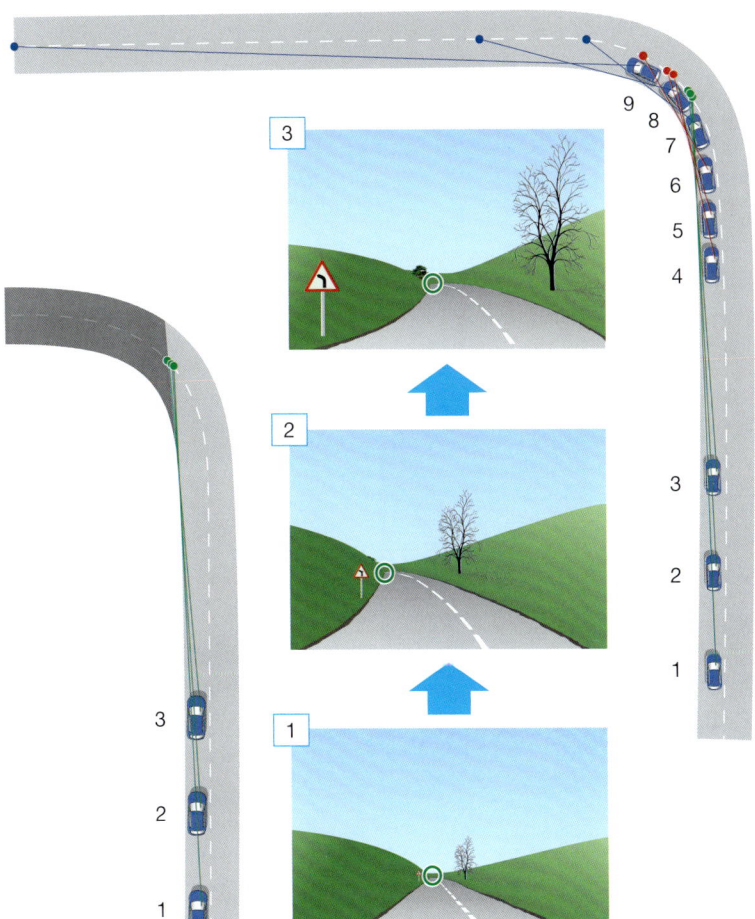

Approaching a left-hand bend

At first the limit point 〇 ● appears to remain stationary.

Adjust your speed so you can stop safely within the remaining distance.

As you approach the bend, take information about the sharpness of the bend and carefully assess the appropriate speed for cornering.

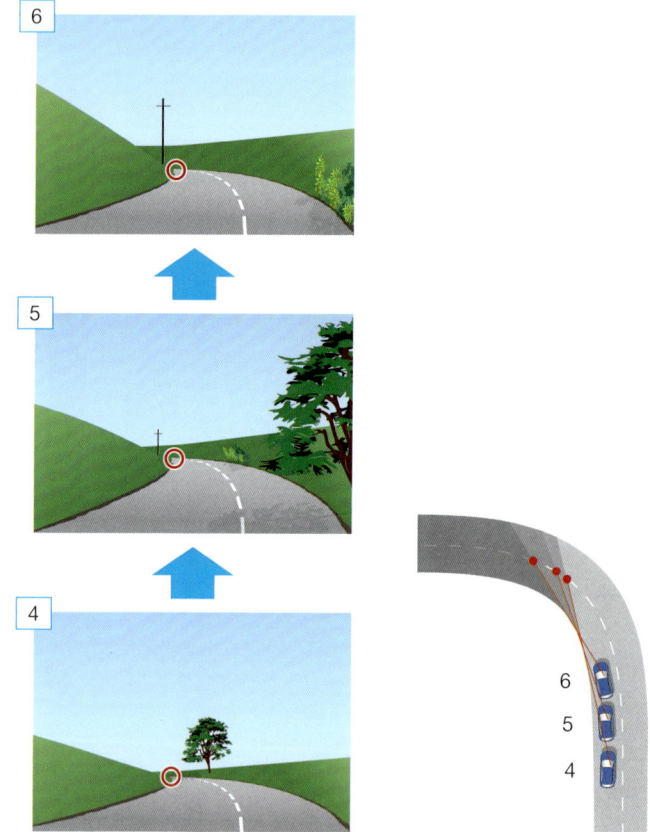

Just before you enter a left-hand bend

Just before you enter the bend the limit point ○ ● begins to move round at a constant speed. Adjust your speed to the speed of this movement.

You now have the correct speed to go round the bend. Select the gear to match this speed before entering the bend. Use the accelerator to maintain a constant speed for maximum stability through the bend.

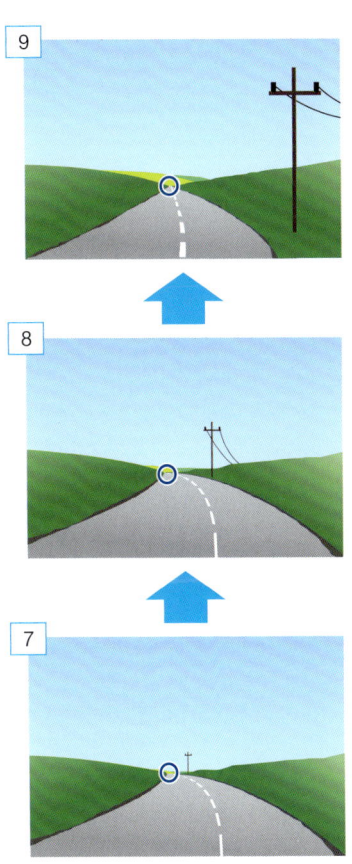

Going through a left-hand bend

As the bend starts to straighten out your view begins to open up, and the limit point ○ ● starts to move away more quickly.

You can then accelerate steadily as you straighten your steering.

The limit point technique is self-adjusting – as road visibility and conditions deteriorate you need more distance in which to stop, and so you must reduce your speed to compensate.

Use the limit point *as well as* other observation links – get into the habit of looking across or beyond the bend as you approach it. You may spot a hazard just *after* the bend – for example, a warning sign or a chevron marker indicating a further bend. In this case, it would be inappropriate to use the limit point alone to set your speed.

Where a road isn't wide enough for two vehicles to pass, consider doubling your stopping distance to give an oncoming vehicle enough space to stop as well. On a left-hand bend on a single-track road, the limit point is where the two kerb lines meet.

> **Practise matching your speed to the movement of the limit point.**
>
> Try this on different types of bend – from very gradual to hairpin – and note how using the limit point enables you to adjust to the characteristics of each bend. Always adjust your speed so that you can stop safely within the distance you can see to be clear.
>
> Make a special point of using the limit point to set your speed for bends and corners on roads you know well. It's on familiar routes that your attention is most likely to wander.
>
> For exclusive video content that illustrates the limit point and other important concepts, see the Roadcraft e-learning course:
> **www.safedrivingforlife.info/shop/roadcraft-elearning**

The double-apex bend

Some bends have been deliberately engineered with a tightening curve or 'double apex'. This has proved a cause of serious collisions on left-hand bends, particularly for motorcyclists. In this type of bend, the curve that the driver initially sees on the approach to the bend continues to tighten so the final curve is much sharper. If you plan for the whole bend on the basis of the curve that you see initially, you run the risk of ending up in the path of oncoming traffic.

Careful observation and using the system of car control to match your speed to the limit point should help you to accurately negotiate deceptive bends like the one below.

> On an unfamiliar bend, be prepared if necessary to adjust your steering as you travel around the bend.

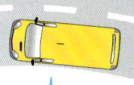

The curve is much tighter where the yellow van is.

If the driver of the blue car has adjusted speed and steering for the visible part of the curve, the car will be travelling too fast and risks running wide into the path of oncoming traffic as the curve tightens.

Using a cross view

You can plan a corner by using a cross view. As you approach the corner, first assess the direction of the corner, find the limit point, and then look across in the same direction as the corner for clues as to where the road goes. This can help you identify upcoming hazards, such as other road users, oncoming traffic, further bends, junctions and speed limit changes.

In this example, by scanning the road ahead, you can see a bend to the left and, by looking down the nearside of the red car, identify the limit point.

By using a cross view, you may be able to see where the road goes after the bend. In this example, you can see the red vehicle as it exits the bend. You can now also see that the road turns to the right following the left-hand bend.

You can now return your focus to using the limit point to negotiate the left-hand bend.

By using a cross view prior to the first left-hand bend, you can adopt an early position for the next right-hand bend. Assess the right-hand bend, then follow with a cross view, which, in this example, shows the red car having negotiated the right-hand bend and possibly braking for the 30 mph limit ahead.

Using a process of multiple cross views allows you to link bends and create a flow, rather than dealing with each bend in isolation.

How to use the system for cornering

Information

On the approach to a corner or bend, you should be constantly scanning the road for information, especially about:

- traffic in front and behind
- the road surface and the effect of weather conditions on it
- the limit point.

Make effective use of lateral information. Whenever you can, look across the bend through gaps in hedges or between buildings for more information. Use the curved line of hedgerows and lamp posts to give you information about the severity of the bend. Look for early warning of other hazards as well.

> Match your speed to the speed at which the limit point moves away from you, provided you can stop safely within the distance that you can see to be clear on your own side of the road.

Position

When positioning your vehicle for cornering, you need to consider:

- safety
- stability
- getting the best view
- reducing the tightness of the bend.

Safety

Safety is the overriding consideration. Position yourself so that you're least likely to come into conflict with other road users. Look out for hazards (for example, pedestrians) to your nearside and oncoming traffic to your offside. Be mindful of the width of your vehicle.

> Always be prepared to sacrifice your road position for safety.

Getting the best view

Your position will determine how much you can see when you enter a bend. Put the car in the best position for you to see, with due regard to safety. The position that gives you the clearest view is different for a left-hand bend and right-hand bend.

- **Right-hand bends** – position yourself towards the left of your road space, where appropriate. But watch out for poor condition of the nearside road surface, blind junctions or exits, and adverse camber.

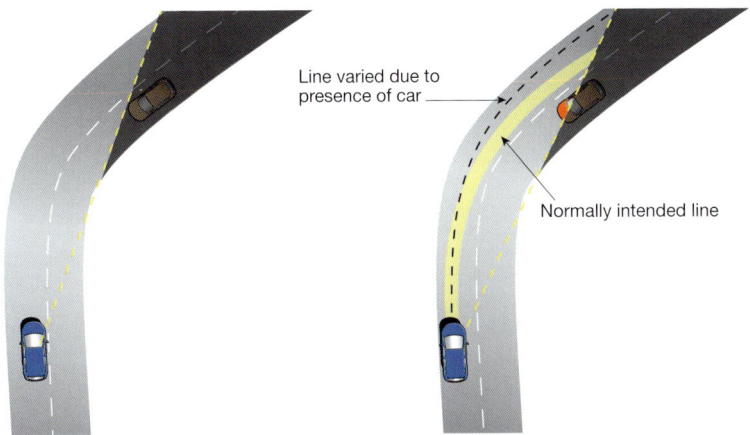

> For right-hand bends, the nearside gives an earlier view into the bend.

- **Left-hand bends** – position yourself towards the centre line so that you get an early view round the bend. Before you take this position, consider:

  > approaching traffic or other offside dangers which need a greater margin of safety

  > whether your position might mislead other traffic as to your intentions

  > whether you'll gain any advantage at low speed or on an open bend.

Don't position yourself in a way that causes concern to other road users. Be prepared to modify your road position in the interests of safety.

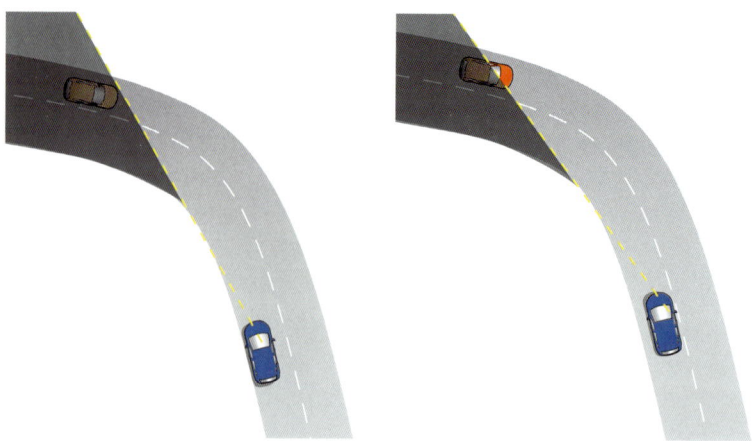

For left-hand bends, a position towards the centre of the road gives an earlier view.

Speed

When you're in the correct position for the bend, use the limit point to judge the safe speed to drive round the bend. Where the bend is a constant curve, the limit point remains at a constant distance from you. Keep your speed constant. If the curve changes, re-assess your speed and re-apply the system.

To assess the correct speed for a bend, also consider:

- the severity of the bend
- the view into the bend
- your vehicle's characteristics
- road and road surface conditions
- traffic conditions
- weather conditions
- road width.

Remember your aim is to be able to stop safely within the distance you can see to be clear on your own side of the road, not to take the bend as fast as possible.

Gear

When you've achieved the correct entry speed, choose the appropriate gear for that speed. Select the gear that gives you the greatest flexibility to leave the bend safely.

See Chapter 6, page 113, Using the gears.

Acceleration

Where the bend is a constant curve, the limit point remains at a constant distance from you. Apply gentle pressure to the accelerator to maintain a constant road speed through the curve, if you can.

> Remember, if the bend tightens, the limit point will appear to move closer, so reduce your speed accordingly to stay within a safe stopping distance.

If there are no hazards, start to accelerate when the limit point begins to move away and you begin to straighten your steering.

As you continue to straighten your steering, increase acceleration to match the limit point. Accelerate until you reach the speed limit or the appropriate speed for the circumstances.

Safe cornering

Think about your driving behaviour on more open roads. As you plan your approach to corners, what's your priority?

- Does the purpose of your journey make a difference to your decision-making; for example, if you're under time pressure?
- What other human factors might affect your driving decisions?
- How do you think about the correct speed for the bend? Is your aim to maximise speed or to achieve a safe stopping distance?
- Do you make the best possible use of observation links to help plan your approach to a corner?
- Do you position yourself to get the best possible view when cornering, with due regard to safety?

Next time you meet a significant corner on an open road, ask yourself: 'What if there's a pedestrian in the road just beyond my limit point?' Does this alter your driving?

✅ Check your understanding

You should now be able to apply learning from this chapter in your driver training so that you can:

- [ ] explain the principles of safe cornering
- [ ] describe the forces involved in cornering and the factors that affect your vehicle's ability to corner
- [ ] show how to use the limit point to assess your speed for bends and corners
- [ ] show how to plan a corner using cross views
- [ ] show how to position your vehicle for the best view when cornering
- [ ] show how to use the system of car control for cornering.

Chapter 12
Overtaking

Learning outcomes

The learning in this chapter, along with driver training, should enable you to:

- explain the risks of overtaking
- show how to use the following and overtaking position safely
- show how to assess and overtake different types of hazards safely in a wide range of circumstances
- explain how to help other drivers to overtake you.

Developing your competence at overtaking safely

Overtaking is potentially dangerous and you need good judgement if it's to be carried out safely. This comes with experience and practice, but even experienced drivers need to be extremely careful.

Overtaking is hazardous because it requires you to negotiate dynamic hazards (for example, moving vehicles) as well as fixed ones (for example, road layout) and it may bring you into the path of other vehicles. It's a complex manoeuvre in which you need to consider the vehicle(s) you want to overtake as well as a number of other hazards as the vehicle to be overtaken moves among them.

There are three things about these elements to consider:

- the vehicle you're overtaking
- external factors
- the interaction between the vehicle you're overtaking and those external factors.

This chapter describes the general principles of overtaking safely.

> Overtaking is a high-risk manoeuvre because you're potentially putting your vehicle into the path of oncoming traffic. If you're travelling at high speed and collide with an oncoming vehicle, the speed of impact will be the combined speed of both vehicles.
>
> Many overtaking deaths are due to head-on collisions on rural roads. Rural roads are the most dangerous roads per mile travelled for all types of road user.

Is your vehicle capable of overtaking?

Are you familiar with the vehicle's capabilities, characteristics and technologies? Are you driving a high-performance vehicle or large vehicle, for example?

Are you sure that the vehicle will give you enough acceleration?

Can you legally achieve the speed you require to overtake?

Have you assessed your vehicle's capability in relation to the road user you're overtaking? For example, overtaking a long vehicle will require more capability than a cyclist.

Have you taken account of the load you're carrying? Have you got passengers or a full boot?

Passing a stationary vehicle

Passing a stationary vehicle is the simplest possible overtaking situation.

The stationary vehicle is your hazard. Use the system to approach and assess the hazard and to pass it safely. Take account of the position and speed of oncoming traffic, the position and speed of following traffic and the presence of pedestrians or other roadside hazards, especially on the nearside. If the situation allows, leave at least a door's width when passing a stationary vehicle.

See Chapter 10, page 178, Roadside hazards.

Other external factors may affect your decision to overtake. For example, an oncoming vehicle may mean you have to wait before overtaking.

Information

Observe and assess the road and traffic conditions ahead for an opportunity to pass safely. Ask yourself the questions below.

Does the road layout present a hazard?

Is there enough road width for me to pass?

Is the vehicle I'm passing likely to move off?

What's the speed and proximity of any oncoming vehicles?

Is there a possibility of as yet unseen vehicles approaching?

Is there a blind area I can't see into before starting the overtake?

What's happening behind? Are any of the following vehicles likely to overtake me?

What distance do I need to pass and regain a nearside position safely?

Have I noted any relevant road signs, markings and speed limits?

Acceleration

Apply the appropriate degree of acceleration to complete the pass safely and leave the hazard.

Gear

Before you start the overtake, select an appropriate gear that's responsive enough for the overtaking manoeuvre. Be prepared to change gear if necessary.

Speed

Adjust your speed to the size of the space you're travelling through. The narrower the space, the slower you'll need to go.

Position

Adopt your position as early as you safely can, ideally to the offside of the road at least a door's width away from the stationary vehicle. Plan your path when you return to your own side. Check for hazards on the offside.

Overtaking moving vehicles

Overtaking a moving vehicle is more complicated because the situation is a dynamic one which is changing all the time. You need to consider the speed and acceleration capabilities of your own vehicle, the physical features of the road and the relative speeds of other vehicles. You also need a good sense of where your own and other vehicles are in relation to gaps in the traffic.

Whenever you consider overtaking, always ask yourself:

- Do I need to?
- Is it safe in the circumstances?
- Is my vehicle capable of overtaking?

The following pages describe two overtaking situations:

- **a single-stage overtake** where you're able to overtake immediately (approaching, overtaking and returning to your own side of the road) in one continuous manoeuvre
- **a three-stage overtake** where other hazards require you to take up a following position before you can safely overtake.

Overtaking usually involves multiple hazards. Any overtaking situation can change rapidly and become complicated by further hazards (for example, new oncoming vehicles, or slower vehicles further ahead on your side of the road). While you're learning to negotiate these complex hazards, you may have to consider and apply the system more than once in an overtaking manoeuvre. As you gain practice and confidence, you'll learn to view the number of hazards as one complex picture, and to use fewer applications.

The vehicle in front

Assess what sort of hazard the vehicle in front presents.

- Is the driver of the vehicle aware of you?
- Can you predict from earlier behaviour whether the driver's response is likely to be aggressive?
- Does the size or the load of the vehicle prevent the driver from seeing you or prevent you from seeing the road ahead clearly?
- Does the vehicle have left-hand drive (for example, a foreign lorry)?

Consider signalling your intention to overtake to the driver in front. Your road position will help you to do this but take care not to appear aggressive. This can be counter-productive and provoke an aggressive response in the other driver, who might speed up as you try to overtake. If the driver in front appears to be obstructive, consider whether it's worth overtaking at all. If you decide to go ahead, think about how much extra speed and space you need to allow to take into account any actions the driver may take.

If the driver in front isn't aware of you, consider using your headlights to signal that you're there.

Take extra care before overtaking a long vehicle or vehicles with wide or high loads. Assess the road ahead very carefully for any possible dangers. If you can, take views to both sides of the vehicle and make sure you have plenty of space to overtake and return safely to your own side.

The vehicles behind

Assess whether the vehicles behind pose a risk. Note their speed, position and progress, and judge whether any of them may want to overtake you. Look out particularly for motorcycles or fast-moving cyclists, especially in urban areas. Be aware that other following vehicles could overtake the vehicle following you. Use your mirrors to monitor the situation behind you, especially before changing your speed or position. Decide whether you need to signal. If you pull out for a look, the vehicle behind may move into your space.

Other hazards to consider before overtaking

Be aware of hazards that might cause the vehicles you're overtaking to alter their position. The illustrations below show some common overtaking collisions.

The driver of the blue car doesn't realise that the motorcyclist can only see the slow-moving van and may pull out onto the main road.

The driver of the blue car doesn't anticipate that the red car may turn without warning into the side road.

The driver of the blue car doesn't realise the driver of the green car is looking only to their right and may pull out.

The driver of the blue car thinks that the van is going to pass the parked car ahead, but the van is turning right, so will move and alter speed very differently.

The driver of the blue car doesn't anticipate that the tractor may turn without warning into an entrance or gateway.

The driver of the blue car doesn't realise that the red car is approaching. The lorry may slip safely into a return gap, leaving the blue car facing the oncoming vehicle.

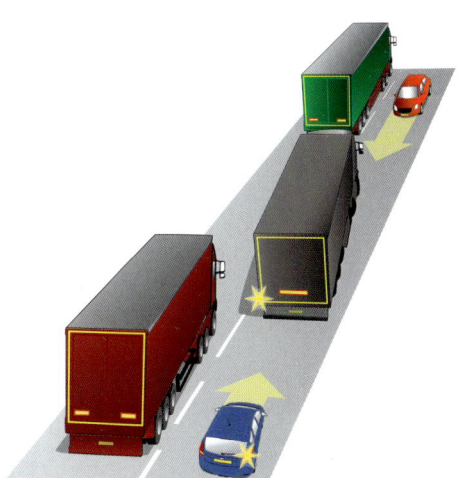

Make sure you have a full view of the road ahead of the vehicle you intend to overtake. Consider the possible actions of the driver of that vehicle and any others that may come into view.

A single-stage overtake

The basic principles of a single-stage overtake are the same as passing a stationary vehicle, but you'll now have additional questions to ask yourself:

What's the speed of the vehicle(s) to be overtaken?

Have I taken into account the speed and performance of my own vehicle?

What's the likely response of the driver and occupants of the vehicle in front?

Information

Observe the road ahead for other actual and potential dangers – physical features, position and movement of other road users and weather/road conditions.

Identify:

- a safe stretch of road along which you have adequate vision to assess the whole overtake
- what's happening behind
- a gap into which you can safely return
- the relative speed of your own vehicle and the vehicle(s) you intend to overtake
- a stretch of road long enough to accommodate the relative speeds of the vehicles – this will be much longer than the distance needed to pass a stationary vehicle.

Consider signalling if it will benefit other road users. Make sure that your signal is clear and can't be misinterpreted.

Think about the likely response of the driver and occupants of the vehicle in front. Consider the need to give information to any other road users.

The next diagram shows a typical single-stage overtake.

> Remember that much of the decision-making will happen *before* you get to the point shown in the diagram. Be aware also that different vehicles give drivers different viewpoints when overtaking.

Chapter 12 – Overtaking 225

Acceleration

Apply an appropriate degree of acceleration to overtake safely.

Gear

Before you start the overtake, select an appropriate gear that's responsive enough for the overtaking manoeuvre. Be prepared to change gear if necessary.

Speed

Consider your speed throughout the manoeuvre. Is it appropriate?

Position

As early as you safely can, take a position to overtake the vehicle in front.

A three-stage overtake

Stage one: following position

Where you're gaining on a vehicle in front but can see it isn't possible to overtake immediately, reduce your speed so that you can follow at a safe distance while you look for a safe opportunity to overtake on a suitable piece of road.

See Chapter 10, page 181, Following position.

In order to overtake in these circumstances, you'll need to observe and assess the road and traffic conditions ahead for an opportunity to overtake safely. When you anticipate one, move into an overtaking position. This is the most complex of the three overtaking stages, so you must ask yourself a number of questions.

- Does the road layout present a hazard?
- Is there enough road width for me to overtake?
- What's the speed of the vehicle(s) to be overtaken?
- What's the likely response of the driver and occupants of the vehicle in front?
- Is/are the driver(s) ahead likely to overtake?
- What's the speed and proximity of oncoming vehicles?
- Is there a possibility of as yet unseen vehicles approaching at high speed?
- What's happening behind? Are any of the following vehicles likely to overtake me?
- What's an appropriate speed to complete the overtake, taking account of the hazards beyond the vehicle I'm overtaking?
- What distance do I need to overtake and safely regain a nearside gap?
- Have I taken into account the speed and performance of my own vehicle?
- Have I noted any relevant road signs, markings and speed limits?

Your priorities may change as you go through the manoeuvre. Continue to observe, plan and process information so that you can adjust your hazard priorities as the overtake develops. Observe what's happening in the far distance, the middle distance, the immediate foreground and behind. Do this repeatedly. Remember that good observation alone isn't enough. Your safety depends on correctly interpreting what you see.

See page 222 for examples of situations where drivers don't correctly interpret what they see.

In some cases, you might plan to take the following position but then find as you close up on the vehicle in front that you have a clear view of the road ahead and there are no additional hazards. In this case, you could go straight into the overtake.

Otherwise, once you think you've found a safe place to do the overtake, start to close some of the distance between you and the vehicle ahead.

Stage two: overtaking position

Once you think you've found a safe place to do the overtake, close some of the distance between you and the vehicle ahead. Position your vehicle to get the best possible view and opportunity by moving into the overtaking position. This is generally closer to the vehicle in front than the following position and you should only use it in readiness for overtaking. Always have due regard for safety. If a hazard (for example, an oncoming vehicle, a road junction) comes into view, move back to an appropriate following distance from the vehicle in front.

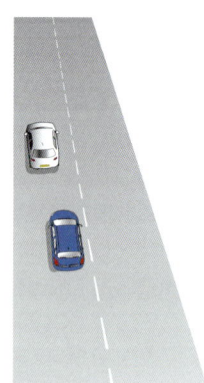

When you're following a large lorry, keep well back and take views to both sides of it.

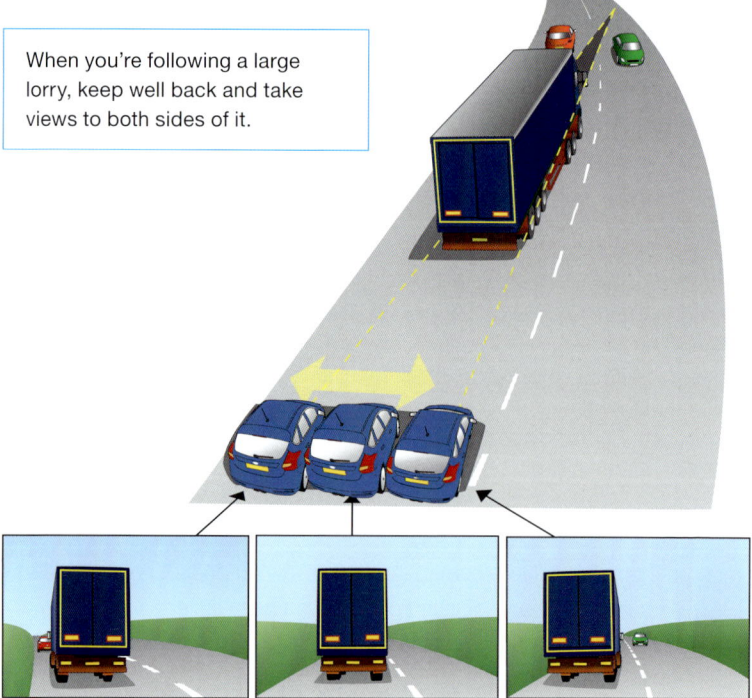

As you move closer to the vehicle in front, the driver is likely to realise that you want to overtake. Be careful not to intimidate the other driver or to appear aggressive by following too closely. This is dangerous and counter-productive. Following too closely may cause the other driver to speed up, making it more difficult to overtake.

From the overtaking position, continue observing until you see an opportunity to overtake.

Stage three: overtaking

Position your vehicle so that you have a clear path beyond the vehicle you wish to pass, without accelerating. Usually this means moving to the right, as in the diagram.

From this position, you have a better view of what's in front of the vehicle you want to overtake.

- Confirm that it's safe to overtake.
- If you see the manoeuvre would not be safe, return to the following or overtaking position as appropriate.
- If you can complete the manoeuvre safely, accelerate past.

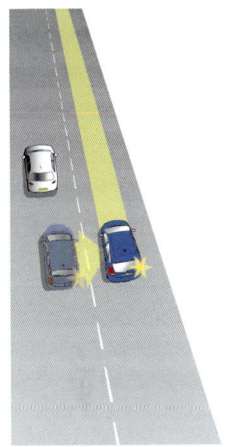

As you accelerate past, continue to assess the hazards ahead of the overtaken vehicle. This may include other vehicles you want to overtake (see below), other road users or physical features such as junctions or bends.

Remember that overtaking is your decision and you can reconsider at any point. But if you decide not to overtake in the light of new information, the vehicle behind could move into your space and leave you marooned. If in doubt, hold back.

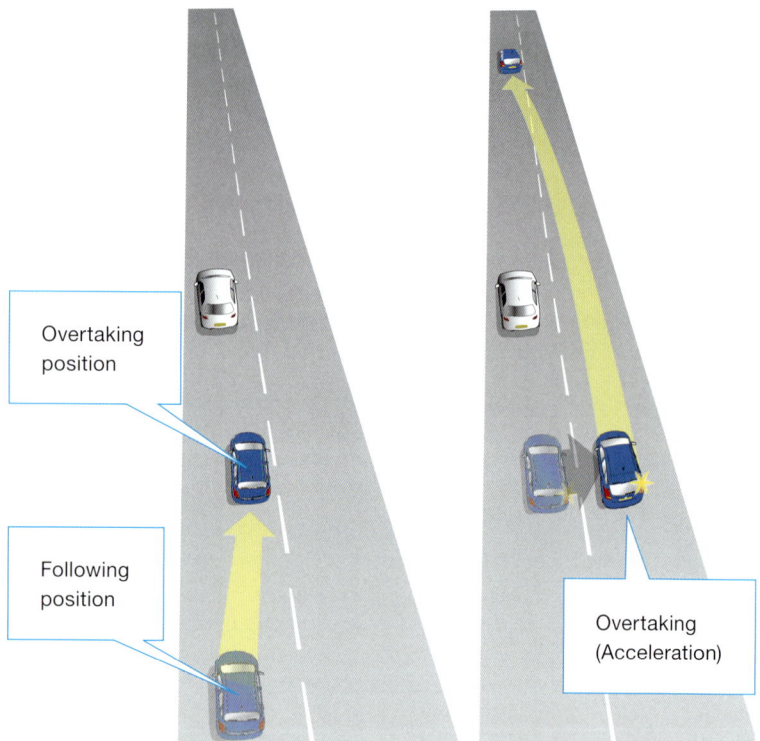

Overtaking vehicles in a line of traffic

Overtaking in a line of traffic is more difficult because it takes more time. You also have to take into account the possible actions of more drivers, both in front and behind. Drivers in front may not be aware that you're there or intend to overtake; drivers behind might try to overtake you. Always signal your intentions clearly to other road users.

Before you overtake, identify a clear gap between the vehicles in front that you can enter safely. This gap may get smaller before you arrive, so choose one that's large enough to allow for this. Don't overtake if you'll have to force your vehicle into a gap.

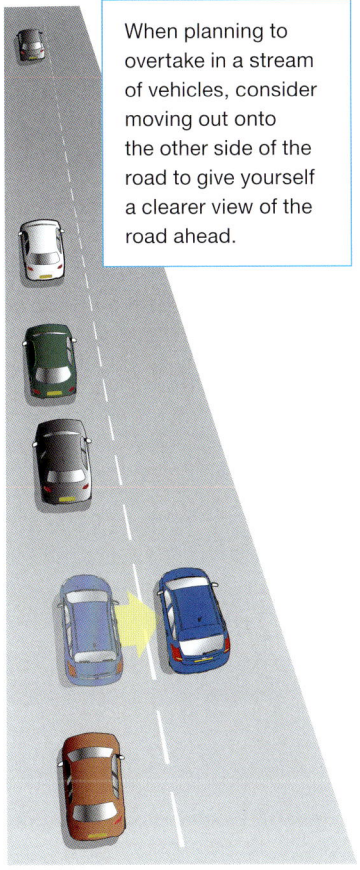

When planning to overtake in a stream of vehicles, consider moving out onto the other side of the road to give yourself a clearer view of the road ahead.

Consider moving out onto the other side of the road to give yourself a clearer view of the road ahead. Hold this position if you can see that the road ahead is clear, and if you can identify a clear return gap and have enough time to reach it. Allow for the possibility that the driver following you might move up into the gap that you've just left. When you reach the first return gap, you may not need to enter it. If it's safe, hold your position while you decide whether you can overtake more vehicles.

Apply the system. If there's more than one vehicle, you may initially wish to plan a series of overtakes as one manoeuvre. However, you'll need to re-appraise each one separately as you approach the vehicle. Do a safety check each time you reach a return gap. Re-apply the system as you complete each individual overtake and check that it's safe to continue to the next one.

Don't be tempted to increase your speed for each overtake in a line of traffic. Remember that you'll need to slow to match the speed of the vehicle ahead of you in the queue when you return or to deal with whatever hazard is ahead if you reach the front of the queue.

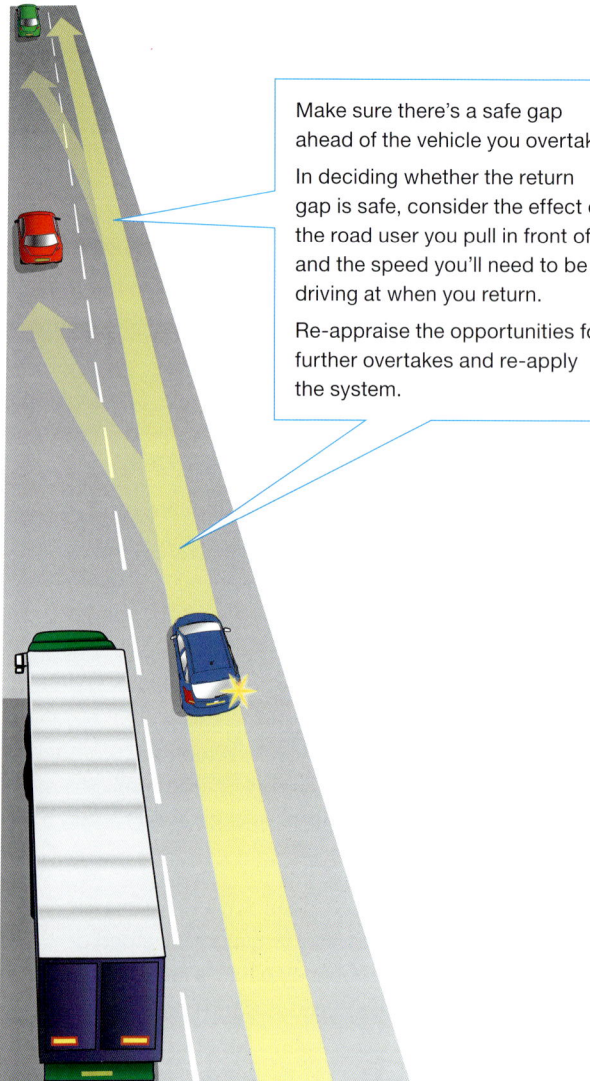

Make sure there's a safe gap ahead of the vehicle you overtake.

In deciding whether the return gap is safe, consider the effect on the road user you pull in front of and the speed you'll need to be driving at when you return.

Re-appraise the opportunities for further overtakes and re-apply the system.

Other overtaking situations

Certain overtaking situations involve particular considerations:

- overtaking on a single carriageway
- overtaking on bends
- overtaking on single carriageway roads marked with three lanes
- overtaking on multi-lane carriageways.

Overtaking on a single carriageway

This is perhaps the most hazardous form of overtaking because you put your vehicle in the path of any oncoming vehicles – so plan this manoeuvre with great care. Remember, you can always reconsider your decision and hold back.

You need to be able to judge the speed and distance of oncoming vehicles accurately to assess whether you can reach the return gap before they do. This can be extremely difficult, especially on long straight roads. The size and type of the oncoming vehicle, for example a tow truck, can give you clues about its possible speed.

As well as looking for vehicles, train yourself to look specifically for motorcyclists, cyclists, pedestrians and horses before you overtake. Drivers often fail to spot the unexpected.

See Chapter 4, page 66, Looking but not seeing.

Next time you plan to overtake on a single carriageway road, review your decision-making. Ask yourself:

- Do I need to overtake?
- How will I assess the speed of any oncoming vehicles?
- Have I checked for pedestrians, cyclists or any other unexpected hazards?
- Will my overtaking manoeuvre put me in the path of oncoming vehicles?

Overtaking on bends

Overtaking on bends is potentially dangerous and you should always ensure that you have the available view to do this safely. In certain circumstances, it's possible to get a good clear view of the road through the bend before you enter it. If you're sure there are no other hazards, position yourself to overtake before the road straightens out. The diagrams that follow give some examples of how to consider making an overtake using this information.

Left-hand bends

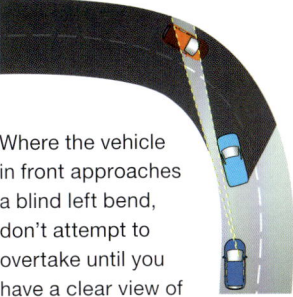

Where the vehicle in front approaches a blind left bend, don't attempt to overtake until you have a clear view of the road ahead.

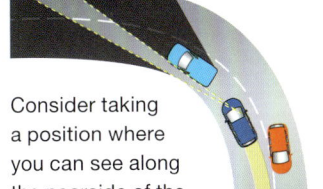

Consider taking a position where you can see along the nearside of the vehicle as it passes through the bend. Never rely on the nearside view alone.

Overtake if the road is clear and it is safe to do so. If conditions are not favourable, drop back.

Right-hand bends

Where the vehicle in front is approaching the apex of a right-hand bend with a restricted view, take a position well to the nearside.

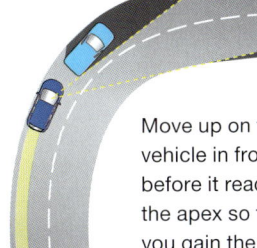

Move up on the vehicle in front just before it reaches the apex so that you gain the earliest possible view along its offside.

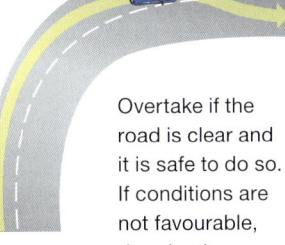

Overtake if the road is clear and it is safe to do so. If conditions are not favourable, drop back.

Overtaking on single carriageway roads marked with three lanes

Single carriageway roads marked with three lanes are potentially very dangerous as traffic in both directions shares the centre lane for overtaking. Never try to overtake if there's the possibility of an oncoming vehicle moving into the centre lane. Avoid overtaking when you would make a third line of moving vehicles, unless you're sure it's absolutely safe to do so.

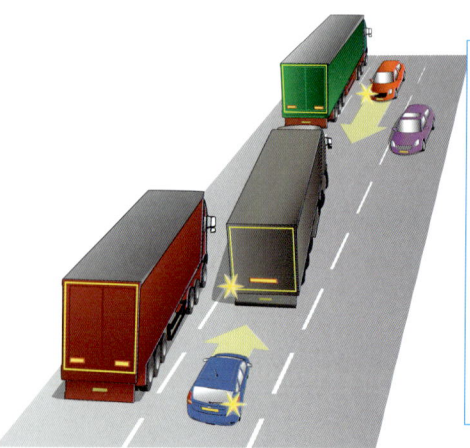

Don't be tempted to follow another vehicle through an apparently safe gap on a three-lane single carriageway. Always identify a safe return gap of your own. The vehicle in front may slip safely into a small return gap leaving you in the middle lane facing oncoming vehicles.

When you are planning to overtake, always look out for the 'lurker' who closes right up unseen behind other vehicles and then sweeps out to overtake. Never assume that the drivers of vehicles behind an oncoming lorry will stay put. They could well pull out just when you do.

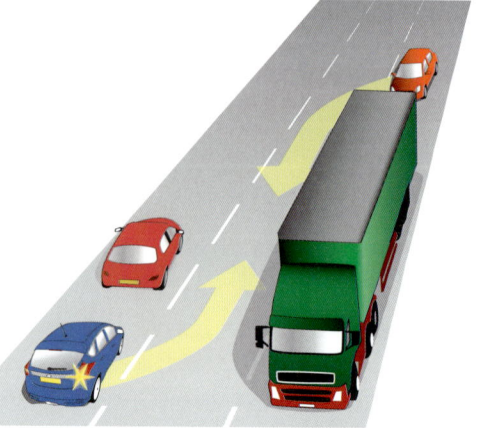

Overtaking on multi-lane carriageways

On multi-lane carriageways, it can be more difficult to judge the speed of traffic approaching from behind.

Before overtaking, check the intentions of drivers in the nearside lanes. If a vehicle is closing up on the one in front, the driver may pull out without signalling or only signal after the vehicle starts to move out. Watch the distance between the wheels of the vehicle and the lane markings. If the gap narrows, the vehicle could be moving out. Follow these key principles:

- Overtake on the nearside only if traffic in all lanes is moving in queues.
- Never use the hard shoulder for overtaking.
- Take particular care when planning to overtake large vehicles at roundabout exits and on left-hand bends.
- On carriageways with three or more lanes, maintain your observation of the gaps between vehicles. A shortening gap may indicate a vehicle preparing to overtake into a lane closer to you.

See Chapter 13, Driving on motorways and multi-lane carriageways.

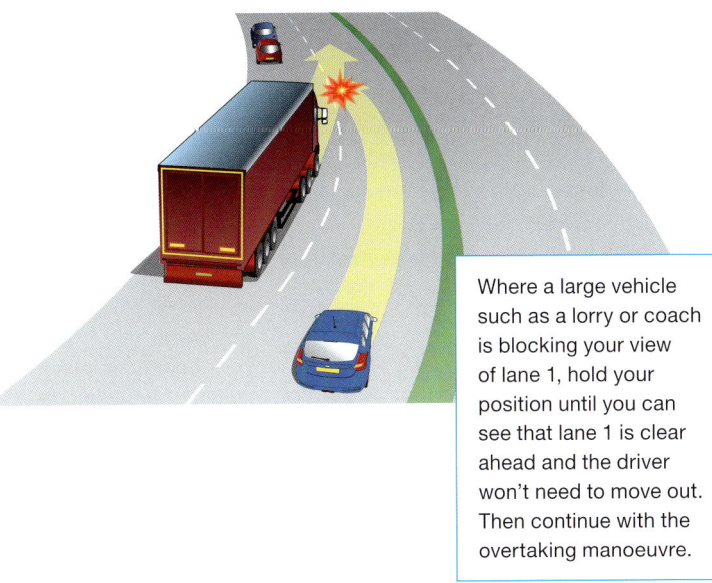

Where a large vehicle such as a lorry or coach is blocking your view of lane 1, hold your position until you can see that lane 1 is clear ahead and the driver won't need to move out. Then continue with the overtaking manoeuvre.

The range of hazards

Before overtaking, consider the full range of possible hazards that each situation presents. You've already considered the hazards presented by the vehicle in front and any vehicles behind, and the hazards associated with particular types of carriageway, but the road conditions and other road users present hazards too, for example:

- pedestrians
- cyclists and motorcyclists
- oncoming vehicles not yet in view
- the road layout and conditions
- the road surface.

You'll also need to note any relevant road signs, markings and speed limits before attempting to overtake.

Some of these hazards are discussed in more depth below.

Cyclists, motorcyclists and horses

Although cycles don't take up much road space, they have a tiny tyre contact area and may have limited tyre grip. They're inherently unstable – they get blown around both by weather and passing traffic and are susceptible to hazards on the road surface such as potholes. They also have limited braking capacity. Cyclists have little physical protection, usually have no mirrors, may be wearing earphones and may be untrained in riding safety.

When you overtake a cycle:

- **Allow the cyclist space to manoeuvre** – at least 1.5 metres, but more if you're travelling at a high speed relative to the cycle. Be aware that you may need to increase this clearance in a larger vehicle.
- **Overtake only on the offside except in complex traffic systems** – and then only on the nearside with care.

- **Don't overtake a cycle then turn in across its path** – the cycle has limited braking capability and this is inconsiderate in any case. Judge the cyclist's speed with care – it's easy to underestimate this.

At traffic lights with advanced stop lines for cycles, you may need to overtake shortly after starting off. The cyclist may be in the centre of the road and may weave as they pick up speed, so be prepared to give them additional space.

Give motorcyclists plenty of room too. If you're too close, displaced air flow could destabilise them. The larger your vehicle, the more clearance you'll need to give.

Allow horses plenty of room and avoid using warning equipment. Be prepared to stop if necessary. Speed or the sound of a horn can startle horses. The British Horse Society recommends that drivers pass horses at no more than 10 mph and allow at least 2 metres of space when passing.

Road layout and conditions

When you plan to overtake, look for possible hazards in the layout of the road ahead. Watch out for nearside obstructions or junctions, including pathways, tracks, entrances and farm gates. Vehicles, pedestrians or animals could emerge from these causing the vehicle(s) in front of you to veer towards the centre of the road. Look for right-hand junctions and entrances concealing vehicles or other hazards that could move out into your path.

Look for lay-bys on both sides of the road and watch out for vehicles pulling out of them. Drivers pulling out of a lay-by on the other side of the road may not see you because they're watching what's happening behind rather than in front of them.

Assess the width of the road and look out for any features that could obscure your view, such as vegetation, bends, hidden dips, hill crests and hump bridges. There may be fast-moving vehicles approaching you on the sections of road you can't see.

Make sure you've observed the whole stretch of road necessary to complete the manoeuvre, and know that it doesn't include any other hazards. Look especially for hazards that might cause the vehicles you're overtaking to alter their position. Make full use of road signs and road markings, especially those giving instructions or warning you of hazards ahead.

See Chapter 5, page 93, Road signs and markings.

The road surface

Before you overtake, observe the condition of the road surface for anything that could throw your vehicle off course or affect your visibility (for example, loose gravel). Watch out for surface water, which could cause a curtain of spray at a critical moment. Be aware that bad weather can affect how your vehicle holds the road and how well you can see the road.

See Chapter 5, pages 86, Weather conditions, and 89, Road surface.

Human factors in overtaking

Overtaking is a particularly hazardous element of any driving task you may need to perform. Human factors affect not just you but also the other drivers you encounter. The interaction between all those factors and the changing environment outside your vehicle as you move along will influence your decision about whether to overtake.

Overtaking safely

What human factor risks should you consider? Ask yourself:

- What human factors might affect my ability to accurately perceive hazards before overtaking?
- How might human factors interfere with my ability to overtake safely (for example, 'red mist', 'noble cause' risk-taking, thrill-seeking tendencies)?
- Does the specific purpose of the journey affect my decisions to overtake? Should it?

Helping other road users to overtake

Helping other road users to overtake eases tensions and contributes to a cooperative driving culture that increases safety. Use your mirrors and be alert to the intentions of drivers behind you. If another driver or rider is overtaking you, try to make it easier by leaving enough distance between you and the vehicle in front to give them a safe return gap, but don't suddenly reduce speed to achieve this.

Be aware that other drivers may try to overtake you when you keep to the legal speed limit. This is more likely as you slow down to enter, or as you're about to leave, a lower speed limit area.

Overtaking: key safety points

- Only overtake if you can see far enough ahead to be sure it's safe.
- Avoid causing other vehicles (overtaken, following or oncoming) to alter position or speed.
- Before you overtake, assess whether your vehicle is capable of the overtaking manoeuvre you're planning.
- Before starting to overtake, always ensure you can move back to the nearside in plenty of time.
- Always be ready to re-assess if a new hazard comes into view.
- Only overtake in situations where you won't come into conflict with other road users.
- Make sure that you can complete your overtake legally.
- When possible, avoid overtaking three abreast to leave yourself a margin of safety.
- On multi-lane carriageways, only overtake on the nearside if there are queues of traffic and offside queues are moving more slowly.
- Never use the hard shoulder for overtaking.
- Consider signalling if it will benefit any other road user. Make sure that your signal is clear and can't be misinterpreted.
- Always be patient and leave a margin of safety to allow for errors.

✓ Check your understanding

You should now be able to apply learning from this chapter in your driver training so that you can:

- [ ] explain the risks of overtaking
- [ ] show how to use the following and overtaking position safely
- [ ] show how to assess and overtake different types of hazards safely in a wide range of circumstances
- [ ] explain how to help other drivers to overtake you.

Chapter 13

Driving on motorways and multi-lane carriageways

Learning outcomes

The learning in this chapter, along with driver training, should enable you to:

- show that you can join and leave a motorway or multi-lane carriageway correctly
- show that you can use the appropriate lane for traffic conditions
- show that you can safely adapt your position and speed for overtaking, motorway junctions and other hazards, including weather conditions
- demonstrate correct use of the hard shoulder
- explain the human factor risks in motorway driving and show how you manage these.

Driving on multi-lane carriageways

Safe driving on motorways and other fast-moving multi-lane carriageways depends on developing your awareness of the extra hazards that arise on these roads and rigorously applying the driving competences and methods explained in *Roadcraft* to them.

Despite the high speed and volume of motorway traffic, there are fewer collisions on motorways for each mile travelled than on other roads. But motorway collisions are more likely to be fatal because of the high speeds involved.

However, other fast-moving multi-lane roads such as dual carriageways combine traffic moving at equally high speed with additional hazards; for example, junctions to the right and left, roundabouts, slow-moving vehicles and the absence of a hard shoulder.

See page 263, Additional hazards on fast-moving multi-lane carriageways.

Much of this chapter applies to all multi-lane carriageways, but motorways have specific features that you'll need to take into account:

- slip roads for entering and leaving the motorway (not always present on other multi-lane carriageways)
- dangers created by the presence of the hard shoulder
- dangers created by the absence of a hard shoulder on some motorways, which means that there could be stranded vehicles on the carriageway or vehicles pulling into or out of emergency refuge areas
- legal restrictions on which types of vehicle can use motorways, and the lane restrictions and speed limits for each type.

It takes time to develop accuracy in assessing speeds and stopping distances in a fast-moving driving environment. Always drive well within your own competence and aim to steadily develop your experience so that you're comfortable and confident within your existing speed range before moving on to higher speeds. Plan how you're going to address the fast-moving traffic conditions before you start your journey. Always take into account the size and limitations of your vehicle.

 Remember that higher speeds on fast-moving roads use more fuel. Smooth acceleration and braking reduce fuel consumption.

See Appendix 3, Fuel-efficient driving, page 295.

Layout of the carriageway

Here we use the numbering system used by the police and other emergency services to refer to the lanes on motorways and other multi-lane carriageways.

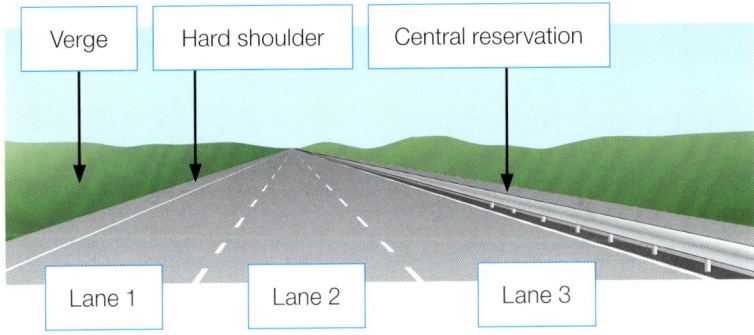

The nearside lane is lane 1, the next is lane 2 and so on. On a traditional three-lane motorway, lane 1 is the lane next to the hard shoulder and lane 3 is the lane next to the central reservation. The hard shoulder isn't counted as a carriageway lane.

See page 256, Using the hard shoulder.

New motorway layouts

An increasing proportion of the motorway network (smart motorways) uses technology to monitor and manage flow from regional centres. In addition to traditional motorways, there are two newer types of motorway:

- All lane running (ALR) – the full width of the road is available to drivers, with emergency refuge areas at intervals.
- Controlled motorways – with three or more lanes, a hard shoulder and variable speed limits.

Joining the motorway

Joining the motorway at a slip road or where motorways merge is potentially hazardous and you should use the system of car control to approach and join. Slip roads are designed to give drivers the time and space to merge smoothly with traffic on the main carriageway without causing other drivers to alter position or speed. If the slip road is raised, take advantage of the high viewpoint to observe the traffic flow and to plan your approach.

Drivers on the motorway have priority and may not be able to move over to allow you to enter lane 1, but looking early, planning and using your acceleration sense will assist you in merging safely. Only poor planning or exceptionally heavy traffic should cause you to stop in the slip road.

Slip roads have one or more lanes. If you're travelling in the outside lane of the slip road, consider how your speed and position will affect vehicles in the inside lane. If you overtake a vehicle on your nearside just before you join the motorway you could block its path on to the motorway. You risk colliding with it if you can't move straight into lane 2 of the motorway.

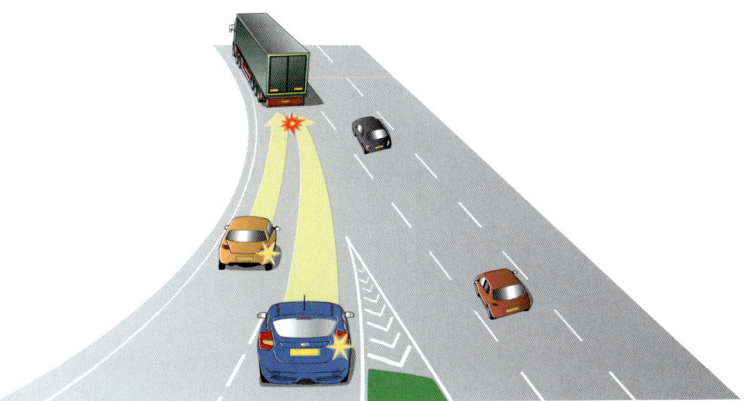

Do not overtake a vehicle that is on the inside lane of the slip road if you will block its path on to the motorway.

Use the system

As you enter the motorway, process information about the traffic on the slip road and motorway so that you're in the correct position, at the correct speed and in the correct gear to accelerate onto the motorway smoothly and safely.

Signalling

Well before you enter lane 1, decide whether you need to signal to let motorists on the motorway know that you intend to join the traffic flow.

Before you join the motorway, check over your shoulder to make sure there's nothing in your blind spot.

Acceleration

Allow yourself time to adjust to the higher motorway speed and to gauge the speeds of other vehicles.

Driving on the motorway

Good observation is key to safe motorway driving. Due to the speeds involved, it's vital to extend your observation:

- look ahead and behind you all the way up to the road horizons
- scan ahead, to the sides and to the rear frequently and thoroughly
- use your mirrors regularly – you should always know what's happening behind you
- be aware of your own and other drivers' blind spots and be prepared to move your body and alter vehicle position to observe what's happening in those areas
- monitor what's happening to your vehicle – regularly check that the instruments are giving normal readings and listen to the sound of your engine and to the noise of the tyres on the road surface
- check your speed regularly – it's very easy to increase speed without realising.

On your next motorway journey, practise extending your observation.

Make a point of scanning as far as the road horizon, front and back. Use your mirrors frequently. Regularly scan to the sides as well.

Aim to give yourself the longest possible time in which to react. Active scanning helps enhance your level of awareness, which in turn increases your overall safety.

Adapting to higher speeds

At 70 mph, you travel 31 metres (102 feet, about three coach lengths) per second. To give yourself as much time to react as possible:

- extend your observations in all directions and to the road horizons

- anticipate early and maintain a safe following distance – in good weather the two-second rule is a good guide but in bad weather you must allow a much greater distance
- use all controls smoothly, particularly steering, when travelling at high speed
- give other drivers enough time to see your signals before making a manoeuvre
- only use a headlight flash if it's necessary to alert other road users to your presence.

Lane discipline

You need good lane discipline for safe motorway driving. There are no slow or fast lanes. Overtake only to the right, except when traffic is moving in queues and the queue on your right is moving more slowly than you are.

Don't overtake by using a lane to your left.

Overtaking

Before you overtake, watch out for:

- slower vehicles moving out in front of you
- faster vehicles coming up behind you.

Apply the system of car control to overtake safely on motorways and other multi-lane carriageways, paying special attention to taking, using and giving information.

Taking information

Scan regularly so that you're continually aware of what the surrounding traffic is doing. You should know which vehicles are closing up on other vehicles in front, and which vehicles are moving up behind. Constantly monitor opportunities to overtake and match your speed of approach to coincide with an opportunity. Make allowances for the additional hazards presented by lane closures and motorway junctions.

Look for early warnings that other drivers intend to overtake:

- relative speeds
- head movements
- body movements
- vehicle movement from the centre of the lane towards the white lane markers.

You're likely to see all these before the driver signals; many drivers only signal as they start to change lanes.

 Over a motorway journey of reasonable length (say 20 miles), practise spotting the warning signs described above to predict when other drivers are about to change lanes.

Use this anticipation to help your planning.

Think carefully before overtaking on left-hand bends where there are mainly heavy or large goods vehicles in lanes 1 and 2. A car may be hidden between the heavy goods vehicles and about to pull out into lane 3. Make sure you can stop safely within the distance you can see to be clear. Don't attempt to overtake unless you're sure you can see all the vehicles in lane 2.

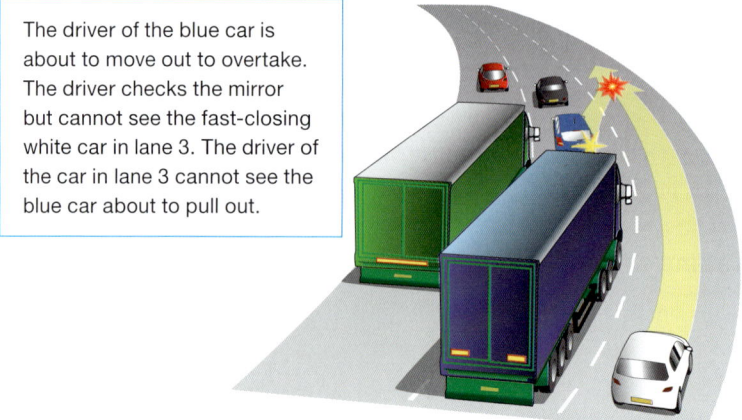

The driver of the blue car is about to move out to overtake. The driver checks the mirror but cannot see the fast-closing white car in lane 3. The driver of the car in lane 3 cannot see the blue car about to pull out.

Just before you overtake, carefully check the position and speed of the vehicles behind. For example, before you move into lane 2 to overtake a vehicle in lane 1, check there are no fast-closing vehicles moving back into lane 2 from lane 3.

As you move from lane 1 to lane 2, beware of vehicles moving up behind you into lane 2 from lane 3.

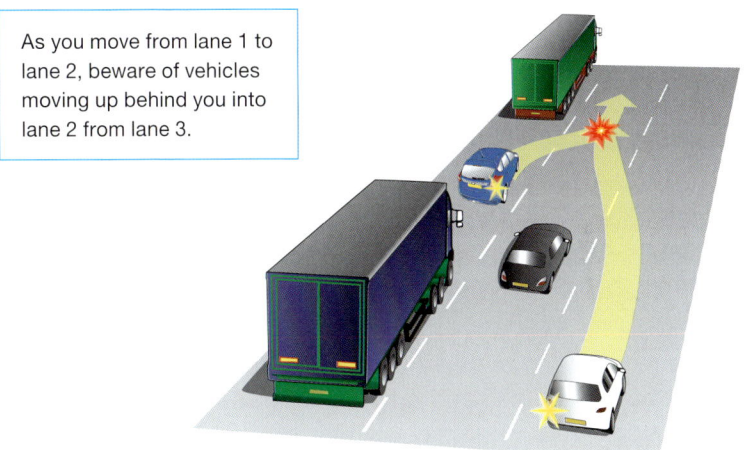

Move your head to increase your view either side of your blind spot. Re-check the position and speed of vehicles to the front and then consider the information that you need to give to the surrounding traffic.

Giving information

Avoid sitting in the blind spot of a vehicle you're trying to overtake. If you find that you're unable to overtake, drop back slightly so that you're visible to the driver.

Consider alerting other drivers to your presence especially if you're travelling at speed. If you decide a headlight flash would be helpful, give it in plenty of time for the other driver to react. Give a single flash: decide on the length of flash according to your speed and the response of other drivers. Take care not to appear aggressive to other drivers, and avoid dazzling oncoming drivers. Be aware that flashing headlights could be misinterpreted by other drivers as an invitation to move out in front of you.

Indicator signals

Consider indicating before changing lanes. Let the indicator flash long enough for other drivers to see and react to it.

When you've passed the vehicle or vehicles in front, return to the appropriate lane when you see an opportunity. But don't keep weaving in and out.

Leaving yourself room to manoeuvre

If you're travelling in lane 2 and traffic in your lane ahead has come to a standstill, consider extending the distance you would normally leave between your vehicle and a stationary vehicle ahead. If traffic is flowing freely in lane 1 there's a particular danger from left-hand-drive lorries approaching from behind and pulling into lane 2 to overtake the lorry ahead.

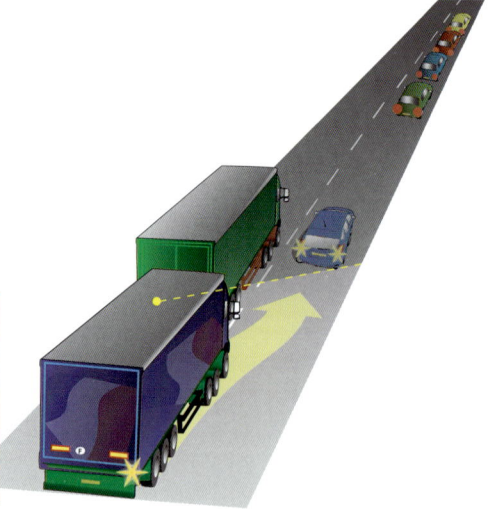

The sight line from the left-hand-drive lorry means the driver will not see your vehicle until almost totally out into your lane.

Being overtaken

Anticipate what the drivers behind you intend to do by their lane position and their speed of approach. This will help you to avoid potentially dangerous situations. As the other vehicle overtakes you, be aware that you're in the overtaking driver's blind spot.

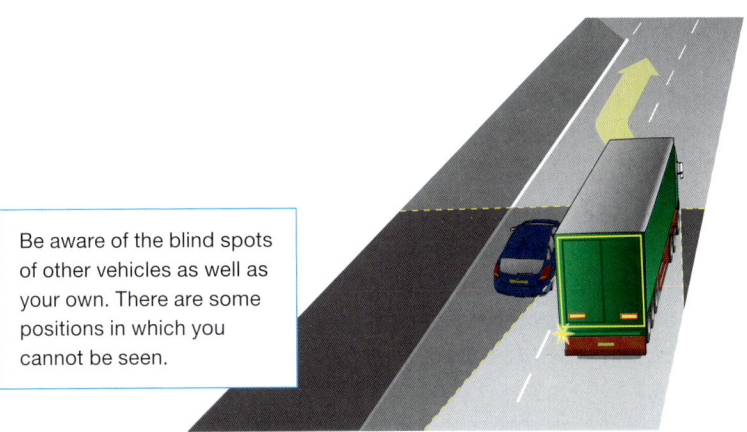

Be aware of the blind spots of other vehicles as well as your own. There are some positions in which you cannot be seen.

Motorway junctions

At junctions and service areas, you're likely to meet variations in traffic speed and more vehicles changing lanes. Watch for drivers who only change lanes for an exit at the last minute.

When you see a motorway exit, anticipate a slip road ahead and the possibility of traffic joining the motorway. If you're on the main carriageway, check your mirrors early and allow traffic to join the motorway by making slight adjustments to your speed or by changing lane. Vehicles on the motorway have right of way so don't do this if it would force other drivers to change their speed or position.

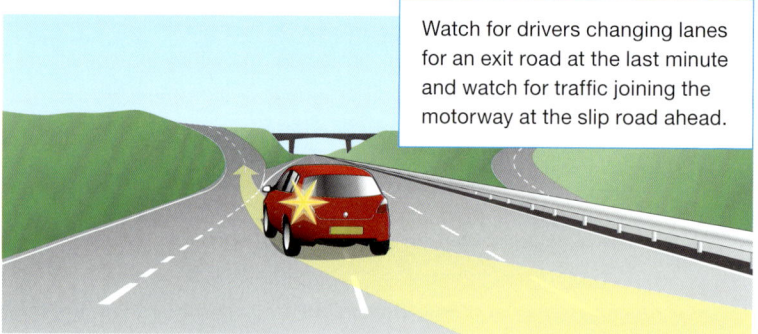

Watch for drivers changing lanes for an exit road at the last minute and watch for traffic joining the motorway at the slip road ahead.

Using the hard shoulder

The hard shoulder forms part of a motorway; on a traditional motorway, it's intended for emergency use only. It must only be used in accordance with the *Highway Code* and, for emergency services drivers, the most recent professional guidelines. Stopping on the hard shoulder is dangerous both for the occupants of the stationary vehicle and for other motorway users because there's a high risk of collision. Never use the hard shoulder for overtaking unless assigned to an emergency incident.

On stretches of smart motorway, you may find that the hard shoulder is being used permanently as a running lane; that is, 'all lanes running' (ALR), or as an additional lane during periods of congestion. In these conditions, be extra vigilant and watch out for stationary vehicles in any of the live lanes. Also, look out for vehicles pulling into or out of emergency refuge areas, which are spaced at regular intervals along the carriageway and marked by blue signs with an orange SOS telephone symbol.

Entering or leaving the hard shoulder

When you move onto the hard shoulder, or into an emergency refuge area, be aware that the road surface may contain loose gravel and other debris, which could reduce the available grip for stopping.

When you leave the hard shoulder or an emergency refuge area, carefully observe the traffic approaching from behind. Depending on the volume of traffic, choose an appropriate moment to move off. If you're leaving the hard shoulder, build up vehicle speed to match the vehicles in lane 1 **before** you move on to lane 1 of the carriageway.

Leaving the motorway

Plan your exit. Make sure you know your exit junction well in advance. Assess the road and traffic conditions as you approach the junction and use the information provided by road signs and markings.

The diagram shows a typical sequence of information given at motorway exits. Note that some motorways have signs at different points, so always read distance marker signs carefully.

As you approach your exit junction, look for the advance direction signs and use the system of car control to plan and carry out your exit. If the motorway is busy, consider joining lane 1 earlier rather than later. If a signal is necessary, always allow plenty of time for other drivers to react. Indicate at the 300-yard countdown marker.

There is usually a route direction sign at the point where the exit road splits from the main carriageway.

A third directions sign at the beginning of the exit road adds principal destinations ahead.

There are countdown marker posts before the start of the exit road. Each bar represents 100 yards to the exit.

At half a mile from the exit a direction sign repeats the information.

One mile from the exit, a direction sign gives the junction number and the roads leading off the exit with the town or destination names.

Avoid braking on the main carriageway if possible. Plan to lose unwanted speed in the exit road – which acts as a deceleration lane. But be aware that other road users may not do this and may start to slow down before reaching the exit road. On busy motorways, watch out for vehicles leaving the motorway at the last minute from lanes 2 or 3 and cutting across your path.

Driving at high speed affects your perception of speed when you leave the motorway:

- check your speedometer regularly to help you adjust to the slower speeds of ordinary roads
- plan for the point at which you'll meet two-way traffic
- be ready for acute bends at the end of motorway exit roads
- watch out for oil or other deposits which can make these areas exceptionally slippery.

Bad weather conditions on fast-moving roads

Chapter 5 explains how weather conditions affect your ability to observe and anticipate. This section looks at planning for bad weather conditions at higher speeds.

See Chapter 5, page 86, Weather conditions.

Bad weather reduces visibility and tyre grip so it's more dangerous at high speed because you need a much greater overall safe stopping distance.

You should always be able to stop safely in the distance you can see to be clear on your own side of the road.

When you can't see clearly, reduce your speed and consider using headlights and fog lights. You must use them if visibility drops below 100 metres (328 feet). The gap between motorway marker posts is about

100 metres so use these to assess how far you can see. Bear in mind that fog lights can mask your brake lights and dazzle the driver behind so switch them off as soon as visibility improves.

Fog

Fog reduces your perception of speed due to the lack of visual reference points. Do not rely on auto lighting systems. Consider manually switching on dipped-beam headlights.

In poor visibility, some drivers may reduce their following distance in order to keep the vehicle lights ahead in view. Be aware also that not all vehicles will be displaying the appropriate lights.

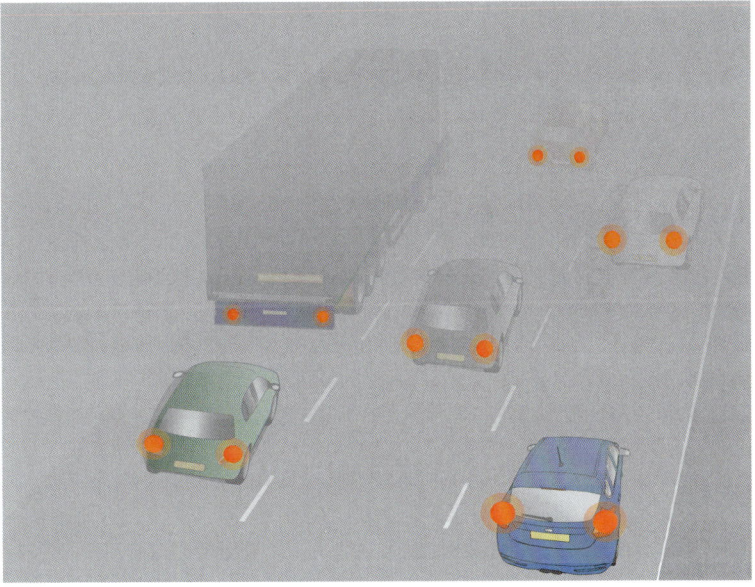

Fog reduces your perception of speed and risk because you can't see. At the same time, it encourages you to drive close enough to keep in sight the vehicle lights ahead.

Adjust your speed to ensure that you can stop within the range of visibility. The denser the fog, the slower your speed. Driving in fog can be very tiring and stressful. If you start to feel tired, take a break at the next available rest area.

Rain

High speed increases the risk created by rain and standing water on the road surface. This is because your vehicle's tyres have to displace water more quickly. If they're unable to do this, a wedge of water will form between the tyres and the road, resulting in aquaplaning. During such conditions, remain vigilant to the possibility of unexpected sections of deep water and adjust your speed on the approach.

See Chapter 8, page 162, Aquaplaning, for further advice.

After a long, hot, dry spell a deposit of tyre and other dust builds up on the road surface. These deposits create a slippery surface especially during and after rain. Avoid heavy braking, steering or accelerating or you could lose tyre grip.

Snow, sleet and ice

Snow and sleet reduce visibility and tyre grip. At speed, spray thrown up by the wheels of the vehicle in front reduces visibility further, and when ruts develop in the snow it may be difficult to steer. In heavy snow, consider whether your journey is really necessary.

Reduce speed and increase following distances in icy conditions, especially if the road surface isn't gritted.

High winds

Sections of carriageway that are raised above the surrounding countryside are affected by high winds. Be prepared for particularly strong gusts of wind as you leave a cutting, enter or emerge from under a bridge, cross a valley or go into open country. Take particular care on viaducts and bridges.

In windy conditions high-sided vehicles can suddenly veer. They also tend to act as wind breaks buffeting smaller vehicles as they draw past them. Keep a firm grip on the steering wheel with both hands.

High-sided vehicles displace air flow, which tends to pull smaller vehicles towards them during overtaking. As the smaller vehicle moves in front, it breaks free of the suction and tends to veer out. Correct this with a firm grip and appropriate pressure on the steering wheel.

Bright sun

Bright sun low in the sky can cause serious dazzle, especially on east/west sections of road: use your visors to reduce dazzle. If the sun is shining in your mirrors, adjust them to give you the best visibility with minimum glare. If you're dazzled by bright sun, other drivers may be too, so allow for this when overtaking.

Other hazards

Debris

Regularly scan the road surface for debris that may have fallen from vehicles. This can damage tyres and cause other vehicles suddenly to alter position.

Lane closures

Roadworks are a regular feature of motorway journeys. Contraflow systems aren't dangerous in themselves but become dangerous when drivers ignore advance warnings. All roadworks are signed on approach and you should know the sequence of signs. Keep to the mandatory speed limits through roadworks, even when conditions seem to be suitable for a higher speed.

Merging with other traffic requires judgement and courtesy. It's sensible for vehicles from each lane to merge alternately. But these situations often create conflict and result in collisions. Allow a reasonable following gap and never close up to prevent other vehicles merging.

Matrix signs and signals warn of lane closures or other changes in driving conditions ahead. On a smart motorway, look out for a red X or reduced speed limit on the overhead gantries. You may not immediately be able to see the need to slow down or change lanes but don't assume the sign is a mistake. The incident may be some distance further along the motorway.

Additional hazards on fast-moving multi-lane carriageways

On multi-lane carriageways, you need to watch out for a range of additional hazards that aren't present on motorways:

- slow-moving traffic
- traffic lights
- roundabouts
- right-hand junctions
- crossroads
- traffic moving into the right-hand lane to turn right
- traffic entering the carriageway from the central reservation
- traffic crossing the carriageway
- pedestrians crossing the carriageway
- entrances and exits other than road junctions (for example, to services, petrol stations, restaurants, pubs)
- left-hand junctions with only a short (or no) slip road
- public footpath crossing the carriageway – indicated by an overlap in the central reservation safety barrier.

Human factors in motorway driving

The nature of motorway driving increases a number of human factor risks:

- tiredness or boredom on long journeys, resulting in poor concentration
- frustration arising out of stop–start progress in dense traffic
- complacency in low-density traffic making drivers less alert to possible hazards
- the behaviour of drivers leaving or joining the motorway from service stations or slip roads.

Stop at the earliest opportunity if you find yourself unable to maintain the high level of concentration needed to drive safely at high speed.

Ask yourself whether your physical state and degree of alertness is optimal for motorway driving before you set off.

Have you ever found your concentration flagging on a motorway journey? What do you do to increase your alertness?

Is your approach always effective? How could you manage your fatigue better?

How do feelings of stress affect your motorway driving? Think about whether your brain can deal with the distraction from stress as well as drive safely.

How might dealing with difficult or demanding motorway situations increase your mental workload?

What can you do to reduce the risk of errors and increase your safety in these situations?

See Chapter 1, Becoming a better driver, and Chapter 4, Information, observation and anticipation.

✓ Check your understanding

You should now be able to apply learning from this chapter in your driver training so that you can:

- [ ] show that you can join and leave a motorway or multi-lane carriageway correctly
- [ ] show that you can use the appropriate lane for traffic conditions
- [ ] show that you can safely adapt your position and speed for overtaking, motorway junctions and other hazards, including weather conditions
- [ ] demonstrate correct use of the hard shoulder
- [ ] explain the human factor risks in motorway driving and show how you manage these.

Chapter 14
Emergency response

Learning outcomes

The learning in this chapter, along with driver training, should enable you to:

- list the exemptions in law available to emergency response drivers and explain their implications for your driving plan
- explain the importance of going through a process of risk assessment before and during an emergency call
- demonstrate the correct use of your vehicle's emergency warning equipment
- demonstrate good practice in emergency response driving across a range of traffic situations.

What is an emergency response?

Officers are deemed to be in an emergency response when they're using emergency warning equipment to facilitate progress, at which time they may make use of exemptions afforded to them by legislation.

Drivers who are trained to nationally agreed police driver training programme standards are entitled to make use of legal exemptions. However, it's essential that these are appropriate and used only in circumstances that can be justified. There's no legal definition of what would or would not constitute justification for making use of police exemptions.

Officers who hold a basic driving authority aren't permitted to take advantage of any legal exemptions.

The Road Traffic Regulation Act 1984 and The Traffic Signs Regulations and General Directions 2016 exempt emergency vehicles from:

- observing speed limits
- observing keep left/right signs
- complying with traffic lights (including pedestrian-controlled crossings).

Other exemptions are available under local Traffic Regulation Orders. These will be covered by your instructor. Use of any of these exemptions must be safe and proportionate to the prevailing circumstances.

> Be aware that some motorists over-react or react unpredictably when they encounter emergency response vehicles – for example, by stopping their vehicle in an unsuitable place such as next to traffic islands, on blind hill crests, on the apex of bends or opposite an oncoming vehicle that has also stopped. At busy junctions, motorists are likely to take more time to react to the presence of emergency response vehicles.

Using the national decision model

To help emergency response drivers make decisions and to provide a framework in which decisions can be examined and challenged, both at the time and afterwards, the police service has adopted a national decision model (NDM).

At its centre is the Code of Ethics, the touchstone for all decision-making. Using the model encourages you to act in accordance with the Code and use your discretion where appropriate. It also reduces risk aversion and weighs the balance of resourcing against demand, threat and risk.

See www.college.police.uk/app/national-decision-model/national-decision-model

Risk assessment

Before you begin your response to an emergency call, you should go through a process of risk assessment.

Here are some of the questions you need to ask yourself:

Does the situation necessitate an emergency response?

What human factors might increase my risk on response (for example, stress, operational distractions, peer pressure)? How do I manage these effectively?

Is my vehicle suitable?

Am I justified in making use of traffic law exemptions?

How far will I have to travel?

Are other units closer?

Do I need to use lights and sirens?

What speed is safe and proportionate for the circumstances, including traffic, time of day, lighting and weather?

An emergency call is an ever-changing environment so continue with this process of risk assessment throughout the response.

While incidents are graded in line with national requirements, as set out in the National Call Handling Standards, drivers responding to calls are responsible for assessing the response required. You must decide if the use of legal exemptions and/or the vehicle's emergency equipment is warranted and you may be called upon to justify your actions at a later stage.

Responding to an emergency

Use of emergency warning equipment

The emergency warning equipment is primarily used to:

- provide advance warning to other road users
- help your progress through traffic
- protect officers at the scene of incidents
- help in stopping motorists, by identifying your vehicle as a police vehicle.

Most drivers seeing or hearing the warning of an approaching emergency service vehicle will try to give way but the use of warning equipment doesn't give you protection or right of way. You may take advantage if other road users and pedestrians give way to you – but only if it's safe to do so. Bear in mind that unwarranted use of emergency warning equipment can undermine its value.

Never assume that your warning will be seen or heard by other road users.

Sirens

Assess when and where to activate your emergency equipment. In normal circumstances, you should activate your emergency lights before using your sirens.

Think carefully before activating your sirens if you're close to other road users, particularly cyclists, pedestrians or animals.

If, in the light of your risk assessment, you decide not to use your emergency warning equipment ('silent approach'), take extra care because other road users may be less aware of your vehicle's presence.

When using sirens, it's often not noise but a *change* in noise that gets a reaction. It's appropriate to use a long tone between hazards. But changing to a short tone on the approach to a hazard is likely to maximise the benefit of the warning.

Use a different tone to other emergency vehicles when travelling in a multi-vehicle response. The public may see one vehicle but they may not expect a second or third.

Consider switching off the sound system in stationary traffic. This often takes the tension out of the situation and gives others time to consider what they might do to help.

Headlamp flashers

The automatic headlamp flashers on most emergency vehicles use an alternating flash pattern. This makes it more likely that the vehicle will be seen but also increases the possibility of dazzling other road users.

Automatic headlamp flashers must not be used during the hours of darkness.

Blue lights

Some vehicles have both rotating and strobe lights in the roof light bar. Strobe lights are particularly effective on multi-lane roads such as motorways, but only show to the front or rear. If you're responding on roads with junctions, make yourself more conspicuous by using the rotating blue lights and/or intersection lights.

Speed limits

Police drivers can use statutory exemptions from speed limits but you must be able to stop safely within the distance you can see to be clear on your own side of the road. During an emergency response, never compromise safety in order to save time. It is far better to arrive later than not at all.

Keep in mind that members of the public will observe you if you exceed the speed limit or use an inappropriate speed. Inappropriate speed or misuse of exemptions is likely to result in negative public perceptions of response driving.

The following scenario shows why you always need to correctly assess the appropriate speed. The police vehicle is approaching at 30 mph the rear of a parked lorry which is 9 metres long. As the police car passes the rear of the lorry, a pedestrian steps out from in front of the lorry directly into the path of the police vehicle.

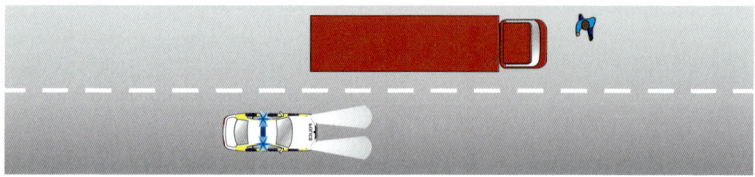

By the time the driver starts braking, the vehicle will have struck the pedestrian

Approaching traffic light-controlled junctions

When you pass red signals, you should treat them as STOP and/or GIVE WAY signs. Do not proceed until you're sure that the way is clear, that no other road user will be endangered and that no other driver will be forced to change speed or course to avoid a collision.

When you approach traffic lights, gather information about the road layout and consider the movements of other road users – both those you can see and those you can't.

Your risk assessment must include not only the red phase but also the green phase. This is important. Your speed of approach must enable you to stop if necessary – for example, if the traffic light signals change from green to red, or if another emergency vehicle going to the same incident is using their exemption and entering the junction through a red light.

On the approach to traffic lights, take a position to ensure the best view. Select the least obstructed path, with due regard to safety and making yourself as visible as possible to other road users.

Assess the position and movement of all traffic on the approach. When it's safe to do so, move forward at a speed that will allow you to maintain good observation and the ability to stop. Look out especially for the presence of cyclists or motorcyclists who are vulnerable and difficult to see among other vehicles.

If your entry speed into the junction is too high, other motorists may over-react and brake sharply. This could result in a 'shunt' type collision.

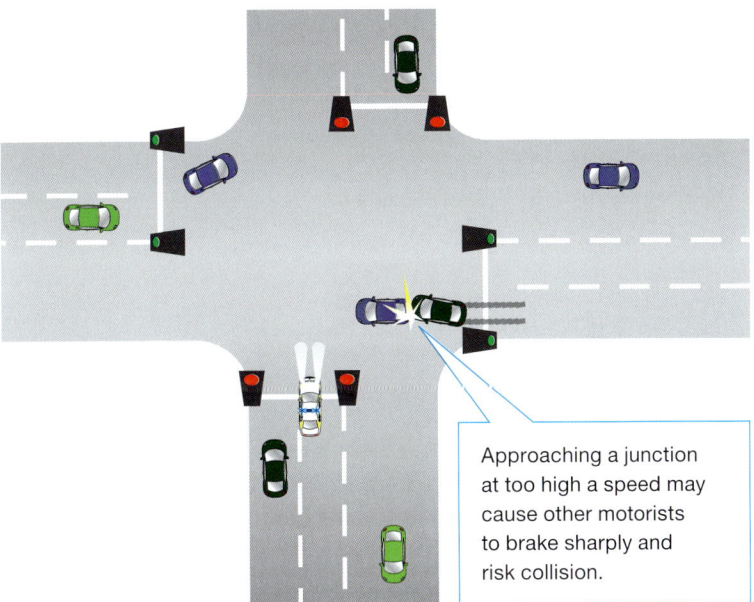

Approaching a junction at too high a speed may cause other motorists to brake sharply and risk collision.

Police drivers exercising the exemption to pass a red traffic light must avoid causing a member of the public to contravene the red light.

If vehicles are occupying all the entry lanes at the stop line on your approach to a set of red lights, consider one of the following options:

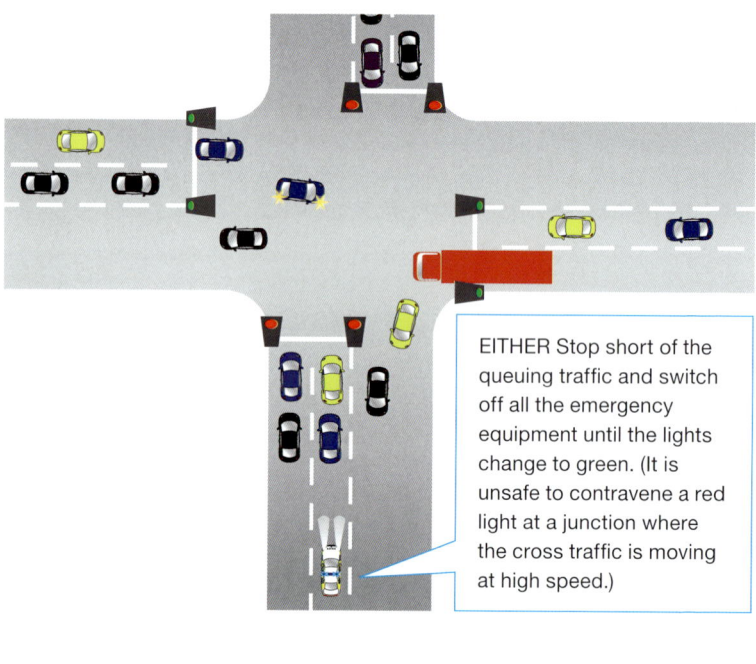

EITHER Stop short of the queuing traffic and switch off all the emergency equipment until the lights change to green. (It is unsafe to contravene a red light at a junction where the cross traffic is moving at high speed.)

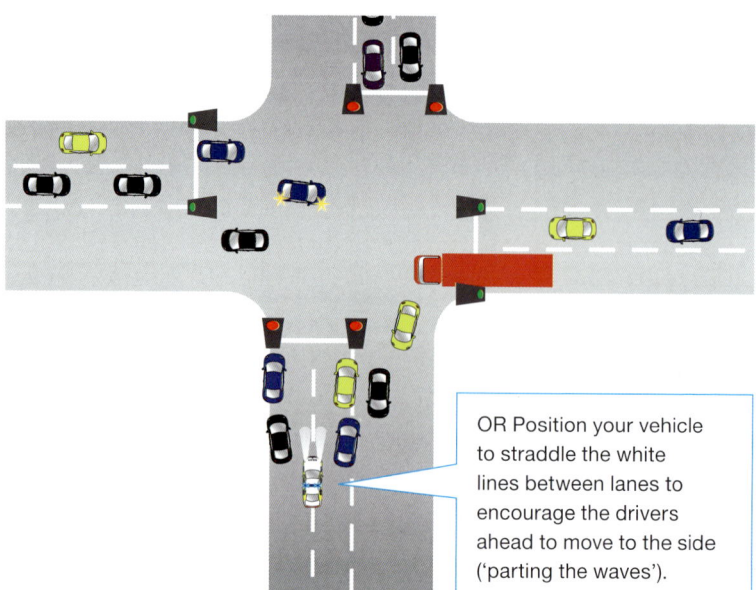

OR Position your vehicle to straddle the white lines between lanes to encourage the drivers ahead to move to the side ('parting the waves').

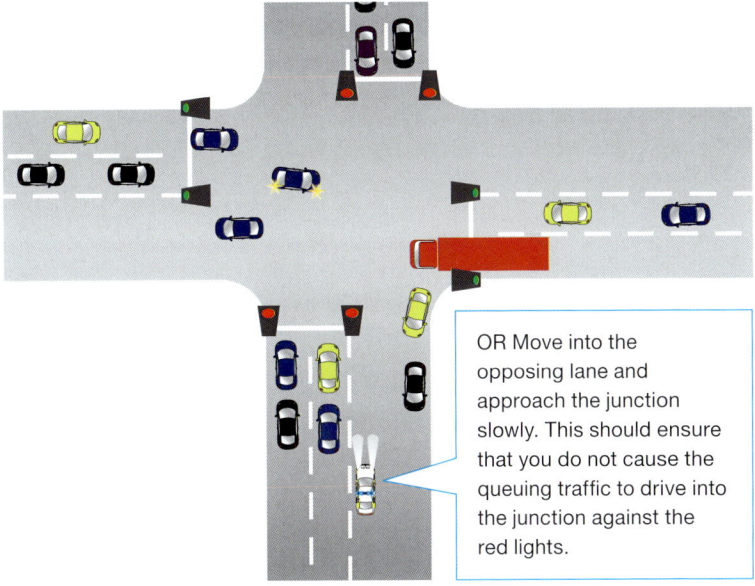

OR Move into the opposing lane and approach the junction slowly. This should ensure that you do not cause the queuing traffic to drive into the junction against the red lights.

Certain traffic light junctions are too dangerous to cross while the lights are red. These are normally where views are restricted, on multi-lane carriageways or where the speed of cross traffic is high.

Approaching traffic light-controlled pedestrian crossings

The advice on approaching traffic light-controlled junctions also applies to pedestrian crossings. As you approach, gather information about the road layout and the presence and movement of pedestrians.

Your speed of approach should allow you to stop safely within the distance you can see to be clear. Pedestrians may be hidden by any vehicle on the approach. When a pedestrian has moved onto the crossing, you must give way to them.

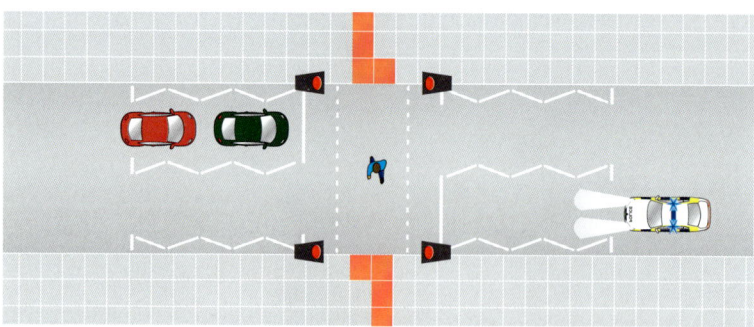

> Where a pedestrian has moved onto the crossing, hold back so as not to intimidate them.

Contravening keep left/right signs

If you exercise the exemption to contravene keep left/right signs, you'll be in an unexpected position so you need to be aware of additional hazards.

For example, where there's a central refuge for pedestrians, they may be looking in the other direction as they cross the road and may step into the path of the emergency response vehicle.

Positioning to see and be seen

During daylight, the best visual warning equipment to use on the approach to other road users is the flashing headlamp/white light-emitting diode (LED) units. To get the greatest advantage, position your vehicle to make the most of these lights.

Where it's safe to do so, position your vehicle early towards the offside. This can help you to get early views and it also allows oncoming drivers and drivers ahead of you to spot you earlier.

> Be prepared to surrender this position if an oncoming driver doesn't react appropriately.

The position shown below also gives a better view of the road and other dangers ahead. The driver of the vehicle directly ahead of the emergency response vehicle will be aware that it's attempting to overtake rather than requiring them to stop.

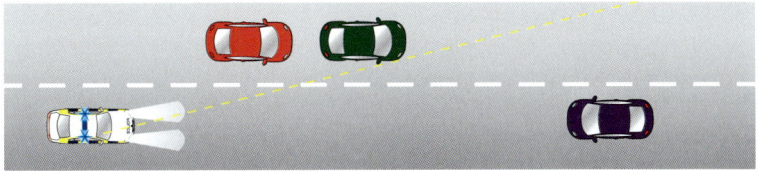

> Always ensure that a safe gap is available on the nearside should oncoming drivers not react appropriately.

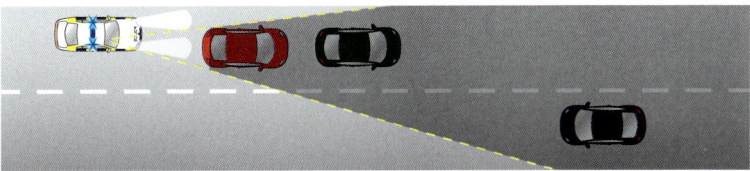

> This position results in a restricted view for both the police driver and the oncoming driver.

Approaching and passing vehicles

Vehicles ahead

When approaching traffic travelling in the same direction, travel at a speed and following position that allows you to respond to heavy or sudden braking by the vehicles ahead.

Seek evidence that the drivers ahead are aware of your presence before you attempt to pass them. Look for the nearside indicator operating or vehicle movement into the nearside or offside. Observe the driver's head and body movements. Never assume that other drivers have seen and/or heard your vehicle.

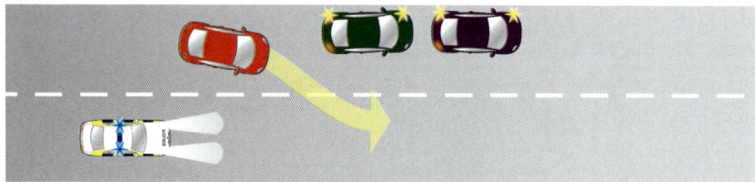

> The drivers of the two lead vehicles have slowed down in response to the police vehicle's presence. The driver of the red vehicle is unaware of the police vehicle and moves to overtake them, pulling out into the path of the police vehicle.

Oncoming vehicles

When the driver of an oncoming vehicle has given way to your approaching vehicle, always remain vigilant for other oncoming vehicles suddenly pulling out from behind the lead vehicle. Your speed should allow you time to stop should an oncoming vehicle suddenly present itself in your vehicle's path.

This is especially important if the lead vehicle is large – for example, a large goods vehicle, van or bus.

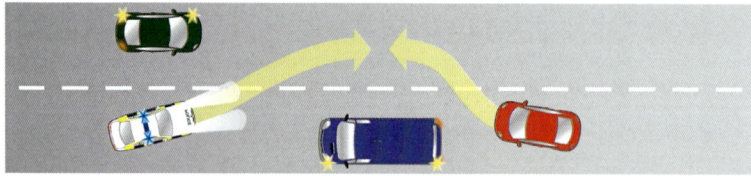

> Vehicles behind the lead oncoming vehicle may be unaware of your presence and attempt to overtake the lead vehicle into your path.

Overtaking slow-moving vehicles across junctions

When moving past slow-moving or stationary vehicles, be aware of the additional hazards presented by road junctions and adjust your speed accordingly.

Nearside junctions

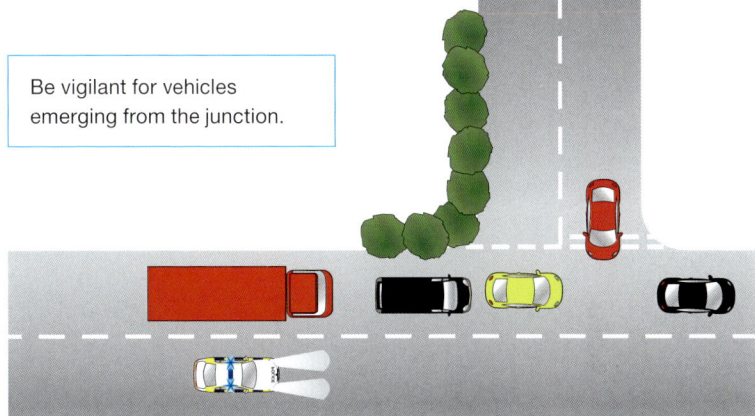

Be vigilant for vehicles emerging from the junction.

Offside junctions

Any driver turning left from an offside junction will emerge into the path of the police vehicle. On the approach to offside junctions with limited or no view, take up a position that allows you to stop or regain the correct side of the road. Never assume that the driver of the vehicle waiting to emerge will look to the left before entering the road.

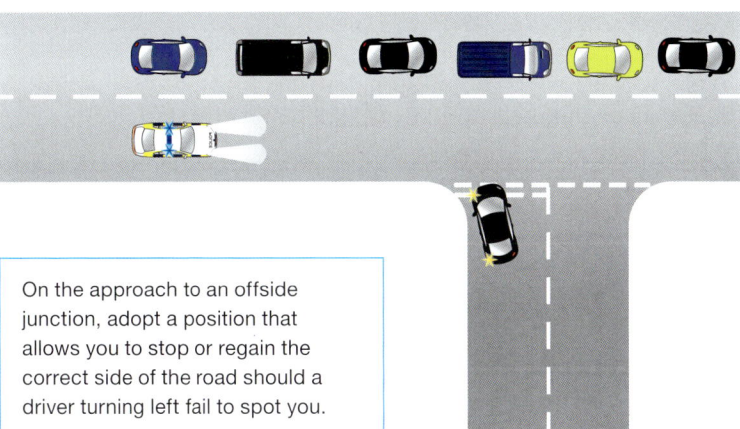

On the approach to an offside junction, adopt a position that allows you to stop or regain the correct side of the road should a driver turning left fail to spot you.

Interpreting other drivers' signals

It's common for motorists to flash their headlights to signal to others their intention to give way in all kinds of driving situations.

In the scenario shown below, there are three drivers who may perceive that the driver of the green car is signalling to them their intention to give way:

- the driver of the red vehicle waiting to emerge from the minor road
- the driver of the black vehicle waiting to turn right
- the police driver.

In situations such as this, take extra care and reduce your speed until you've safely negotiated the hazard.

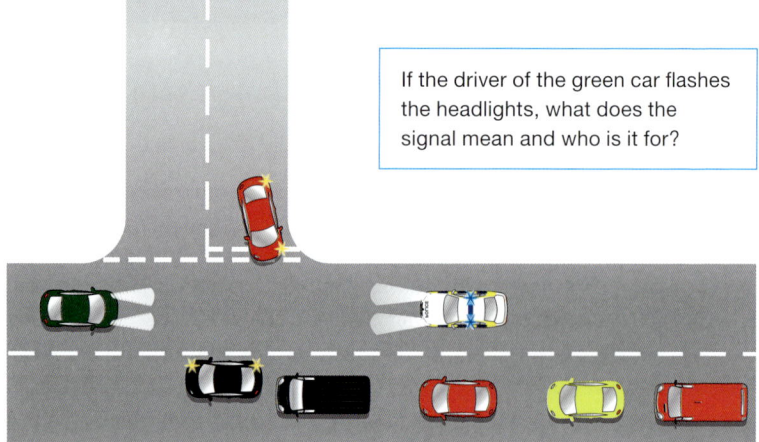

If the driver of the green car flashes the headlights, what does the signal mean and who is it for?

Stationary vehicles at or near an incident

Police drivers approaching a scene may become distracted searching for the exact location of the incident. This may mean that their attention is drawn away from the road immediately ahead so increasing risk.

Drivers who have been stationary for some time may try to do a U-turn or leave their vehicle. Pedestrians may also be walking between the stationary vehicles.

Responding on multi-lane roads

On multi-lane roads equipped with central reservations, such as dual carriageways and motorways, your positioning will vary according to the volume and speed of vehicles ahead.

In very congested conditions where vehicles are either stationary or travelling at low speed, it's best practice for police drivers to straddle lane markings to allow the traffic ahead to spread left and right. This is often referred to as 'parting of the waves'.

Be aware that some of the drivers ahead may not react as expected. Your approach speed must enable you to react to any vehicle crossing your path.

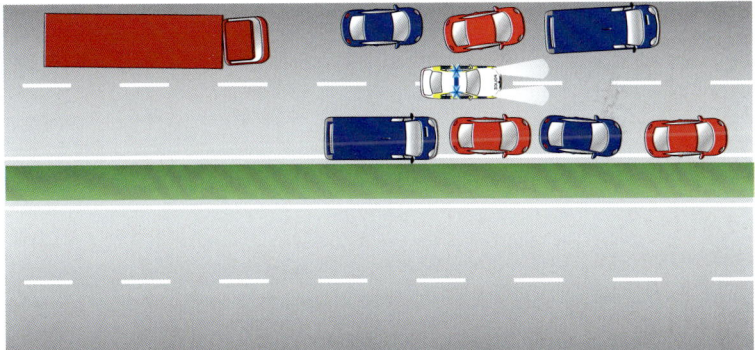

'Parting of the waves'

Where traffic is free flowing, travel in the outer lane and allow vehicles ahead to move into the nearside lanes – but without placing drivers under undue pressure to do so. Look out for vehicles in lanes on the nearside ahead suddenly moving into the outer lane.

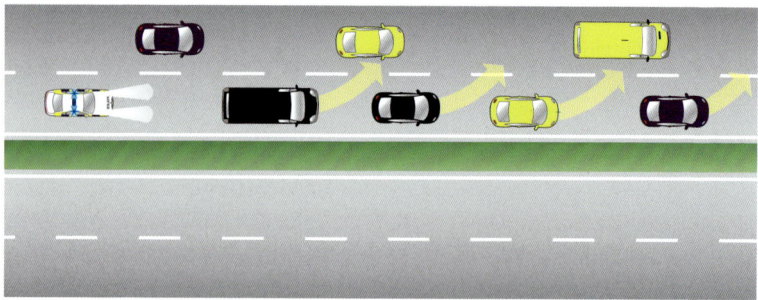

Travel in the outer lane of a multi-lane carriageway if the traffic is flowing freely.

Approaching roundabouts

A roundabout is a one-way system for which there's no exemption.

Approach roundabouts in the same manner as you would red traffic lights. Choose a low approach and entry speed so as not to cause drivers on the roundabout to over-react or brake hard.

If there are vehicles occupying all the approach lanes to the roundabout, use the same procedures as for a traffic light junction. Consider the following options to minimise the risk of drivers ahead entering the roundabout into the path of other vehicles.

Options

- Turn off all the emergency equipment and hold back.
- Straddle the lane markings to cause a 'parting of the waves'.
- Subject to view and safety, use the opposing carriageway. Bear in mind that drivers exiting the roundabout may have a late view of your vehicle.

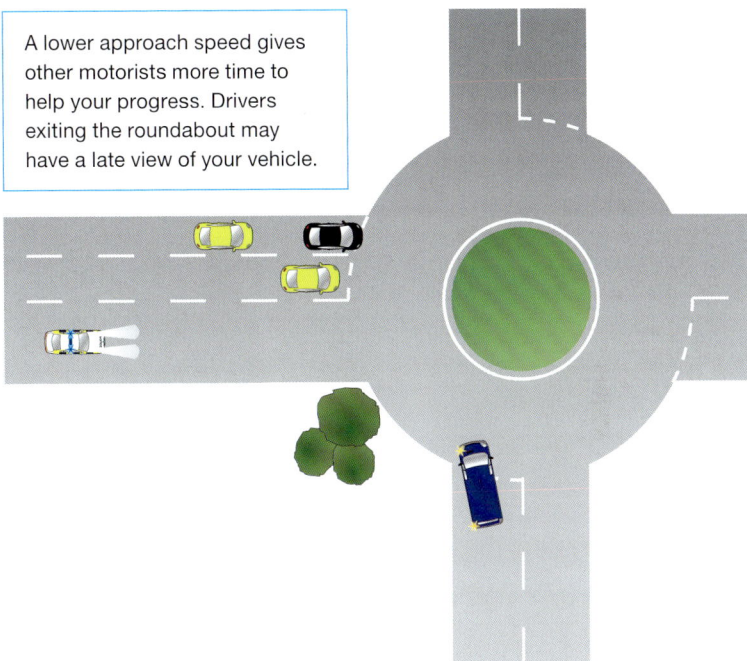

A lower approach speed gives other motorists more time to help your progress. Drivers exiting the roundabout may have a late view of your vehicle.

Passing on the nearside of other vehicles

Other drivers may find it hard to visually locate a police vehicle that is travelling along the nearside of stationary or moving vehicles. The natural response of a driver hearing a siren is to move to the nearside to help the emergency vehicle's progress. Be aware of this as you formulate your driving plan. Drive at a speed that enables you to stop your vehicle safely if the vehicle ahead moves to the nearside.

Anticipate by carefully observing other drivers. For example, watch for hand movements on the steering wheel, indicators, brake lights and movement of the wheels. These clues can provide early warning of potential movement to the nearside.

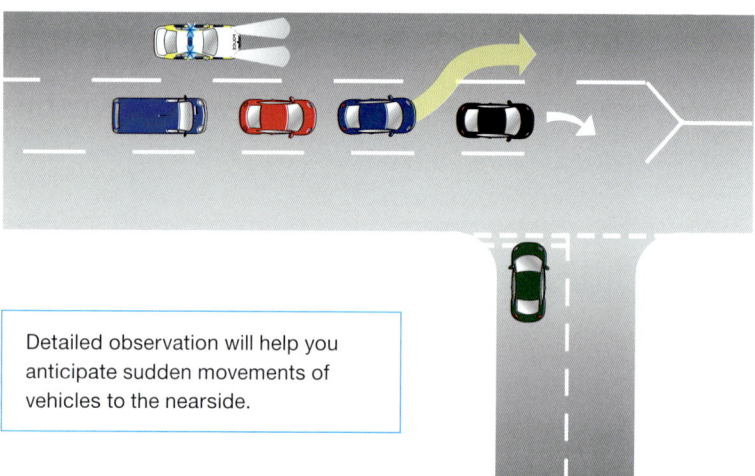

> Detailed observation will help you anticipate sudden movements of vehicles to the nearside.

Multi-vehicle response

Multiple vehicles travelling together in response mode are more hazardous than a single vehicle. The public sometimes only react to the lead vehicle, and once it has passed may resume their journey into the path of additional vehicles.

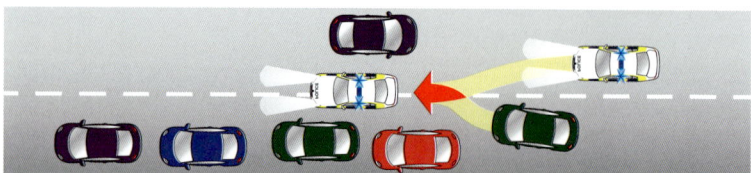

> Be aware that other drivers may not anticipate the presence of additional responding emergency vehicles.

Depending on the circumstances, you may need to extend the reactionary gap between emergency vehicles, both to reduce the pressure on the emergency vehicle drivers and to allow members of the public time to realise that there's more than one emergency vehicle approaching.

Alternatively, you may choose to close the gap to reduce the risk of traffic pulling out between the emergency vehicles.

If the vehicles have to remain together, for example when escorting an ambulance, make sure the vehicles are using a different siren sound.

Even if you're not part of a multi-vehicle response, always be aware of the possible presence of other emergency vehicles attending the same incident or a different one.

Vulnerable road users

Cyclists

Cyclists are very hard to see and may also react unexpectedly when a vehicle on an emergency call is approaching. The natural reaction of a cyclist on hearing the sirens is to look over their shoulder towards the emergency vehicle. This can cause wobbling and instability. Make sure you leave an appropriate safety margin when passing cyclists.

Motorcyclists

Look out for motorcyclists. Riders have restricted peripheral vision due to the wearing of crash helmets.

Be aware that sudden heavy braking on a motorcycle is hazardous for the rider. It may cause the motorcyclist to lose control of their machine, especially on wet or slippery road surfaces.

Also, be aware that cyclists and motorcyclists travel along both the nearside and offside of slow-moving or stationary traffic, and look out for them.

Pedestrians

Where pedestrians are present, drive at a speed that enables you to stop if a pedestrian steps into the road. Older people and children find it especially difficult to judge the speed and distance of approaching vehicles.

In bad weather, pedestrians tend to hurry, walking or running on slippery surfaces. Hoods, umbrellas and the use of personal audio equipment may hamper their awareness of your presence.

Horses and other animals

Horses are easily startled by noise, movement or bright colours and may rear up or bolt, risking injury to the rider or horse. If there's a horse on the road, promptly deactivate all the emergency equipment and reduce your speed. Wait for an opportunity to pass safely. Adopt a slow speed and a position as far away from the animal as possible.

Do not speed up or reactivate the emergency response equipment until you've achieved a safe distance from the animal.

Be aware of the possible presence of other animals, particularly in rural areas and where animals are being transported in livestock vehicles. Look out for hazard warning signs depicting animals and make use of this information in your driving plan.

✅ Check your understanding

You should now be able to apply learning from this chapter in your driver training so that you can:

- ☐ list the exemptions in law available to emergency response drivers and explain their implications for your driving plan
- ☐ explain the importance of going through a process of risk assessment before and during an emergency call
- ☐ demonstrate the correct use of your vehicle's emergency warning equipment
- ☐ demonstrate good practice in emergency response driving across a range of traffic situations.

Appendices

1   Are you fit to drive?

- I AM SAFE checklist

2   Is your vehicle fit to drive?

- Roadworthiness/pre-driving checklist
- POWDER checklist
- Inside the vehicle checklist
- Testing the brakes

3   Fuel-efficient driving

- Key principles of fuel-efficient driving

4   Goals for Driver Education

Appendix 1 Are you fit to drive?

Even before you get in a vehicle, you should always assess whether you're fit to drive.

I AM SAFE checklist

Do a self-check using the I AM SAFE* checklist. Ask yourself these questions:

- [ ] **I**llness – Do I have an illness or symptoms that might affect my ability to drive?
- [ ] **A**ttitude – How do I feel about this journey? Am I fully focused on the driving task? What human factors do I need to take account of?
- [ ] **M**edication – Am I taking any medication that might affect my performance?
- [ ] **S**leep – Am I suffering from lack of sleep/fatigue?
- [ ] **A**lcohol – Have I had a drink? Am I still affected by alcohol?
- [ ] **F**ood – Am I hungry or thirsty? Could low blood sugar or dehydration affect my judgement?
- [ ] **E**motion – Am I angry, depressed, or stressed? Could this lead me to take risks?

*There are many versions of this checklist. Follow the one you find most useful.

Appendix 2 Is your vehicle fit to drive?

If you haven't driven the car before, refer to the vehicle handbook.

Roadworthiness/pre-driving checklist

Before you start to drive a vehicle for the first time each day, you should ensure that it's roadworthy. Always carry out the following pre-driving checks.

Identify the type of vehicle you're going to drive:

- [ ] front-/rear-/four-wheel drive
- [ ] fuel type: petrol/diesel or electric vehicle
- [ ] gearbox type (manual/automatic)/position of gear selector
- [ ] safety features – anti-lock braking system (ABS)/electronic stability/traction control/adaptive suspension systems
- [ ] parking brake operation
- [ ] position of controls and auxiliaries
- [ ] window glass – mirrors and lenses are clean
- [ ] security of carried items – rear seat/boot space
- [ ] fire extinguisher present and in date
- [ ] first aid kit present.

POWDER checklist

Petrol (or charge) Ensure that you have sufficient fuel/AdBlue or electric charge for your journey.

Oil Oil level. Secure oil filler cap and dipstick.

Water Radiator water level including coolant/anti-freeze mixture. Include washer fluid levels (front and rear).

Damage Visual examination of exterior, looking for insecure items and/or damage.

Electrics Verify operation of electrical systems.

- Lights – mandatory running lights (main and dipped beam)
- Brake and reversing lights
- Indicators and hazard warning lights
- Number plate light (rear)
- High-intensity lights
- Emergency warning lights (blue, headlight flash, rear red)
- Interior – instrument warning lights
- Audible warning systems (horn/two-tone horns)
- Windscreen wipers (front/rear).

Rubber Wheels – wheel nuts secured to correct torque setting. Tyres – tread depth/free from cuts, bulges, tears/pressure/compatibility.

Inside the vehicle checklist

Switch on the ignition. Note the warning lights. Start the engine.

- After systems become operational, check your instruments.
- If any checks could not be completed before ignition or start up, do them now.
- Carry out a static brake check (see below).
- Adjust the seat/head restraint/steering wheel.
- Adjust the mirrors – inside and out.
- Do a visual inspection of all gauges and warning lights.
- Check the seat belt isn't frayed, twisted, locks when tugged, fastens and releases freely.

As soon as possible after moving off and in a safe place, carry out a moving brake test (see below).

Check gauges and warning lights at intervals during all subsequent journeys, taking action if necessary.

Testing the brakes

Check the brakes both before you move off and when the vehicle is moving, provided it's safe to do so.

The stationary test

Check that the brake pedal moves freely and gives a firm positive pressure that can be maintained for 3 to 4 seconds. In some newer cars, the engine won't start without a foot on the brake. Physically check that the parking brake secures the vehicle.

The moving test

The purpose of the moving brake test is to:

- check that the vehicle pulls up in a straight line under progressive braking
- learn how much to press the brake pedal in that particular vehicle
- identify any unexpected problems.

Brakes are the most important part of the vehicle and a moving brake test is vital when you move off in an unfamiliar vehicle that you may need to drive in demanding conditions at higher speeds.

Check the brakes at around 30 mph, using a non-retarding gear (third or fourth).

Test the foot brake as soon as possible after moving off. Always consider the safety and convenience of other road users before you do a moving test:

- Check the road is clear behind you.
- Declutch (to avoid engine braking interfering with the test).
- Gripping the wheel lightly, brake gradually and progressively, not harshly.
- Feel for anything unusual (for example, a tendency to pull to one side, any vibration or pulsing through the brake pedal) and listen for anything unusual (for example, noise from the brakes could mean they are binding).
- Release the pedal before you reach a standstill to check that the brakes release fully and aren't binding.

Appendix 3 Fuel-efficient driving

The emissions produced by vehicles cause damage to the environment and reduce air quality. Driving in a fuel-efficient way benefits not only the environment, but also you the driver, other road users and your vehicle.

Key principles of fuel-efficient driving

- **Enhanced hazard perception and awareness** – looking well ahead and anticipating potential hazards decreases fuel consumption by reducing unnecessary acceleration and braking.
- **Selective use of gears** – it's generally more efficient to change gears upwards sequentially, but if the revs have climbed high enough it's more fuel efficient to skip a gear and block change. In an EV or vehicle with automatic transmission, select the 'eco' option to prioritise range over performance.
- **Progressive use of controls** – smooth use of all controls (accelerator, brakes, steering) saves fuel.
- **Compliance with speed limits** – consider reducing your speed where possible to save fuel.
- **Prepare to stop, plan to go** – by using engine braking/torque, using vehicle momentum and avoiding unnecessary stops.
- **Use technology** – correct use of cruise control, stop–start features and in-vehicle technology can all contribute to reduced emissions, but systems may need to be switched off under certain operational conditions. Check your vehicle handbook for full information.
- **Effective pre-driving checks** – for example, check tyre pressures. Incorrect tyre pressure could result in increased tyre wear, affecting stability and stopping distance. Under-inflation can increase fuel consumption and emissions. Keep windows closed to reduce turbulence and drag. Switch off air conditioning/climate control if environmental circumstances permit.

Adapt to changing conditions. Always prioritise safety over fuel efficiency.

For further information, see the DVSA publication, *The Official DVSA Guide to Driving – the essential skills*.

Appendix 4 Goals for Driver Education

The European framework Goals for Driver Education (known as the 'GDE matrix') sets out the competences that driver training should focus on to produce the safest possible drivers.

The four levels of competency needed in all driving tasks	Knowledge and skills you have to master	Things that increase risk: be aware of and avoid these	Self-assessment for continuous improvement
4 Human factors before you get in the vehicle (for example, your personality, confidence, attitudes and mood)	What are your life goals and values? How do you behave on your own and in a group? How do your beliefs and personality affect your driving?	How do you react to peer pressure? In life, do you tend to take risks or avoid them? What personal tendencies or habits could increase your risks as a driver?	Think about yourself, your lifestyle and values. Are you impulsive? Are you always aware of the motives for your actions? What tendencies or attitudes do you need to manage when driving? Are you competitive? Do you find speed exciting? Do you get irritated by other road users?

3 The purpose of the journey	Each journey is different, with a different purpose and set of circumstances. This is about weighing up each journey in context.	What do you need to plan for? What's the purpose of this journey? Is it urgent? Are you under pressure? Or is it routine and tedious? What are the driving conditions likely to be?	Have you planned adequately for this journey? How do you respond to time pressure? What action do you take to manage tedium or monotony? What could you learn from this journey for next time?
2 The traffic situation – including road and weather conditions	This is about observing, signalling, reading the road, assessing safety margins, obeying the rules, anticipating danger and positioning your vehicle to make safe progress.	Be aware of hazards in the specific driving conditions. Are there vulnerable road users? Are you going too fast to stop safely? Are you allowing for weather conditions?	During the drive, ask yourself: are you always in the correct gear and position for your speed? Do you anticipate hazards and deal with them safely? After the drive, assess what you did well, what you did less well and how you could improve.
1 Controlling your vehicle	This is about the physics of driving: knowing the vehicles you drive and how to control them; for example, using the accelerator, brakes and gears smoothly and safely.	What are the characteristics of the vehicle you're driving? For example, does it tend to oversteer or understeer? What safety features are fitted? What do they do if activated?	During the drive: can you manoeuvre the vehicle accurately? After the drive: did it spring any surprises on you? Were you in perfect control throughout? What did you do well, what did you do less well and how could you improve?

For a detailed description of the GDE framework as a theoretical basis for driver education, explaining each competency level, its content and its implications for driver education, see Hatakka *et al.* (2002) and Peräaho *et al.* (2003).

There was a proposal to add a fifth level (social environment) to the GDE framework, but this has not been formally incorporated into the model. For further information, refer to Keskinen *et al.* (2010) in the bibliography. This would focus on cultural and social groups, and their associated values and norms, which impact on the attitudes and behavioural intentions of drivers identifying with a particular group. This in-group mentality may be of particular relevance to emergency services drivers.

Bibliography

Brake and Direct Line (2018) *Direct Line & Brake Reports on Safe Driving: Speed*.

Briggs, G.F., Hole, G.J. and Land, M.F. (2016) Imagery-inducing distraction leads to cognitive tunnelling and deteriorated driving performance, *Transportation Research Part F*, 38, 106–117.

Briggs, G.F., Hole, G.J. and Turner, J.A.J. (2018) The impact of attentional set and situation awareness on dual tasking driving performance, *Transportation Research Part F*, 57, 36–47.

Briggs, G., Savigar-Shaw, L. and Wells, H. (2024) 'Why aren't you using Bluetooth?!' Officer understanding of the dangers of handheld and handsfree mobile phone-use by drivers, *The Police Journal: Theory, Practice and Principles 2024*, 0(0), 1–17.

Burdett, B.R.D., Starkey, N.J. and Charlton, S.G. (2017) The close to home effect in road crashes, *Safety Science*, 98, 1–8.

Chu, H.C. (2016) Risk factors for the severity of injury incurred in crashes involving on-duty police cars, *Traffic Injury Prevention*, 17, 5, 495–501.

College of Policing (2024) *Police Driving: Authorised professional practice*.

DeGuzman, C.A. and Donmez, B. (2021) Knowledge of and trust in advanced driver assistance systems, *Accident Analysis & Prevention*, 156, 106–121.

Deng, M., Wu, F., Gu, X. and Xu, L. (2021) A comparison of visual ability and its importance awareness between novice and experienced drivers, *International Journal of Industrial Ergonomics*, 83, 103–141.

Department for Transport (DfT) (2024) *Reported Road Casualties Great Britain, annual report: 2023*.

DfT (2024) *Reported Road Casualties Great Britain: Motorcyclist factsheet 2023*.

DfT (2024) *Reported Road Casualties in Great Britain, Provisional Estimates: Year ending June 2024*.

DfT (2024) *Reported Road Casualties in Great Britain: Younger driver factsheet, 2023.*

DfT (2024) *Road Safety Factors: Initial analysis.*

Dorn, L. (2023) *Skill Decay, Distraction and Driver Stress.*

Driver and Vehicle Standards Agency (DVSA) (2013) *National Standard for Driving Cars and Light Vans.*

DVSA (2023) *The Official DVSA Guide to Driving – the essential skills.*

Endsley, M.R. (2020) Situation awareness in driving, in Fisher, D.L., Horrey, W.J., Lee, J.D. and Regan, M.A. (eds) *Handbook of Human Factors for Automated, Connected and Intelligent Vehicles*, London: Taylor and Francis.

Filtness, A.J. and Anund, A. (2023) A practical human factors method for developing successful fatigue countermeasures, in Rudin-Brown, C.M. and Filtness, A.J., *The Handbook of Fatigue Management in Transportation: Waking up to the challenge* (pp. 65–78), Oxford: CRC Press.

Hatakka, M., Keskinen, E., Gregersen, N.P., Glad, A. and Hernetkoski, K. (2002) From control of the vehicle to personal self-control; broadening the perspectives to driver education, *Transportation Research Part F*, 5(3), 201–215.

Health and Safety Executive (HSE) (2025) *Employers – driving and riding safely for work.*

Hembroff, C.C., Arbuthnott, K.D. and Kratzig, G.P. (2018) Emergency response driver training: Dual-task decrements of dispatch communication, *Transportation Research Part F*, 59, 222–235.

Home Office (2021) *The Law, Guidance and Training Governing Police Pursuits: Government response.*

Horswill, M.S., Hill, A., Buckley, L., Kieseker, G. and Elrose, F. (2023) Further down the road: The enduring effect of an online training course on novice drivers' hazard perception skill, *Transportation Research Part F: Traffic psychology and behaviour*, 94, 398–412.

Horswill, M.S., Taylor, K., Newnam, S., Wetton, M. and Hill, A. (2013) Even highly experienced drivers benefit from a brief hazard perception training intervention, *Accident Analysis & Prevention*, 52, 100–110.

Hsaio, H., Chang, J. and Simeonov, P. (2018) Preventing emergency vehicle crashes: Status and challenges of human factors issues, *Human Factors*, 60, 7, 1048–1072.

International Transport Forum (ITF) (2016) *Zero Road Deaths and Serious Injuries: Leading a paradigm shift to a safe system*, OECD Publishing.

James, S. M. and Vila, B. (2015) Police drowsy driving: Predicting fatigue-related performance decay, *Policing: An International Journal of Police Strategies and Management*, 38(3), 517–538.

Keskinen, E., Peräaho, M., Laapotti, S., Katila, A. and Hernetkoski, K. (2010) *Proposal for Driving Instruction in Three Stages to Acquire a B-category Driving Licence*, University of Turku, Finland: Trafi Publications 7/2010.

Koski, A. and Sumanen, H. (2019) The risk factors Finnish paramedics recognize when performing emergency response driving, *Accident Analysis & Prevention*, 125, 40–48.

MacKillop, D. (2012) *Single Vehicle Accident on Rural Left-hand Bends*, personal communication.
The 'double apex bend' illustration and caption on page 205 are adapted from this paper with kind permission of the author.

National Police Chiefs' Council (NPCC) (2022) *National Roads Policing Strategy, 2022–2025*.

Oviedo-Trespalacios, O., Tichon, J. and Briant, O. (2021) Is a flick-through enough? A content analysis of Advanced Driver Assistance Systems (ADAS) user manuals, *PLoS ONE,* 16(6), e0252688.

Pammer, K., Raineri, A., Beanland, V., Bell, J. and Borzycki, M. (2018) Expert drivers are better than non-expert drivers at rejecting unimportant information in static driving scenes, *Transportation Research Part F*, 59, 389–400.

Peräaho, M., Keskinen, E. and Hatakka M. (2003) *Driver Competence in a Hierarchical Perspective; Implications for Driver Education*, University of Turku, Traffic Research.

Robbins, C. and Chapman, P. (2019) How does drivers' visual search change as a function of experience? A systematic review and meta-analysis, *Accident Analysis & Prevention*, 132, 105–266.

Royal Society for the Prevention of Accidents (RoSPA) (2022) *Road Safety Factsheet: Overtaking factsheet.*

RoSPA (2023) *Road Safety Factsheet: Inappropriate speed factsheet.*

RoSPA (2024) *Road Safety Factsheet: Driver fatigue and road collisions.*

Sharp, G. (1997) *Human Aspects of Police Driving*, Scottish Police College.

Taylor, Y., Merat, N. and Jamson, S. (2019) The effects of fatigue on cognitive performance in police officers and staff during a forward rotating shift pattern, *Safety and Health at Work*, 10, 67–74.

Useche, S.A., Cendales, B., Montoro, L. and Esteban, C. (2018) Work stress and health problems of professional drivers: a hazardous formula for their safety outcomes, *PeerJ*, 6, e6249.

Winston, C., Maheshri, V. and Mannering, F.L. (2006) An exploration of the offset hypothesis using disaggregate data: The case of airbags and antilock brakes, *Journal of Risk and Uncertainty*, 32(2), 83–99.

Yazdi, H., Wickman, C., Aust, M.L., Selbing, I., Kowalski, L. and Axelsson, J. (2024) Understanding frustration triggers and emotional responses in driving situations, *Scientific Reports*, 14, 28613.

Young, M.S. and Stanton, N.A. (2023) *Driving Automation: A human factors perspective*, Oxford: CRC Press.

Zahabi, M., Nasr, V., Mohammed Abdul Razak, A., Patranella, B., McCanless, L. and Maredia, A. (2023) Effect of secondary tasks on police officer cognitive workload and performance under normal and pursuit driving situations, *Human Factors*, 65(5), 809–822.

Index

Bold page numbers indicate illustrations, *italic* numbers indicate tables.

acceleration 105–6
   bends 110–11, **112**
   car control system 44, 45, 46, 47, 48
   in car control system 41, 44
   competence in 108–9
   control of the vehicle **107**, 107–113, **112**
   cornering 211
   fuel/power source 113
   joining motorways 249
   overtaking stationary vehicles 219
   releasing the accelerator 123–4
   sense 109–10
   single-stage overtaking 225
   skidding and 159
   tyre grip **103**, 103–5, **104**
   vehicle balance and **107**, 107–8
advanced driver-assistance systems (ADAS) 23–33, **26**, *26, 27*
   features at a glance **26**, 26–7, *26, 27*
   features in more detail 28–32
alertness 4, 76
animals, emergency response and 286
anti-lock braking systems (ABS) 152–3
anticipation 4, 58–9, 62–3
   human factors and 76–9
   night driving 82–6
   planning and 60, **61**
   road signs and markings 93–7, **94**
   road surface 89–93, **90**
   skidding 158
   speed, choice of 71–4
   weather conditions 86–8, **89**
aquaplaning 162, **162**
arm signals 172
attention distribution 4
attention overload 18
attitude towards driving 3
automatic transmission 118–20
   developing your competence at using 120
   road conditions 122–3
autonomous emergency braking (AEB) systems 26, 28, 131, 153
autonomous vehicles 32

bad weather conditions 87, 258–62, **259**, **261**
bends
   acceleration round 110–11, **112**
   brakes/braking 129–30
   overtaking on 234–5, **235**, 252, **252**
   positioning 182
   see also cornering
blue lights 271
brakes/braking
   anti-lock braking systems (ABS) 152–3

autonomous emergency braking (AEB) systems 131, 153
control of the vehicle 123–32, **125**, **128**, **129**
corners and bends 129–30
emergency brake assist (EBA) 27, 30, 131, 153
emergency braking 131
engine braking 123–4
fuel/power source 113
hazards, approaching 130
lights 170
normal braking 124, **125**
overlapping braking and gear changing **49**, 49–51, **50**
parking brakes 132
regenerative 106–7
releasing the accelerator 123–4
retarders 106, 123
safe stopping distance 126–9, **128**, **129**
skidding and 159
testing 294
two-second rule 128–9, **129**
tyre grip **103**, 103–5, **104**, **125**
using the brakes 124

camber 194, **195**
car control system
   acceleration 41, 44, 45, 46, 47, 48
   application of 43–8, **44**, **45**, **46**, **47**, **48**
   collision prevention 36
   cornering 190–1, 207–11
   flexible use of 42
   gears 41, 44, 45, 46, 48
   hazard approaching and negotiation 37–8
   information processing 38, 39, 40–1, 44, 45, 46, 47, 48
   integration of competences 36, **37**
   left-hand turns 44, **44**
   low-speed manoeuvres 140–3, **141**, **144**
   mirrors 39
   overlapping braking and gear changing **49**, 49–51, **50**
   phases of 38
   position 41, 44, 45, 46, 47, 48
   potential hazards 48, **48**
   right-hand turns 45, **45**
   roundabouts **46**, 46–7, **47**
   signals 39
   speed 41, 44, 45, 46, 48
   TUG (take, use and give information) 39
carelessness, collisions and 6
cat's eyes 85, **85**
central position 177

centre of gravity 154
collisions
    causes of **6**, 6–7
    drivers most likely to have 7–8
    prevention via car control system 36
competences for police drivers 4–5, **5**
    car control system 36, **37**
    European Goals for Driver Education (GDE) 10, 296–8
continuous improvement 5, 20
control of the vehicle
    acceleration **107**, 107–113, **112**
    accelerator 105–6
    automatic transmission 118–20
    braking 123–32, **125**, **128**, **129**
    competence in 102
    electric vehicle transmission 120–2
    engine braking 123–4
    gears 113–17, **115**
    regenerative braking 106–7
    retarders 106
    safe stopping distance 126–9, **128**, **129**
    slowing down and stopping 123–32, **125**, **128**, **129**
    steering 132–7
    technology 105
    tyre grip 102–5, **103**, **104**
    vehicle balance 104, **104**, 125
cornering
    acceleration 211
    brakes/braking 129–30
    camber 194, **195**
    car control system 190–1, 207–11
    competence in 190
    cross views, using **206**, **207**, 206–7
    double-apex bends 204–5, **205**
    forces **191**, 191–2, **192**
    gears 211
    left-hand bends 197, **201**, 201–3, 209, **210**
    limit points 196–204, **198**, **199**, **200**, 021, **202**, **203**
    positioning 208–9, **209**, **210**
    right-hand bends **198**, 198–200, **199**, **200**, 208, **209**
    roadworthiness of vehicles 193
    safe 212
    sharpness of bends 196–205, **198**, **199**, **200**, **201**, **202**, **203**, **205**
    specifications, vehicle 193
    speed 210
    superelevation 194, **195**
    tyre grip **191**, 191–2
    understeer and oversteer 193–4
    vehicle characteristics 193–4
courtesy signals 172–3
cross views **206**, 206–7, **207**
crossroads, positioning at **184**, **184**, **185**
cycles/cyclists
    emergency response and 285

expectation of seeing 66–7, **68**
    overtaking 238–9

dazzle 84
dipped headlights 82–3
    bad weather 87
distraction 57–8
    due to multi-tasking 13
drivers
    qualities of good 3
    as role models 3
    vulnerability of **6**, 6–9, 10–12

electric vehicle transmission 120–2
    developing your competence at using 122
    road conditions 122–3
electric vehicles 108, 113, 117–18, 120–3, 154, 170
electronic stability programmes 154
emergency brake assist (EBA) 131, 153
emergency braking 131, 153
emergency response
    approaching and passing vehicles 277–9, **278**, **279**
    headlamp flashers 271
    interpretation of signals 280, **280**
    keep left/right signs, contravening 276
    legal exemptions 268, 269
    multi-lane roads **281**, 281–2, **282**
    multi-vehicle response **284**, 284–5
    national decision model (NDM), using the 269
    nearside of vehicles, passing on 283, **284**
    oncoming vehicles 278, **278**
    overtaking across junctions 278–9, **279**
    pedestrian crossings 275, **276**
    positioning 276–7, **277**
    reactions of motorists 268
    risk assessment 269–70
    roundabouts 282, **283**
    sirens 270–1
    speed limits 271–2, **272**
    stationary vehicles at incidents 280–1
    traffic-light junctions 272–5, **273**, **274**, **275**
    vehicles ahead 277, **278**
    vulnerable road users 285–60
    warning equipment, use of 270–1
engine braking 123–4
environment, driving **89**
    local road knowledge 97
    night driving 82–6
    road signs and markings 93–7, **94**, *95*, **96**
    road surface 89–93, **90**
    see also weather conditions
errors
    driver, collisions and 6
    of perception 57
European Goals for Driver Education (GDE) 10, 296–8

expectancy, errors in hazard perception and 57

familiar roads 97
feedback as part of learning 18
fit to drive
   brakes testing 294
   I AM SAFE checklist 290
   inside the vehicle checklist 293
   POWDER checklist 292
   pre-driving checklist 291–4
   roadworthiness of vehicles 291–4
flashing headlights 171–2, 253
focus of attention 57–8
fog 259–60, **259**
following positioning 181, **181**
fuel-efficient driving 295

gears
   accurate use of 114–17, **115**
   automatic transmission 118–20
   car control system 44, 45, 46, 48
   in car control system 41, 44
   control of the vehicle 113–17, **115**
   cornering 211
   economic progress 116
   moving off from stationary 114
   overlapping braking and gear changing **49**, 49–51, **50**
   overtaking stationary vehicles 219
   rapid progress 116
   single-stage overtaking 225

habit, errors in hazard perception and 57
hard shoulders 256–7
hazards
   anticipation 62–3
   approaching and negotiation of in car control system 37–8
   brakes/braking on approaching 130
   expectation of seeing 66–7, **68**
   night driving 82–6
   observation 59–60, **60**
   perception of 18, **19**, 57
   peripheral vision 68, **69**
   planning beyond the next hazard 64–5
   positioning when approaching 178–86
   prioritising 63
   roadside 178–80
   scanning the environment 65–6, **66**
   speed, choice of 71–4
   types of 59
   warning lights 169
   zones of visibility 69, **69**, **70**
   see also overtaking
headlights 82–4, **84**
   bad weather 87
   flashing 171–2, 253
hierarchy of road users 3

horns 170, **171**
horses
   emergency response and 286
   overtaking 239
human factors
   alertness 76
   anticipation and 76–9
   combating stress 15
   distraction due to multi-tasking 13
   impact on driving 2
   levels of the driving task 10–11, *12*, 296–8
   motorways 263–4
   'noble cause' risk taking 16
   observation and 76–9
   operational stress 14–15
   overtaking 241
   'red mist' 16–17
   stress, driving 13–14
   time pressures 16
   tiredness 76–8

I AM SAFE checklist 290
indicators 168–9, **169**
information processing
   anticipation 58–9, 62–3
   car control system 38, 39, 44, 45, 46, 47, 48
   decision-making 55
   errors of perception 57
   feedback 55
   focus of attention 57–8
   improving 55–8
   input 54
   memory storage 58
   model of **54**, 54–5
   motorways 251–5, **252**, **253**, **254**, **255**
   observation 59–60, 60, 62
   output 55
   planning 60, **61**
   reaction time **56**, 56–7
inside the vehicle checklist 293

journeys
   purpose of 16
   risk assessment of 11, **11**, *12*, 297
judgements
   errors in 7
   making 5
   poor, collisions and 6

keeping your distance 74–5, **75**, 181, **181**

lane closures 262
lane discipline on motorways 251
learning
   from experience 8–9
   feedback 18
   overconfidence after training 18–19
   self-assessment 19–21

training and practice 18–19
left-hand bends 197, **201**, 201–3, **202**, **203**, 209, **210**
left-hand turns, car control system and 44, **44**
levels of the driving task 10–12
lights 82–4, **84**
 bad weather 87
 blue lights 271
 brake lights 170
 flashing headlights 171–2, 253
 hazard warning lights 169
 headlamp flashers 271
 interpretation of signals 280, **280**
limit points 196–204, **198**, **199**, **200**, **021**, **202**, **203**
local road knowledge 97
low-speed manoeuvres
 car control system 140–3, **141**, **144**
 competence at 140
 confined spaces 144–5
 guides, using 141, 146
 observation **141**, 141–2
 parking 146–7
 planning 142
 reversing 143–5, **144**
 steering 143, **144**

manoeuvres at low speed *see* low-speed manoeuvres
memory storage 58
micro climates 88
mirrors in car control system 39
motorcycles/cyclists
 emergency response and 285
 expectation of seeing 66–7, **68**
 overtaking 238–9
motorways
 bad weather at high speeds 258–62, **259**, **261**
 debris 262
 emergency response **281**, 281–2, **282**
 flashing headlights 253
 hard shoulders 256–7
 hazards 246–7
 human factors 263–4
 information processing 251–5, **252**, **253**, **254**, **255**
 joining 248–9, **249**
 junctions 255, **256**
 lane closures 262
 lane discipline 251
 layout of carriageway **247**, 247–8
 leaving **257**, 257–8
 new layouts 248
 observation on 250
 overtaking 251–5, 252, 253, 254, 255
 signals 253–4
 slip roads 248–9, **249**
 speed, adapting to higher 250–1

moving brake test 294
multi-lane carriageways
 bad weather at high speeds 258–62, **259**, **261**
 emergency response **281**, 281–2, **282**
 hazards 246–7, 263
 layout of carriageway **247**, 247–8
 overtaking 237, **237**
 see also motorways
multi-tasking 4, 8
 distraction due to 13

national decision model (NDM) 269
nearside position 177
night driving
 dazzle 84
 following other vehicles 83
 hazards 82–6
 lights 82–4, **84**
 reflective studs and markings 85, **85**
 vehicles and 82
 you, impact on 82
'noble cause' risk taking 16

observation 59–60, **60**, 62
 expectation of seeing 66–7, **68**
 human factors and 76–9
 improving 65–75
 keeping your distance 74–5, **75**
 links 97–9, **98**
 local road knowledge 97
 low-speed manoeuvres **141**, 141–2
 motorways 250
 night driving 82–6
 peripheral vision 68, **69**
 road signs and markings 93–7, **94**
 road surface 89–93, **90**
 scanning the environment 65–6, **66**
 speed, choice of 71–4
 weather conditions 86–8, **89**
 zones of visibility 57, **69**, **70**
offside position 177
operational stress 14–15
overconfidence after training 18–19, **19**
oversteer and understeer 160–1, 193–4
overtaking
 bends 234–5, **235**
 capability of the vehicle 217
 competence in 216
 cyclists 238–9
 hazards **222**, 222–3, **223**, 238–40, **239**, **240**
 helping others to overtake 241
 horses 239
 human factors 241
 junctions during emergency response 278–9, **279**
 in line of traffic 230–2, **231**, **232**
 motorcyclists 238–9

Index

motorways 251–5, **252, 253, 254, 255**
moving vehicles 220–1
multi-lane carriageways 237, **237**
risks of 216
road layout and condition **239**, 239–40, **240**
road surface 240, **240**
safety points 242
single carriageways 233–4
single-stage 223–5, **225**
stationary vehicles 217–19, **219**
three-lane single carriageways 236, **236**
three-stage 226–30, **228, 229, 230**

parking 146–7
parking brakes 132
pedestrian crossings, positioning at 186
pedestrians, emergency response and 285–6
perception, errors of 57
peripheral vision 68, **69**
planning 5, 60–1, **61**
  beyond the next hazard 64–5
  low-speed manoeuvres 142
  skidding 158
positioning
  for advantage 177, **177**
  bends 182
  brow of a hill, approaching 186
  car control system 41, 44, 45, 46, 47, 48
  central 177
  competence in 176, **176**
  cornering 208–10, **209, 210**
  crossroads 184, **184, 185**
  emergency response 276–7, **277**
  following 181, **181**
  hazards, approaching 178–86
  nearside 177
  offside 177
  overtaking stationary vehicles 217
  pedestrian crossings 186
  roadside hazards 178–80
  single-stage overtaking 223
  stopping behind other vehicles 185, **186**
  traffic lights 186
  turning 182–3, **183**
  view into nearside junctions 180, **180**
potholes 24, 90, 238
POWDER checklist 292
practice as part of learning 18–19
pre-driving checklist 291–4
pull–push method 134–5, **135**

rain 260
reaction time **56**, 56–7
recklessness, collisions and 6
'red mist' 16–17
reflective studs and markings 85, **85**
regenerative braking 106–7
regression effects 57
response time 56, **56**

retarders 106, 123
reversing 143–5, **144**
right-hand bends 198, 198–200, **199, 200**, 208, **209**
right-hand turns
  car control system 45, **45**
road conditions 38, 96, 122–3, 157–8, 239–40
road layout and condition, overtaking and **239**, 239–40, **240**
road signs and markings 85, 93–7, **94**, 95, **96**
road surface 89–93, **90**, 264, **264**
road users, hierarchy 3
roadworks 262
roadworthiness of vehicles 193, 291–4
role models, drivers as 3
rotational steering **136**, 136–7
roundabouts
  car control system 46–7
  emergency response 282, **283**

safe stopping distance 71, 126–9, **128, 129**
satnav 83
scanning the environment 65–6, **66**
self-assessment 2, 5, 19–21, 36
sharpness of bends 196–205, **198, 199, 200, 201, 202, 203, 205**
signals
  arm signals 172
  brake lights 170
  in car control system 39
  competence in 166
  courtesy signals 172–3
  flashing headlights 171–2, 253
  hazard warning lights 169
  horns 170, **171**
  indicators 168–9, **169**
  interpretation of other people's 167, 280, **280**
  joining motorways 249
  motorways 253–4
  purpose of 166
  responding to other people's 173, **173**
signs and markings 85, **85**, 93–7, **94**
single-stage overtaking 223–5, **225**
sirens 270–1
situational awareness 5, **5**
skidding
  anticipation of road conditions 158
  causes of 156, **156**, 158–61, **159, 160, 161**
  condition of vehicles 157
  minimising risk of 157–8
  weather conditions 157–8
slip roads 248–9, **249**
snow, sleet and ice 260
speed
  bad weather at high speeds 258–62, **259, 261**
  car control system 44, 45, 46, 48

in car control system 41, 44
choice of 71–4
collisions and 7
cornering 210
emergency response 271–2, **272**
hazard anticipation and 71–4
motorways, adapting to higher speed on 250–1
overtaking stationary vehicles 219
safety and 72–3
single-stage overtaking 223
skidding and 159
underestimation of 6–21
see also low-speed manoeuvres
stability, vehicle
  anti-lock braking systems (ABS) 152–3
  aquaplaning 162, **162**
  attitude to safety technology 151
  autonomous emergency braking (AEB) systems 153
  controlling 150
  electronic stability programmes 154
  emergency brake assist (EBA) 153
  safety systems 150–5
  skidding 155–61, **156**, **159**, **160**, **161**
  traction control systems (TCS) 153
stationary brake test 294
steering
  control of the vehicle 132–7
  holding the steering wheel 134, **134**
  low-speed manoeuvres 143, **144**
  pull–push method 134–5, **135**
  rotational **136**, 136–7
  seat position 133
  skidding and 160
  technique 133
  tyre grip 103–5
  understeer and oversteer 160–1, **161**
stress
  combating 15
  driving 13–14
  operational 14–15
sun, bright 262
superelevation 194, **195**
surfacing materials 91

tailgating 8–9, **9**
technology, control of the vehicle and 105
three-stage overtaking 226–30, **228**, **229**, **230**
time pressures 16
tiredness 76–9
traction control systems (TCS) 153
traffic
  competence in dealing with 11, 12, 297
  traffic lights, positioning at 186
training
  overconfidence after 18–19, **19**
  as part of learning 18–19
transmission systems 117–23

automatic 118–20
electric vehicles 120–2
road conditions 122–3
TUG (take, use and give information) 39
turning, positioning for 182–3, **183**
two-second rule 128–9, **129**
tyre grip 102–5, **103**, **104**, 125, **125**, **191**, 191–2

understeer and oversteer 160–1, **161**, 193–4

variety of driving tasks 4
vehicle balance 125
  acceleration and **107**, 107–8
  control of the vehicle 104, **104**
  different types of vehicles 107–8
vehicles
  autonomous 32
  cornering and 193–4
  electric 108, 113, 117–18, 120–3, 154, 170
  knowledge of 11, 12, 297
  night driving 82
  roadworthiness of 291–4
  safety technology and equipment 19
  transmission systems 117–23
  see also control of the vehicle; fit to drive; stability, vehicle
visibility zones 69, **69**, **70**
vulnerability as a driver
  awareness of 10–12
  collisions **6**, 6–8, 12
  hierarchy of road users 3
  learning from experience 8–9
  levels of the driving task 10–11, 12

warning equipment, use of 270–1
water on the road 92–3
weather conditions 86–8, **89**
  bad weather at high speeds 258–62, **259**, **261**
  fog 259–60, **259**
  rain 260
  road surface in winter 92
  skidding 157–8
  snow, sleet and ice 260
  sun 262
  water on the road 92–3
  wind 260–1, **261**
wind 260–1, **261**
work, driving as part of, collisions and 7–8

young drivers, collisions and 7

zones of visibility 69, **69**, **70**

Bluline
The Police Healthcare Scheme

First 3 months FREE

The not-for-profit healthcare scheme for police officers, police staff and their families

Bluline gives you access to fast, professional diagnoses and top quality medical treatment, helping you get better, faster. Specifically designed for the police and managed by police officers, you are at the heart of everything we do.

- Excellent value for money
- Fast, accurate diagnosis
- Top quality medical treatment
- Claiming is quick and easy
- Designed for the police
- Managed by police officers

To find out more visit:
www.blulinehealth.co.uk

Or call us on
01905 796 682

BLULINE
POLICE HEALTHCARE SCHEME

Roadcraft

e-learning course and app

Enjoy flexible learning with the Roadcraft e-learning course and app!

The Roadcraft e-learning course takes all the content from the bestselling book and combines it with the power of digital learning.

Students benefit from:

- end-of-chapter assessments
- supplementary videos that demonstrate key concepts, such as road positioning
- voiceovers that enhance the experience of auditory learners
- a certificate of completion.*

Find out more at **safedrivingforlife.info**

The Roadcraft app allows you to keep building your knowledge on the go, even without an internet connection.

*Only available upon successful completion of the e-learning course

The Stationery Office Limited is registered in England No. 3049649 at 18 Central Avenue, St Andrews Business Park, Norwich, NR7 0HR.